# Pink Hats and Ballots

# Pink Hats and Ballots

## An Ecofeminist Analysis of Women's Political Activism in the Age of Trump, Coronavirus, and Black Lives Matter

Lydia Rose and Teresa M. Bartoli

LEXINGTON BOOKS
*Lanham • Boulder • New York • London*

Published by Lexington Books
An imprint of The Rowman & Littlefield Publishing Group, Inc.
4501 Forbes Boulevard, Suite 200, Lanham, Maryland 20706
www.rowman.com

6 Tinworth Street, London SE11 5AL, United Kingdom



British Library Cataloguing in Publication Information Available

**Library of Congress Cataloging-in-Publication Data**

Names: Rose, Lydia, 1965- author. | Bartoli, Teresa M., 1963- author.
Title: Pink hats and ballots : an ecofeminist analysis of women's political activism in the age of Trump, coronavirus, and black lives matter / Lydia Rose and Teresa M. Bartoli.
Description: Lanham : Lexington Books, 2021. | Includes bibliographical references and index.
Identifiers: LCCN 2021018608 (print) | LCCN 2021018609 (ebook) | ISBN 9781793626554 (cloth) | ISBN 9781793626561 (epub) | ISBN 9781793626578 (pbk)
Subjects: LCSH: Ecofeminism—United States. | Women—United States—Political activity—History—21st century.
Classification: LCC HQ1236 .R59647 2021 (print) | LCC HQ1236 (ebook) | DDC 304.20820973—dc23
LC record available at https://lccn.loc.gov/2021018608
LC ebook record available at https://lccn.loc.gov/2021018609

∞™ The paper used in this publication meets the minimum requirements of American National Standard for Information Sciences—Permanence of Paper for Printed Library Materials, ANSI/NISO Z39.48-1992.

*For*
*Minnie and Joe*

********

*For Abdel Kader Adjiri and Sabrina Adjiri, the two most important people in my life and the ones who support me unconditionally through the daily struggles of researching, writing, and completing this project and every project I take on. Sabrina, thank you for knitting me a pink hat on the way to DC!*

*Of course, none of my accomplishments would have been possible if I were not first raised by the most awesome parents along with my sisters and brother who have been and are my best friends throughout my life. I miss and pray for you all every day.*

*My parents were my first teachers that taught me to be an ecofeminist, to participate politically, and to pray to God for strength and perseverance. Yeah, they didn't use that word "ecofeminist" but I've embraced that name for their teachings and praxis.*
*—Lydia Rose*

********

*For:*
*Bob Garcia, Jr.*
*in gratitude for your unwavering support through every writing project*
*and*
*Katherine Anne Garcia, Jessica Clarise Garcia, and Phillip Robert Garcia*
*Thank you for your love and encouragement*
*throughout the writing of this book.*
*I dedicate this book to you and your children*
*with prayers, love, and an enduring faith in our democracy.*
*—Teresa Bartoli*

# Contents

# Acknowledgments

I, Lydia Rose, would like to acknowledge Anthony J. Lemelle, Jr. He was instrumental in helping me find a voice for my research and analysis as I earned a PhD and embarked on a career in academia. I am saddened that I no longer have the opportunity to discuss my work with him, but I could hear his voice as I read each chapter being developed and produced. I also want to thank Gwen Yarbrough for reading the first draft of the chapters and providing wonderful feedback and encouragement—Thank you!

I, Teresa Bartoli, would like to acknowledge Donna Miller. Her educational influence on my life propelled me toward higher levels of education and provided me with the foundation to achieve my goals within education and in my personal life. I will always be grateful.

Our families were critical in helping us get this project completed during the COVID-19 pandemic. We are happy to have accomplished our goal of finishing this research and writing this book during the global pandemic, but like all work, we wish we had more time. We will address the additional issues in the next book.

We would like to thank Courtney Lachapelle Morales and Shelby Russell in reaching out to us for this project and guiding the publication of this book.

# Introduction

## *Pink Hats and Ballots—Women's Increase in Political Participation and Activism*

The distinguished feminist scholar Patricia Hill Collins once noted that ordinary people bring about most activism. On January 21, 2017, approximately seven million ordinary people worldwide, many of whom had never protested before, participated in the historic 2017 Women's March (Chenoweth and Pressman 2017). The activists that day included over nine thousand women in Alaska who braved sub-zero temperatures and severe snowstorms to march together outside with parkas, pink hats, and protest signs (Hillman 2017; Chenoweth and Pressman 2017). That same day, a group of women in Los Angeles, too sick to leave a hospital, participated in a sister March in their cancer ward (Morley 2017).

The 2017 Women's March marked the beginning of a powerful movement that would inspire women across the country to run for local, state, and national political offices in 2018 and transform the US Congress with diversity and the largest number of women representatives ever elected. Empowered by the Women's March, women began to share their experiences with sexual abuse, causing a resurgence of the #MeToo movement and resulting in men of power being held accountable for their sexual misconduct in the workplace. Women's political activism would maintain momentum for the next few years, demonstrated through continued protests against oppression and participation in politics that continued through 2020 to the historic election of the first woman vice president, Kamala Harris.

The current surge of women's political activism in the age of Trump, the coronavirus pandemic, and the Black Lives Matter movement reveals that ordinary people's extraordinary level of commitment to political activism has the power to transform society. The historically significant surge of women's political activism raises two vital questions. What compelled a historic number of women to become active in political protests and running for elected government positions? Secondly, how are the many diverse issues addressed at the 2017 Women's March, the campaigns of women running for political office in 2018, and the 2020 Black Lives Matter protests linked together in a united cause?

*Pink Hats and Ballots* is a research monograph that addresses and answers these questions, identifying the dramatic shifts in dominant social and political ideology, ignited by Donald Trump, as the catalyst for the surge in women's political activism. An analysis of the many diverse issues addressed by the Women's March, the 2018 Midterm Elections, and the Black Lives Matter movement confirms that current women's issues are interconnected and are grounded in ecofeminism. Ecofeminism is a multi-dimensional praxis in this work, emphasizing equity, diversity, inclusion, and consensus. In terms of praxis, ecofeminism is fluid, non-hierarchical, and aims to eliminate any participation barriers. Ecofeminism is a means to seek answers to questions that are holistic. Ecofeminism is a movement that serves to inform and contribute to feminist and environmental justice scholarship.

Our research on the current surge of women's political activism began at the 2017 Women's March in Washington, D.C. An analysis of speeches, chants, and posters/signs identified the themes and issues addressed at the march. One of the most compelling and consistent suggestions made at the march promoted the idea that women needed to become politically active and become candidates for public office. A year later, women won 60 percent of the Congressional seats up for election, making the 2018 Midterm Election an extraordinary event, with the largest number of women ever elected to Congress. Data regarding the political candidates revealed that the successful women candidates, many of whom had never previously run for political office, campaigned on political platforms consistent with ecofeminist values, the same values promoted at the Women's March. The results of our research were presented at the 2019 American Sociological Association meeting in New York. That original paper became the foundation for this book.

*Pink Hats and Ballots* uniquely brings together ecofeminism and politics to analyze, examine, and explain the extraordinary levels of women's political activism in the age of Trump. The analysis of women's political activism (2016–2020) is an exploration into an unprecedented time in history, revealing insights and understanding about shifting political ideologies, the influence of social media on current social movements, the current social and political issues, and the compulsion to become politically active beyond voting. The research revealed that, unlike feminist movements of the past that sought equality, the current women's movement is firmly grounded in ecofeminism, involving multiple social and environmental ecosystems and the resistance to oppression while striving for equitable social transformation.

Chapter 1, "Shifting Ideologies and Ecofeminism," examines the relationship between the current surge of women's political activism and the dramatic shift in dominant social and political ideology that became prevalent with the presidential campaign of Donald Trump. This chapter explores the political polarization that preceded Trump's entry into politics, tracing the shift to the 2000 Presidential election, the emergence of the Tea party, and the rise of Donald Trump as a presidential candidate and then as the elected president of the United States.

Chapter 2, "A Socio-Historical Overview of Ecofeminism," traces ecofeminism's development over the last 100 years. This chapter provides an in-depth overview of ecofeminism as a philosophy and political movement for scholars who are new to this field of study. Ecofeminism is the theoretical framework of this book.

Chapter 3, "The Denigration of Women and Minoritized Groups," provides an ecofeminist analysis of the historical events that exemplified the dramatic political and social shift in the United States beginning in 2016. Many of the events that occurred in the United States from 2016 to 2020 were extreme, and at times, unbelievable. This chapter describes and analyzes federal policy changes, presidential rhetoric, and the real-life harms and consequences to women and minoritized groups within the United States. This chapter examines the political environment that evoked the current surge in women's political activism, providing the rationale for political resistance.

Chapter 4, "Environmental Justice and the Exploitation of the Environment," examines the shift toward environmental exploitation through federal policy changes that eliminated environmental protection and resulted in significant harm. This chapter explores the intimate connection between environmental issues and women, people of color, and minoritized groups. An examination of the social justice issues embedded in the connections between the exploitation of the environment and oppression of women, children, and minoritized groups, provides the rationale for understanding women's political activism.

Chapter 5, "The Battle Cry: Resistance and a Surge in Women's Political Activism," describes how the nature of inequity and identity leads to resistance and evolves to the point of action through participation in social movements. A description and analysis of the grassroots movement that led to the Women's March on Washington, D.C., demonstrate the ways modern social movements develop and gain momentum through social media and manifest in political protests out in the streets. An analysis of the pink hats worn by activists at the Women's March demonstrates the power of resistance symbolism. This chapter traces women's activism in protests to becoming candidates in political campaigns, explaining how women (many who had never previously participated in politics) dominated an election, gained control of the House of Representatives, and transformed Congress with diversity.

Chapter 6, "Pernicious Political Tactics: COVID-19 and Voter Suppression," examines the COVID-19 pandemic, analyzing how the pandemic altered life in the United States and resulted in disproportionate burdens to minoritized groups. This chapter also uncovers political suppression during the pandemic.

Chapter 7, "Police Brutality and the Black Lives Matter Movement," examines 2020's increased momentum of the Black Lives Matter movement. An ecofeminist analysis of systemic racism, police brutality, and policing history in the United States provides insights into addressing government-sanctioned oppression. This chapter traces the history of the Black Lives Matter movement as activism aimed at ending oppression. This chapter documents the police killing of George Floyd that resulted in continued worldwide protests and culminating in Black Lives Matter becoming the largest social movement in US history.

The extraordinary surge of women's political activism during the age of Trump, the coronavirus, and the Black Lives Matter movement has demonstrated elevated engagement levels and active participation in democracy. Through participation in continuing protests, multiple social movements, and political candidacy on all government levels, women have become a force in US politics. The research and the data tell a story. The current surge of women's political activism is a story about America and democracy. It is a story about the power of political participation in social transformation and the essential element that protesting has in a healthy democracy. This chapter of feminism's history reveals that the phenomenal increase of women's political activism is grounded in the knowledge that environmental issues are inherently feminist issues. That a healthy society cannot condone oppression, and that inclusion, equity, and justice are the inherent values that define an authentic working democracy. The research and data tell a story about the power of pink hats and ballots.

# *Chapter 1*

# Shifting Ideologies and Ecofeminism

> With unabashed and audacious intensity, the dominant social and political ideology in the United States was challenged and resulted in a dramatic shift in 2016. . . .
>
> And it all began with a tweet.

While many in society can influence others, no one person has the power to independently alter the social and political landscape of an entire country. The conditions in the United States were ripe for Donald Trump's rise to power and, with it, a presidency of explicit racism, sexism, environmental exploitation, and the most anti-progressive government policy changes seen in years. The current surge in women's political activism began in 2016 with the Women's March organizing and launching multiple social movements. These social movements were a direct response to the dramatic shift in the dominant social and political ideology that began with the presidential campaign of Donald Trump.

Discerning the motivation for political activism contributes to the understanding of the rise of multiple social movements that seek social transformation. Understanding the shift in the social and political ideology in the United States provides insights into the rise of political activism in general and about the Women's March as an ecofeminist social movement. This chapter traces the growing tensions and polarization in America, leading to 2016's dramatic shift in the dominant social and political ideology that provoked the surge of women's political activism.

## A RATIONALE FOR THE STUDY OF WOMEN IN POLITICS AND SOCIAL MOVEMENTS

The study of democracy is the study of social and political transformation. The founders of the United States established a constitution, setting social values as a guide for the ultimate goals and hopes for democracy based on rule by the people. Democracy is an ongoing process of social and political transformation that is continuously changing. Achievements in a democracy are made by those who participate both within and outside of government institutions. The justification for studying women's participation in politics and social movements is grounded in activism's role in democracy and social discourse. The significance of women's political activism during Trump's presidency (2016–2020), Covid-19, and the Black Lives Matter movement is established by the role of women in leading and organizing the current social movements. Most compelling about women's political activism during this period is both the historic number of participants and the historic number of demonstrations and protests that began with the Women's March in 2017.

## PARTISAN POLARIZATION IN VALUES AFFECTING EQUITY, DIVERSITY, AND THE ENVIRONMENT

In the years leading up to the dramatic changes in 2016, American values and beliefs had grown increasingly polarized along political party lines. The notable beginning of this recent rise in polarization can be traced to the 2000 presidential election between George W. Bush and Al Gore; this was a presidential race so close that the results were unknown 36 days after the election. The election came down to Florida's results, where chaos and controversy surrounded the recounting of ballots by hand and debating the hanging chads. Although Florida law dictates that all votes must be counted, the Supreme Court upheld Florida's decision to stop counting the ballots and declare Bush the winner by a mere 537 votes. Former vice president Al Gore won the popular vote in the 2000 presidential election, but George W. Bush became the president as his victory in Florida established his win of the electoral college. Accusations of fraud and voter suppression fueled growing resentments throughout the United States. The 2000 presidential election not only put a spotlight on a significant flaw in the electoral college regarding the popular vote but began a trend of growing polarization that would continue to escalate with the election of the next president.

The landmark election of Barack Obama in 2008 was viewed as a turning point in American democracy as the first Black American president suggested the realization of a transformed America. Issues of equity, diversity, and the environment were brought to the forefront. Obama's term as president began in the midst of the Great Recession, the most severe financial crisis in the United States since the Great Depression. The Obama agenda focused on reviving the economy, prioritizing inclusion and diversity throughout all government agencies, and providing environmental protections that included addressing climate change. Federal policies were aimed at issues of wealth inequality, such as providing accessible health care for all Americans, improving public education, and strengthening social security. Obama's elegant manner revealed a high level of education, intellect, and dedication to service while shattering prevalent racial stereotypes. It would soon become clear that federal policies based on equity, diversity, and protection of the environment were not embraced by all Americans.

Many viewed Obama's election as the beginning of a post-racial America, but when the world's wealthiest billionaire brothers devised a plan to challenge and eliminate corporate taxation and government regulations, it would unleash and expose a level of outrage and racial resentment that would intensely escalate America's polarization and embolden mainstream racism. The Koch brothers' plan was simple: empower and control a nationwide uprising to demand that national political policy conforms to their personal political agenda based on "drastically lower personal and corporate taxes, minimal social services for the needy, and much less oversight of industry—especially environmental regulation" (Mayer 2010). In order to empower and control an uprising, the Koch brothers enlisted support from two industry giants and began financing and organizing small political groups throughout the United States that began provoking and stoking public anger over increased taxation used to support social programs.

Just one year after Barack Obama's inauguration, mass gatherings of angry protesters emerged from across America to oppose President Obama and his policies. They called themselves the "Tea (Taxed Enough Already) Party." The Tea Party introduced the politics of anger as very vocal and enraged protesters gathered with signs to fight and resist taxation. In 2009, the "summer of rage," hundreds of infuriated and shouting Tea Party supporters took to the streets and town hall meetings carrying signs and "bearing arms" (Peters 2019). Tea Party protesters also began regularly attending President Obama's political events with guns and rifles (Thompson 2009). That summer, among the various guns carried by Tea Party protesters, one man brought a military AR-15 semi-automatic rifle to the convention center where President Obama was giving a speech, a legal right in Arizona where no permit was needed (Kurtz 2009).

The Tea Party protesters presented a narrative that their participants were average American citizens identifying as Republican conservatives who believed in limited government and were standing up against the unfair taxation of hard-working people. However, rather than focusing on fiscal issues, most signs created and carried by Tea Party protesters contained overtly racist messaging aimed at denigrating President Obama. These racist signs and slogans became a staple of the Tea Party rallies (Fantz 2009), uniting them in a racist ideology that displayed resentment at having a man of African descent as the US president. Marilyn Davenport, a member of Southern California's central committee of the Orange County Republican Party and a Tea Party activist, sent out an email to fellow conservatives that was eventually made public. The email contained a photo of a family of apes with President Obama's face photoshopped onto the smallest animal (Adams 2011). The offensive image is situated with America's long history of racism, implying that Black people are less than human.

Aside from racist images and slogans aimed at President Obama, the Tea Party promoted racist rhetoric that embraced prevalent racial stereotypes to re-establish the dominant white racial hierarchy (i.e., white supremacy). Haltinner (2016) examined the ways Tea Party activists frame inequality and uncovered prevalent racial stereotypes embedded in the way the Tea Party framed their ideology of "individual responsibility." Haltinner discovered that although Tea Party activists emphasized their unity under the broad notion that they were "color blind," Tea Party activists promoted the idea that racial inequality was simply the result of individual shortcomings from people of color. Further, Tea Party activists argued that it was "an assault to hard-working white Americans" to pay taxes that are used for social programs that primarily benefit people of color who "take advantage of the system" (Haltinner 2016: 399). These narratives are unfounded in that statistics show that the majority of people in these programs are white (Delaney and Scheller 2015).

As the Tea Party movement gained momentum, it was consistently identified as a conservative grassroots movement within the Republican Party (Peters 2019). Some researchers have argued that the Tea Party provided a "new identity" for Republican conservatism (Williamson, Skocpol, and Coggin 2011). However, this narrative was a facade. The Tea Party movement was neither a grassroots movement nor was their anger and resentment limited to government spending.

An exhaustive investigation revealed that the Tea Party's categorization as a grassroots movement is inaccurate; the movement did not develop organically on a local level, organizing from the bottom up. The Tea Party movement was orchestrated from the top down by the politically powerful Koch brothers, two of America's wealthiest men. Billionaire brothers David and Charles Koch are the owners of Koch Industries, named by Forbes as the second-largest private company in the United States with annual revenues exceeding one hundred billion dollars. Motivation for orchestrating the Tea Party movement emerged from the Koch brothers' goals of seeking drastic reductions of their personal and corporate taxes and eliminating government oversight regarding environmental regulations, likely tied to Koch Industries' designation as one of the top ten polluters in the country (Mayer 2010). The Tea Party movement opposed limited government regulation, including environmental safeguards and protections. (Environmental regulations of polluting industries would directly impact Koch Industries as well as other industrial polluters). The Koch brothers covertly financed the founding of the Tea Party, privately donating to organizations such as Americans for Prosperity, FreedomWorks, and Citizens for a Sound Economy. The funding was for the sole purpose of "educating," organizing, and mobilizing protesters for Tea Party rallies, giving the appearance of an American grassroots movement (Mayer 2010; Fenn 2011; McFadden 2019). The Koch's were assisted by corporations such as Phillip Morris and RJ Reynolds, who were key players in the development of the Tea Party (Fallin, Grana, and Glantz 2014). Mayer (2010) reported that funding the Tea Party's organization and the creation of nationwide protests was not personally about Barack Obama; for the Koch brothers, it was about maintaining their wealth. Any president enacting policies that raised taxes for corporations or the wealthiest one percent, providing social services for the needy, or enacting environmental regulations, would have encountered the Koch's wrath.

The Koch brothers were successful in launching the Tea Party and the nationwide protests that supported their agenda. Although the Tea Party narrative portrayed supporters as hard-working, middle-class Americans fighting for fiscal responsibility from their government, researchers determined from demographic data that Tea Party supporters are predominantly white, male, Republican, and wealthier than the general public (Arceneaux and Nicholson 2012; Zernike and Thee-Brenan 2010). The anger-filled protests of the Tea Party were fueled by racial resentments that appeared to emerge with the election of Barack Obama as the US president. In goading citizens to protest against taxation through the Tea Party movement, the Koch brothers unleashed a level of outrage grounded in racial resentments that would intensely escalate America's polarization and create a political climate where overt racism became mainstream.

The rise of the Tea Party contributed to ongoing political polarization. Researchers began to notice that, as the beliefs and values gap continued to widen between Republicans and Democrats, both major political parties began to shrink. The number of Americans who identified as Independents (38 percent) became more considerable than those affiliated with either the Democratic Party (32 percent) or the Republican Party (24 percent) (Kohut, Doherty, Dimock, and Keeter 2012). The increased polarization of American values and the growing rejection of the two major political parties changed the political landscape that allowed for a dramatic shift in political ideology, leaving the American political system vulnerable to extreme change while providing a unique opportunity for a political outsider.

## SHIFTING THE DOMINANT SOCIAL AND POLITICAL IDEOLOGY

When reality-television celebrity Donald Trump began to question President Barack Obama's citizenship on Twitter in 2011, there was no recognition of Trump's emergence into the political arena. In fact, no one could have predicted at that time that the real estate developer/television celebrity would eventually be elected as the next president of the United States or that he would have such an impact on political and social ideology. Trump tweeted fabricated claims that President Barack Obama was not born in the United States and was not a legitimate citizen (Abramson 2016; Krieg 2016; Benen 2016). Despite public revelations that Trump's claims were based on lies (Krieg 2016; Barbaro 2016), and despite the White House's public release of the official long-form birth certificate of Barack Obama (obamawhitehouse.archives.gov 2011), Trump continued with the lies. Through social media and television interviews, Trump successfully introduced the long-debunked "right-wing conspiracy" theory to mainstream America (Parker and Eder 2016). It would later be revealed that Trump had personally contacted right-wing conspiracy theorist Joseph Farah several times about taking the fictitious and "long-debunked" accusation to the American general public (Parker and Eder 2016).

Donald Trump's false allegations that the sitting American president was not a legal citizen of the United States not only established Trump's unusual emergence into politics but ignited a shift that significantly altered the dominant social and political ideology in the United States. For five years during President Obama's two terms in the White House, Trump remained the most vocal proponent of what came to be known as the "birther" controversy (Dickerson 2011), challenging the legitimacy of America's first Black president. Trump's influence was undeniable as respected mainstream news programs and newspapers began reporting on the unfounded birther controversy. Reporters from the three major television networks interviewed Trump about birtherism, knowing that the claims were untrue, but providing Trump a platform to reinforce doubt about Obama's citizenship. At one point, one in four Americans incorrectly believed that President Obama was not born in the United States (Condon 2011). Birtherism became the foundation of Trump's access into presidential politics as he struck a chord with growing racial resentments while cultivating widespread support among mainstream America and, most notably, with white supremacists and alt-right groups.

Donald Trump had very little in common with former American presidents. Trump lacked knowledge of the law and policy development, and he lacked any previous service, participation, or leadership in government or in the US military. For many years, Trump constantly rotated political party affiliation, registering as a Democrat, a Republican, and an Independent.

By 2016, political leaders and citizens within the United States and around the world witnessed Donald Trump's unforeseen and startling rise to power and were confronted by a presidential candidate who boldly and passionately espoused xenophobic and misogynistic rhetoric. Trump's ascent to becoming the Republican Party's presidential nominee had political and social ramifications as Trump disregarded the established standards of behavior expected from politicians. In US history, no other presidential candidate had ever behaved or spoke in such an explicit, unreserved, and vulgar manner when speaking about women, non-white citizens, and immigrants. Television and radio news programs grappled with unique ways to report Trump's latest profanity-laden statements, while mainstream political discourse was dramatically altered. Racist, sexist, and gender biases that may have previously existed in unspoken thought or relegated behind closed doors were now openly embraced and championed by Trump at campaign rallies promoting patriotism grounded in nationalism. Non-white citizens and immigrants were vilified by Trump, and in the process, hate became mainstreamed. Aggressive and often obscene verbal attacks were reserved for women, particularly political opponents and reporters.

Donald Trump orchestrated a presidential campaign that provided constant and extensive media attention to himself by delivering shocking statements that insulted, ridiculed, and slandered others. In the process, he guaranteed his presence in daily news reports. Many political commentators discussed the political impact of Trump's simply worded insults, use of profanity, as well as his use of misogynistic and xenophobic language. Throughout the presidential campaign, Trump continued a political strategy focused on self-promotion while delivering verbal personal attacks that denigrated other political candidates, and minority groups, without restraint. Donald Trump's behavior and participation in politics marked the beginning of a dramatic shift in dominant American social and political ideology.

Historically, political leaders have been held to a particular standard in regard to behavior and language. While it would have been political suicide for a seasoned politician to speak about individuals, groups, or countries with inflammatory and offensive terms, Trump gained support by claiming that he was fighting against having to be "politically correct." Under the guise of fighting "political correctness," Trump promoted racist narratives as he denigrated American war heroes, American Generals, Gold Star families, and the American political system, as well as non-white citizens, immigrants, citizens from other countries, and leaders from other countries. Trump's use of hate rhetoric and profanity was linked to his inexperience in government and was justified by his supporters who identified his vulgarity as code for someone who "speaks his mind."

Throughout his campaign, Trump spoke to and about women in degrading terms. Trump promoted the narratives of demeaning women and demonizing immigrants, refugees, and racial-ethnic groups. Trump dispersed the messages of hate through the daily use of Twitter and numerous political MAGA rallies that would continue throughout his presidency. The standards of acceptable behavior changed along with the national political discourse. Once devoted to the discussion and analysis of issues related to public policy, the economy, and global affairs, mainstream political dialogue became reiterations of Trump's most recent xenophobic or misogynistic statements. American social and political dialogue became infused with Trump's terms used to denigrate others, as hate became mainstream.

As a presidential candidate, Trump's adverse behavior and history with women became public knowledge. The celebrity businessman had a long record of objectifying and degrading women through years of celebrity interviews. Trump's background revealed numerous allegations of sexual misconduct and included a legal history of sexual assault allegations. Trump's participation in the presidential campaign began to alter mainstream political dialogue as Trump's sexist and racist statements were repeated almost daily by national news outlets. Whether they were prime ministers, political leaders, or presidential candidates, women in powerful positions were repeatedly characterized in a derogatory manner by Donald Trump. By the time the infamous Access Hollywood audiotape surfaced exposing Donald Trump's explicit description of grabbing women "by the pussy," mainstream political dialogue in America had been intensely altered.

Trump's white supremacist agenda was continually demonstrated throughout his presidency and would culminate with the January 6, 2021, insurrection where his supporters stormed the US Capitol building killing a Capital police officer and injuring many others. Trump's election to the White House immediately emboldened white nationalist groups such as the Ku Klux Klan, neo-Nazis, and Proud Boys, creating a surge of alt-right, white supremacist events, and rallies (Gay-Stolberg and Rosenthal 2017). One of the "bloodiest" and most violent of these events occurred in Charlottesville, Virginia, during the first summer of Trump's presidency (Gay-Stolberg and Rosenthal 2017). Self-identified alt-right members and Klansmen attended the "Unite the Right" rally, carrying guns and assault rifles, holding tiki torches and Nazi flags, yelling racial slurs, and chanting anti-Semitic slogans used in Nazi Germany. Neo-Nazis and white supremacists organized the event as a celebration of white nationalism (Parker 2019). In an interview that day, David Duke, the former imperial wizard of the Ku Klux Klan, told reporters that the protesters were "going to fulfill the promises of Donald Trump" to "take our country back" (Gay-Stolberg and Rosenthal 2017). Hostility erupted into bloodshed, causing injury to dozens of individuals and prompting the governor to declare a state of emergency and send the National Guard to join the police. The violence escalated and turned deadly when an avowed neo-Nazi drove his car into a crowd of counterprotesters, killing one young woman and injuring 19 others (Kessler 2020). Trump's support of white supremacist groups would continue for the rest of his term in office. During the 2020 presidential debate with then presidential candidate Joe Biden, Trump used his allotted time to address the white supremacist group, the Proud Boys, calling on them to "stand back and stand by."

Trump's immediate response to the incident was to suggest that "both sides" were equally at fault. Trump then publicly claimed that there were "very fine people on both sides" (Kessler 2020). Trump would later defend his statements declaring, "If you look, there were people protesting very quietly the taking down of the statue of Robert E. Lee." Trump continued his defense by pointing out, "I was talking about people that went because they felt very strongly about the monument to Robert E. Lee, a great general" (Kessler 2020).

The unconventional presidential campaign and election of Donald Trump completely changed mainstream political dialogue while his participation in national politics resulted in a drastic shift in the dominant social and political ideology in the United States, becoming the impetus for a surge in women's political activism. An ecofeminist analysis of Donald Trump's rhetoric and behavior, in addition to the changes in federal policy brought about by Trump and his administration, demonstrates the extreme nature of the shift that proliferated throughout society. The shift ignited by Trump is worthy not only of examination but a vital consideration in the analysis of women's political activism and the extraordinary number of women elected to Congress in 2018.

## ECOFEMINISM: SHIFTING ENVIRONMENTAL AND SOCIAL-ECOLOGICAL SYSTEMS

The dramatic changes in social and political ideology are linked with the increase in women's political activism. To explore this link, the core values of ecofeminism that emphasize nature and all life as valuable are contrasted with the political majority that prioritized capitalistic gain through the exploitation of nature and human life. Ecofeminism was chosen as the theoretical lens for this research because of the non-binary elements of understanding the connections of multiple and layered environmental and social ecosystems. The parallels between the ideals of democracy and ecofeminism are established in the Declaration of Independence: that all people are created equal, are endowed with rights, and that these truths are self-evident. Additionally, social movements and ecofeminist research stress the link between capitalism and oppression of women, people of color, and nature; in this way, an ecofeminist analysis significantly contributes to the scholarship regarding women and their involvement in political structures.

An ecofeminist analysis provides insight into the intersectionality of racism, classism, and sexism that can explain the expansion of political activism. In addition, an ecofeminist framework is made up of multidimensional and interconnected environmental and social ecologies such as those located within the place (urban, suburban, and rural), within identity (race, class, gender, and sexuality), within social statuses (employed, underemployed, unemployed), and within social institutions (family, work, and education). Focusing on multiple and interconnected environmental and social ecologies enables an explanation of the elimination of rights from women and marginalized groups that are grounded in the value of nature and all life, including humans and animals. Ecofeminism emphasizes the intersection and interconnectedness of environmental and social ecologies that allow for insights that are rooted in activism and social change.

Ecofeminist theory recognizes capitalism, patriarchy, and colonialism as a root cause of the oppression and exploitation of women, the minoritized, and nature. Donald Trump's selection as the presidential candidate of a major political party had significant implications for these marginalized groups, as the decision to endorse a wealthy, corporate businessman who had no previous experience in government or public service demonstrated a clear effort to reassert patriarchy, capitalism, and colonialism as core values. With claims of representing "the people" in the fight against the arrogant intellectual elite, Trump's rhetoric throughout the campaign manifested into a presidency based on a renewed political populism that sought the elimination of federal policies that protected women, minoritized groups, and the environment.

The election of Trump to the presidency was a catalyst for the current surge of women's political activism. On January 21, 2017, a massive crowd, estimated at nearly 500,000, descended upon Washington, D.C., for the first Women's March. Across the country, in every state, women marched. At that time, it was the largest single-day protest in the history of the United States and became a global event with sister Marches on every continent, with an estimation of over three million people participating worldwide. The March was an authentic grassroots movement that embraced themes of "resistance," yet the movement itself did not entirely fit the category of a resistance movement; it did not seek civil disobedience nor attempt to disrupt civil order or stability. Demonstrators gathered to support civil rights and gender inequality. The Women's March became a social movement and inspired resistance in the form of change from within existing political systems. The increase of women's political participation would continue for the next four years, inspiring women to become political candidates, resulting in the election of the most women ever elected to Congress in 2018, inspiring movements that would hold men accountable for sexual misconduct, protesting against police violence and systemic racism in the Black Lives Matter movement, and, under the leadership of Stacey Abrams, fight against voter suppression during the COVID-19 global pandemic resulting in 2020's election of the first woman vice president. The new surge of women's political activism revealed the power to shift the course of US politics.

## CONCLUSION

While the existing and growing political polarization in the United States enabled the inexperienced reality-television celebrity to become a legitimate candidate for president of the United States, Donald Trump's participation in politics ignited the dramatic shifts in political and social ideology. Whereas ecofeminist values embrace cooperation, the new ideology practiced domination. In contrast to ecofeminism's connection to democratic ideals, the new ideology supported authoritarianism. The democratic principles created to protect democracy, such as the system of checks and balances, separation of powers, individual rights, and the rule of law were challenged and fell to the wayside.

Trump had connected with growing anger and resentment that manifested into policies that represented much more than a partisan political shift. The social changes created by Trump introduced misogynistic language into mainstream political dialogue and influenced the increase of racist activity. The anti-government president would eventually attack democracy itself, claiming that the 2021 election was not legitimate and inspiring an insurrection in the US Capitol on January 6, 2021. The changes to political and social ideology were reflected by the policies of the Trump administration, which focused on eliminating civil and human rights and exploiting the environment, resulting in health risks and deaths for women and individuals belonging to minoritized groups.

The intense shift in political and social ideology was the catalyst for the current spate of women's activism. The themes addressed at the 2017 Women's March reflected ecofeminist issues while nearly every successful female candidate conducted their campaign with political platforms consistent with ecofeminist values, the antithesis of the political agenda that had dominated American politics since the 2016 presidential election. The following chapters provide insight into the social and political changes that prompted women from all walks of life to engage in political activism through protests and becoming political candidates. This research monograph is not a collection of dates in history, but rather a documentation of key events that shaped and greatly altered the mainstream political and social environments from

2016 to 2020. This "snapshot" of history brings clarity to the context in which demonstrators around the world marched together in protest.

The nature of oppression that was brought about through hate rhetoric and policy changes is examined through an ecofeminist lens. Trump's ability to mainstream hate is analyzed, and his political agenda based on white male supremacy is clearly exposed. An evaluation of Trump's politics involving sexual and gendered violence against women reveals a perspective and behavior based on the denigration of women. An examination of policy changes that eliminated existing rights for women, immigrants, people of color, young people with DACA status, and individuals from the LGBTQ+ community reveal the goal of re-establishing and strengthening a social hierarchy that embraces patriarchy. Many of Trump's policies were officially classified as human rights violations by the United Nations and were in direct violation of international law.

An analysis of the Trump administration's policies toward environmental exploitation exposes authoritarian strategies that included propaganda that reflected a war on science and the takeover of the EPA in order to permit unrestrained environmental destruction that will have long-lasting impacts for decades. The Trump environmental agenda demonstrated a commitment to capitalistic goals over the health and protection of humans and the environment, while the disproportionate burdens of toxic environmental pollution resulted in minoritized groups struggling for environmental justice.

The examination of the rhetoric, events, and policy changes in the United States provides the explanation and motivation for women's political activism. An analysis of the 2017 Women's March and the historic wave of women elected to Congress in 2018 contributes insights into women's resistance and the battle against oppression. The continued activism of women in the era of Trump would endure through a global pandemic, voter suppression, and the intensified crisis of police brutality. To fully understand the connection between ecofeminism and the current women's movement, the next chapter provides a socio-historical overview of ecofeminism presented through feminist activism against the oppression of humans and the environment that inspired the emergence of ecofeminism.

# *Chapter 2*

# A Socio-Historical Overview of Ecofeminism

The primary goal of this chapter is to provide an overview of ecofeminism through its history in feminism. Ecofeminism brings together ecology and feminist goals for a primary purpose: exposing oppression and seeking social transformation to eliminate domination over others and nature. Ecofeminism is in a constant state of development due to the continuous identification of oppressive systems involving environmental and social ecosystems that are multidimensional, intersectional, and interconnected.

This chapter is organized into five sections. In the first section, we situate the development of ecofeminism in the last 100 years, providing a glance of scholarship about women by women, women's statuses, and women's achievement in developing and articulating feminist philosophy and scholarship as feminism. The second section of this chapter addresses ecofeminism as a theoretical approach and movement against domination and oppression. The section outlines the primary theoretical tenets of ecofeminism, the role of gender, ecofeminism's initial focus on patriarchy, hegemonic masculinity, and colonialism. The third section follows ecofeminism's development in exposing systems of unjustified domination, examining the links between gender, race, and class, and the emergence of the theory of intersectionality (Collins and Bilge 2020). The fourth section addresses the critique of ecofeminism as "essentialist." The final section discusses resistance to feminism and environmentalism.

## SITUATING (ECO)FEMINISM IN THE LAST 100 YEARS: THE FOUR WAVES OF FEMINISM

Many people throughout history have worked to change ideas, practices, and beliefs about women, women's statuses, and women's capacity to meet the basics of life or human needs (physiological, safety, love and belonging, esteem, and self-actualization, i.e., Maslow's hierarchy of needs). This intellectual history and knowledge has been gathered, developed, and shared throughout history (e.g., Ramsey 2012 describes women's intellectual history in the Middle Ages). Since the middle of the nineteenth century, the more extensive umbrella term for this intellectual knowledge and history is feminism. This section aims to briefly describe ecofeminism's development through the four waves of feminism. The threads of environmentalism are traced throughout feminism's history, providing a historical context for the emergence of ecofeminism.

Feminism as a body of knowledge is quite complicated and under constant assault, as are women and nature. Historically, feminism is described and divided into waves. (For a concise critique of this metaphor, see Hewitt 2012.) The use of the metaphor "waves" has been heavily critiqued because past research has typically only focused on upper-class and middle-class white women (Mann 2011). However, women of color have always had a presence in American feminist movements, which have included prominent leadership roles. This re-articulation of the four waves of feminism attempts to recognize the significant and valuable contributions of women of color that have often been omitted from feminist history while exploring women's historical engagement with environmental issues that influenced the emergence of ecofeminism.

## First Wave of Feminism (1840–1920)

The first wave of feminism is generally described as the suffrage movement, beginning in the mid-nineteenth century and ending with the ratification of the 19th Amendment. The Amendment granted women the right to vote and participate in politics (Heilmann 2005). This section examines the influences during the first wave of feminism that contributed to the development of ecofeminism. This section also addresses the inherent flaws in designating the 19th Amendment as an achievement for all women, giving the Amendment the historical distinction used to mark the end of feminism's crusade for voting rights and the end of feminism's first wave.

Suffrage, the right of women to vote in political elections, was intimately connected with the abolitionist movement, also known as the anti-slavery movement. While both social movements were led by women, fought against oppression, and sought social reformation, the abolitionist movement led to the suffrage movement's creation. Many leaders and activists of the abolitionist movement became leaders and activists of the suffrage movement. They included many formerly enslaved free Black women such as Harriet Tubman, Maria W. Stewart, Sarah Remond, Harriet Forten Purvis, and Mary

Ann Shadd Cary, Henrietta Purvis, and Sojourner Truth (Harley 2019). As an abolitionist and feminist, Sojourner Truth is considered one of history's most influential advocates for human rights.

Sojourner Truth began advocating for women's right to vote during the abolition movement. Women abolition activists embraced Truth's ideas about voting rights, leading to the suffrage movement's formation. The suffrage movement gained momentum when two abolitionists, Elizabeth Cady Stanton and Lucretia Mott, organized the Seneca Falls Convention, devoted to women's rights. While there were no Black women at the Seneca Falls Convention (Waxman 2020), many prominent free Black women eventually began holding leadership positions at women's rights gatherings throughout the 1850s and 1860s (Harley 2019).

Sarah Remond was recognized as an influential public speaker and was given wide acclaim for her speeches at National Women's Rights Conventions (Terborg-Penn 1997). Sojourner Truth continued advocating for a women's right to vote and began speaking about the painful realities, not only of being a woman but also of being a woman of color. Most notable is Sojourner Truth's speech describing her lived experiences as a slave and a Black woman, working alongside men. In 1851, Sojourner Truth delivered the speech at the Women's Rights Convention in Akron, Ohio. Truth's speech, "Ain't I a Woman," is recognized as one of the most famous human rights speeches in American history. Truth spoke about the discrimination resulting from the interconnecting statuses of gender, race, and class, creating a severe level of oppression unique to women of color. This reality's insights would be articulated years later by feminist women of color through intersectionality theory (Collins and Bilge 2020).

After a decades-long fight, the 19th Amendment to the US Constitution was ratified in 1920 and granted American women the right to participate in politics through the power of voting. Although this was a landmark success for women, the right to vote did not extend to all women. Despite their participation, activism, and roles in the suffrage movement, most Black women would have to wait nearly five decades for the right to vote.

From the beginning of the suffrage movement, Black women had worked together, side by side with white women. These feminist activists had a long history of working together in the abolitionist movement that preceded the suffrage movement. Together, they witnessed the materialization of their goal to end slavery when the 13th Amendment was ratified in 1865. The 14th Amendment, ratified in 1868, granted all formerly enslaved people all the liberties and rights of citizenship guaranteed by the Bill of Rights. However, the proposal of the 15th Amendment, granting African American men the right to vote, would bring awareness of existing racism in the suffrage movement and feminism's history.

Feminist founders Elizabeth Cady Stanton and Susan B. Anthony, who fought so hard for human rights during both the abolitionist movement and the suffrage movement, became enraged that Black men could be granted the right to vote before white women. Both Elizabeth Cady Staton and Susan B. Anthony engaged in racist rhetoric that degraded Black men and dismissed the plight of Black women. Elizabeth Cady Staton began promoting a political ideology that would become the foundation of feminism. Cady began focusing on the unjust situation of "we educated, virtuous white women" that would ultimately identify future women's issues in feminism as those issues affecting white, middle-class women. The racism expressed by Stanton and Anthony would continue within the feminist movement even after their deaths. An example of continued racism was on full display at the first organized women's march on Washington in 1913, known as the "Woman Suffrage Procession." Organizers of the event requested that Black women march at the back of the parade instead of with their state delegations (Staples 2018). Human rights activist and journalist Ida Bell Wells-Barnett famously refused and marched with her delegation from Illinois, as did many Black women. However, many others marched at the parade's back, such as the sorority members from Howard University's Delta Sigma Theta who marched in cap and gown (National Park Service.gov).

Feminist historians added insult to injury by highlighting and marking the achievement of women's voting rights, with the ratification of the 19th Amendment, as the end of feminism's first wave, despite knowing that Black women were still not allowed to vote. It would be 45 years later, with the passage of the Voting Rights Act of 1965, that Black women would secure their right to vote in the United States. Historian and legal scholar Martha S. Jones (2020) offers a detailed history of American Black women's political activism and their pursuit of political power in *How Black Women Broke Barriers, Won the Vote, and Insisted on Equality for All.*

The first wave of feminism was more complex than the suffrage movement; environmental issues gained attention, and women became active in conserving and preserving the environment. In the 1800s, several nature conservatory societies emerged but were typically exclusively limited to white male membership. In response, women organized into societies separately based on race (Black women societies and white women societies). Many of these societies took up the cause of conservation, the appreciation of nature and wildlife, and urban environmental pollution—in direct opposition to the urban ills associated with capitalism and the industrial revolution.

The emergence of Black women's clubs in the 1890s had considerable influence on environmental issues. Organized on the local, state, and national level, Black women's clubs focused on social and political reform. Black women's clubs demonstrated that "contrary to widely held racist myths, Black communities have a continuous record of self-help, institution-building and strong organization to which Black women have made continuous contributions" (Lerner 1974: 159). Like white women's clubs, Black women's clubs were led by educated, middle-class women. However, Black women's clubs were much more successful than their white counterparts at crossing the class barrier. Lerner (1974) points out that Black women's clubs focused on education and community improvement, centered on poor women, working mothers, and tenant farm wives. Feminist activists such as Josephine St. Pierre Ruffin, Victoria Earle Matthews, Dr. Susan McKinney, Mary Church Terrell, Mary Margaret Washington, and Ida B. Wells were instrumental in the formation of Black women's clubs (Lerner 1974). These clubs would address the various social and political issues affecting the community were involved in philanthropic activities and engaged in environmental activism. Rather than conservation or preservation, Black women's clubs were committed to addressing environmental conditions, such as organizing clean-up campaigns (Mann 2011).

Around the same time (the late 1800s and early 1900s), an American chemist and feminist, Ellen H. Swallow Richards, also began laying the groundwork for contemporary ecofeminism. Richards was the first woman to be accepted to the Massachusetts Institute of Technology (MIT). She encouraged other women to enter the sciences by establishing the Women's Laboratory at MIT, providing women opportunities in natural sciences. Richard's work in utilizing scientific knowledge to better the environment and women's lived experiences would result in her recognition as one of the earliest ecofeminists (Richardson 2002).

The first wave of feminism included environmental issues that were embedded with racism. Racialized decision-making regarding land use and land abuse would significantly impact racial and ethnic minorities, including indigenous people. In decisions regarding land use, racial-ethnic women's voices and struggles were suppressed (Mann 2011; Collins 1990). By the early 1900s, many nations and traditional colonial powers set aside lands to preserve the wilderness and nature (lands that belonged to indigenous nations).

## Second Wave of Feminism (1960 to 1990)

The second wave of feminism is dated as of the 1960s–1980s. This period highlights how women worked to confront gender segregation using the strategies from the civil rights movements that were taking place in the late 1950s and 1960s, such as sit-ins, demonstrations, and lawsuits (Hickey 2008). The second wave of feminism focused on laying bare, structural misogynistic practices that reinforced a "male code." This male code situated women with a secondary set of rules separate from men. "Men only" places were targeted for sit-ins. Women in the United States began to push for equality and, once again, pushed for an equal rights amendment to the constitution. The work of feminists in the late 1970s and 1980s continued the work of the feminists early in the second wave, bringing forth additional issues related to women and inequality, particularly issues of unpaid labor, sexist practices in employment, and family planning.

Feminist successes in the second wave include "the demand for legal abortion and reproductive rights, equal employment laws, sexual offense bills, equal education, equal opportunity in the workplace, recognition of housework and childcare as unpaid labor/work" (Mohammed 2003). The term "feminism" was not generally used until late into the 1960s, typically identified as Liberal feminism. Liberal feminism assumed that the nature of gender inequality was the primary issue for all women, and much of the work focused on opening doors for women where women were previously barred. However, this struggle was very much particular for the white upper-class and middle-class women.

During this time, women of color brought attention to middle-class feminist agendas and called for attention to women's issues related to class, race, and sexuality. Women of color identified other struggles related to the intersection of race and class that influenced lived experiences of womanhood, inequality, and oppression (Collins 1990).

In addition to focusing on gender and inequality, the second wave of feminism advanced feminist scholarship toward the interconnection between gender, economic development, and environmental change. The groundbreaking work of women scholars and scientists during this time brought to light environmental issues from a new perspective that would eventually impact subsequent research and became influential to the foundation of an articulated "ecofeminism."

Scientist Rachel Carson was already a best-selling author when her book, *Silent Spring* (1962), was published, presenting scientific research to mainstream audiences and bringing attention to harmful pesticides that impacted humans and animals' health in the environment. Carson presented a perspective that valued life, both human and animal, and juxtapositioned it against patriarchy's indifference to capitalism's consequences through the production of poison for financial gain. Carson's book would inspire a global environmental movement and provide some of the basic tenets of ecofeminism. Lewis (1991) maintains that *Silent Spring* "should be counted among the few books that have actually altered the course of history" and that it is clearly a powerful "feminist" work (Lewis 1991: 5).

Economist Ester Boserup's seminal book, *Women's Role in Economic Development* (1970; 2007), examined the relationship between humans and the environment, presenting a perspective that connected issues of gender to economic development (Turner and Fischer-Kowalski 2010). Boserup's pioneering book contributed to the discourse on gender issues and emphasized gender as the primary influence in the division of labor. Boserup examined the negative consequences to women due to colonialism and capitalism, revealing that women overall were disproportionately affected by economic burdens (Benería and Sen 1981).

Researchers began giving increasing attention to the connection between gender roles and attitudes toward nature, specifically analyzing women's impact on the natural environment and women's roles in environmental management within resource-based economies (Resurrección 2017). Women became recognized, not only for environmental management but also for their crucial role in sustainable development. This research brought attention to the ways the environment significantly impacts women, influencing the emergence of "women, environment, and development" (WED) scholarship (Resurrección 2017). As the global community became increasingly concerned with environmental issues, WED perspectives gained attention among donor agencies and non-governmental organizations (NGOs), influencing their policies and approaches to addressing environmental concerns (Leach 2007).

## Third-Wave Feminism (1990–2010)

The third wave of feminism is generally dated from 1990 to 2010 and focused on the complexity and multidimensionality of sex and gender in one's identity and the intersection with race, class, gender, and sexuality. The feminists early in the third wave brought to the forefront issues of sexual violence and sexual abuse of women and the problems of linear and binary thinking and static definitions of gender and sex. In contrast to second-wave feminism (that distinguished between conceptual boundaries and standpoints such as Liberal feminism, radical feminism, Socialist feminism, and others), contemporary third-wave feminists were more accepting of complexity and a multiplicity of gendered identities, untethered by the limiting aspects of boundaries. Such third-wave feminists are distinguished by embracing contradictions, questioning, and redefining gender, sexuality, femininity, and masculinity. Third-wave feminism maintained a rejection of a single unifying feminist agenda or praxis (Snyder 2008; Kinser 2004). Additionally, feminists had varying ideas of social action and consciousness.

## Fourth-Wave Feminism (2010–Present)

The current fourth wave continues to evolve. Feminism in the fourth wave began around 2010 to the present and emphasizes social media use to seek justice against the harm of sexual harassment/assault/abuse and rape culture and incorporates a fluid element of identity and intersectionality (Collins and Bilge 2020). Fourth-wave feminists have generally continued the struggle for empowerment of women and representation of marginalized groups within government and economic practices.

Fourth-wave feminism challenges marginalizing labels and practices and relies on social media as a tool for political activism and for articulating feminist agendas. The non-central stance of fourth-wave feminism emerged from the difficulty of practicing organic intersectionality. Such intersectionality requires constant diligence to represent oneself without speaking for others in generalizations that may ignore or discount the oppressive practices experienced by others. There is a heightened awareness to limit the divisive and counterproductive practices that would disregard the impacts of race, class, age, gender, ability, sex, sexuality, employment, caretaking, nationality, and other marginalizing statuses which work in conjunction with each other to impact one's lived experiences of oppression. Okolosie (2014) highlights the importance of listing and recognizing differences as it allows for fourth-wave feminists to unite against imperialism, capitalism, white supremacy, and patriarchy. Critical self-reflection is the tool in which feminists may work to be allied with others who occupy marginalized identities.

Throughout each wave of feminism, there have been branches of distinct feminist thought that emerged throughout the decades. Ecofeminism is one such branch in the feminist academic field. Alongside the four waves of feminism were different threads of environmentalism. Concern for the environment, beginning with conservation and preservation, has existed hand-in-hand with women's movements since the 1800s. Taylor (2002) describes the environmental timeline of movements in terms of environmental exploitation hallmarks: (1) Exploitive Capitalism (1820–1913); (2) Post Hetch Hetchy Era (1914–1959) (the destruction of Yosemite's Hetch Hetchy valley to store water for San Francisco); (3) Post Carson Era (1960–1979) (the publishing and dissemination of Rachel Carson's *Silent Spring* which brought mass awareness of the detriments of pesticides, particularly DDT); and (4) the Post Three-Mile-Island Nuclear Accident (1980–2002).

Issues of environmentalism and the realities of race, class, and gender inequality and oppression shaped the environmental movement and environmental activism (Taylor 2002), and ultimately, the emergence and development of ecofeminism as a theoretical praxis and movement. Women have been engaged in activism and work to address environmental issues with environmental stewardship as part of each wave of feminism. Unfortunately, ecofeminism is typically described in a linear timeline beginning in the 1970s and developing and growing. While a linear timeline is used to document the development of ecofeminism, we reject the developmental stage theory and embrace an ecological model of discovery, change, and understanding. The ecofeminist thoughts and influences that surfaced and made a presence in modified thinking and action in the 1800s did not necessarily create a basic foundation of thought that was layered with added influences. Rather, ecofeminist knowledge, ideas, and understanding were developed, created, and shared in a manner that allowed for different visions, inclusions, and creations of ecofeminist knowledge. By viewing the construction of a more ecological model of ecofeminism, the variations of activism and social change in the 1990s, 2000s, and 2010s provide the groundwork for a promise of evolving knowledge in this coming decade of the 2020s.

## ECOFEMINISM: A THEORETICAL APPROACH AND MOVEMENT AGAINST DOMINATION AND OPPRESSION

Ecofeminism is a branch of feminism that recognizes and examines the connections between women and nature to seek social and ecological justice. Ecofeminist scholars have determined that humans' and nature's oppression results from the compulsion to dominate and is based on distorted conceptual frameworks. The primary objectives of ecofeminist research are to examine oppression and expose the faulty reasoning used to justify the domination of humans and nature, known as the "logic of domination" (Warren 2000). Ecofeminist theory has established that the roots of ecological and social injustice are so firmly linked that one cannot overcome one type of injustice without addressing the other. Further, the established connections between women and nature demonstrate and confirm that environmental issues are inherently feminist issues (Warren 2000). The purpose of this section is to present an overview of ecofeminism and its central tenets.

As the theoretical framework for this book, ecofeminism can provide increased knowledge and greater awareness of oppression and evaluate social and political changes by analyzing "human systems of unjustified domination" (Warren 2000: 43). Moreover, ecofeminism as a movement can contribute valuable insights about the recent surge in women's political activism, bringing to light how the 2016 shift in dominant social and political ideology produced unjustified domination and led to the historical increase of political participation of women.

Throughout the four waves of feminism, women have devoted themselves to environmental issues. At the same time, feminist scientists such as Ellen Swallow Richards and Rachel Carson laid the groundwork for the emergence of ecofeminism by articulating the importance of the environment to feminism. The term ecofeminism is recognized as being "coined" in 1974 by civil rights activist and feminist Françoise d'Eaubonne in Le Feminisme ou la Mort (Feminism or Death). However, since d'Eaubonne's book was not translated into English until 1994, Noël Sturgeon (1997) credits Ynestra King for originating the word in its US context. Gaard and Gruen (1993) trace the development of ecofeminism to the goals of connecting feminism and ecology.

There are many types of ecofeminism, just as there are many types of feminism, such as Marxist feminism or Liberal feminism. There is, however, general agreement on a central claim of ecofeminism: there are established connections between the domination of nature and women's domination. Warren (1990) explains ecofeminism's position that these crucial connections between the domination of nature and the domination of women are: historical, experiential, symbolic, and theoretical, providing an understanding that is "crucial to both feminism and environmental ethics."

One of the most significant connections between the domination of nature and women's domination is established by the fact that environmental losses are more substantially problematic for women (McKinney and Austin 2015). Women worldwide are more dependent on natural resources for water, food, and shelter. In developing countries, women are the primary providers of water and energy (e.g., firewood) while producing up to 80 percent of the food. Environmental degradation leads to economic loss, displacement, and food insecurity for women. The correlation between the domination of nature and the domination of women is not limited to developing countries. In the United States, the negative consequences of environmental exploitation affect women more than men. The devastating outcomes of environmental damage negatively impact women's sustenance and quality of life, including their health and mortality due to toxic waste left in the land, water, and air by industrial pollution. Ecofeminist researchers have established that there is a clear link between the exploitation of nature and the oppression of women (Murphy 1998) and that "women and children, particularly in poor communities of color," are disproportionately affected by the hazardous consequences resulting from the exploitation of the environment (Warren 2000).

Ecofeminism's scope extends beyond women's domination to include minoritized groups (women, children, poor communities, immigrants, people of color, and LGBTQ+ individuals) and nature (non-human animals, plants, and natural resources). The term "minoritized" is adapted from Benitez's (2010) research on social justice frameworks. "Minoritized" is used to highlight the social oppression experienced by particular groups in society and focuses analysis on the power dynamic among dominant groups and other groups. Ecofeminism analyzes "-isms of domination" (Warren 2000) such as racism, sexism, and classism as human systems of unjustified domination.

Contemporary ecofeminism directs attention to frameworks of analysis that address linked oppressions beginning with gender analysis, researching the ways gender is connected to race, class, age, nature, and other areas of oppression. Ecofeminist analysis identifies the ways dualistic and hierarchical systems of relations result in oppression and dominance over others. Ecofeminist research has brought attention to environmental justice issues embedded within environmental exploitation and examines oppressions such as poverty, food insecurity, inequities in healthcare, racial injustice, and the disproportionate burden of health risks and death caused by environmental degradation such as the climate change crisis and industrial pollution.

Ecofeminism's focus on patterns of domination includes the oppression of non-human animals (Gaard 1993). Animals are used in medical experiments to test beauty products, trained with whips to perform physically demanding tricks for human entertainment, and killed in the name of fashion. In the production of animals for human consumption, animals live an existence of constant abuse before being slaughtered in disturbing and painful methods. Often these methods are used because they reduce the cost of production. Animal cruelty provides consumers better prices for meat.

Why should feminists be concerned about animal rights? Ecofeminism recognizes the essential interconnectedness between humans, non-humans, and the environment. Mies and Vandana (1993) explain that the justification that permits domination over animals and nature is no different from the justification that permits domination over women, reaffirming the ecofeminist position that all forms of oppression are linked. Mies and Shiva (1993) maintain that ecofeminism must recognize the extraordinary strength and integrity of all living things.

Carol J. Adams (1990) examined the interconnections among violence against women, violence against nature, and pornography and revealed profound similarities. Consider the production of milk for human consumption. Cows can only produce milk during lactation, which is the result of giving birth to a calf after a nine-month pregnancy. The practice in modern dairy farms involves keeping cows constantly pregnant by dominating their reproductive system. Acts of sexual violence are routinely performed on dairy cows in the process to forcibly inseminate the animal, beginning after the young heifer becomes one year old. The cycle of milk production involves insemination, pregnancy, giving birth, and lactation. Shortly after giving birth, the cow is forcibly inseminated again. The physical strain on a young dairy cow is not as observable as the emotional distress when the newborn calf is taken from its mother a day after giving birth. Dairy cows are known to frantically cry for days as machines suck milk from their udders. Adams (1990) explains that humans regard animals as inferior species (speciesism) to justify their treatment of animals in the same way that men regard women as inferior to justify their dominance and abuse of women. Ecofeminist research confirms that the domination of reproductive freedom for females (human and animal) is linked to patriarchy and capitalism. Humans behave with a sense of entitlement over the treatment of animals, which is similar to men's sense of entitlement in the treatment of women. The connection between oppressions is revealed in the established discourse where men refer to women using animal metaphors such as chick, cow, dog, or bitch (Adams 1990).

Aside from a theoretical approach, an essential tenet of ecofeminism is that it connects the wholeness of theory and practice (Mies and Shiva 1993). Ecofeminism is a movement, meaning that ecofeminism's primary goal is to expose unjustified domination and seek alternatives to the oppressive and destructive ways humans relate to each other and nature. There is the recognition that oppressions are linked and that the roots of linked oppressions must be addressed. Ecofeminist scholars continue to examine social systems, such as patriarchy, to expose unjustified domination and focus on oppressive conceptual frameworks that use gender, race, class, and other classifications of identity to wrongly justify dominance over others. Ecofeminists acknowledge the interdependence with and dependence upon other humans and nature. Ecofeminism promotes biological and cultural diversity, recognizing its value and necessity for social transformation. Ecofeminists seek social and ecological justice, knowing that social transformation is crucial to ecological survival.

## Gender and the Gendering of Nature

Gender, the impact of gender on oppression, and the impact of gender interconnected with multiple identities are of crucial importance in ecofeminist research. The connection between women and nature can be understood by society's tendency to "gender" the environment. The process of assigning masculine or feminine characteristics to a role, position, object, organization, or even to a phenomenon as vast and extraordinary as nature is a deep-rooted practice. Gendering not only ascribes maleness or femaleness to a phenomenon but also ultimately results in the determination of levels of worth, power, and advantage. The gendering of the environment has produced a view of nature as "feminine," inferring that women are naturally linked to nature. This section examines the development of gender as a human classification, the impact of gendering nature, and the interconnections between the domination of women and the domination of nature.

Historically, societies have typically characterized human females based on biological attributes. Gender emphasized the distinction between biology and social construction and became an important focus during the second wave of feminism. Psychologist Robert Stoller (1968) is recognized as identifying that biological characteristics (sex) differentiate from behaviors based on cultural and social distinctions (gender), although observations of the distinctions were made many years earlier. In the early 1930s, anthropologist Margaret Mead identified the contrast between sex (as a biological description) and behaviors (exhibiting social roles within cultures) in her research of Samoan societies. Mead (1928) discovered that the social roles of men and women differed from culture to culture, leading to the conclusion that the physical body does not determine behavior or intrinsic social roles.

By the 1970s, the term "sex" was employed to exemplify biological traits and "gender" to distinguish the amount of femininity and masculinity exhibited by a person. Rubin (1975) acknowledged that the vast distinctions between men and women are not simply a product of biology but "shaped by human, social intervention" (1975:165). This understanding of gender was embraced by feminism and the term "woman," as gender was further examined through the range of characteristics influenced by culture, social roles, and gender identity. Whereas sex is a fixed, essentialist designation, the socially constructed process of gender provides greater understanding and knowledge about the existing spectrum of masculine/feminine gender identities (an individual's internal sense of masculinity/femininity, e.g., transgender) and of the range of sexual orientations (an individual's enduring physical and/or emotional attraction to another person. e.g., gay, straight, lesbian, bisexual). Ecofeminists focus on gender as a product of social construction. Gender as a social construct, serves to counter biological determinism while contributing to the study of oppressive systems that dominate others based on gender identity. Gender identity is typically interconnected with other identities.

Recent feminist scholarship and research on gender have expanded our understanding of gender beyond vague ideas about what it means for gender to be "socially constructed." In *Gender Trouble*, Feminist scholar Judith Butler introduced the theory of gender performativity (1990) to explain "gender as an enactment that performatively constitutes the appearance of its own interior fixity" (Butler 1990: 70). In other words, your gender is constructed through your repetitive performance of gender. Butler (1995) maintains that all individuals, no matter where on the spectrum of sexuality, engage in repeated acts and behaviors producing the impression of being a particular gender. *In Bodies That Matter*, Butler (1995) argues that no one is a gender; gender is a phenomenon that is constantly being produced and reproduced. This view of gender renders biological sex inconsequential to gender identification; biological sex is absorbed into the social construction of gender. Gender is established by the repetition of acts that are often impacted by society's dominant conventions of gender. The theory of gender performativity does not view gender as a choice. Rather, gender performativity explains the oppressive power of society's gender norms (e.g., what is expected, social policing of behaviors) on an individual's gender, which is in constant production and reproduction. The theory of gender performativity provides a specific understanding of the phenomena of gender and invaluable insights about human behavior and interaction with society.

Long before the distinctions were made between sex and gender in the characterization of individuals in society, the gendering of non-human entities was common practice. While this practice involves agreement and is shaped by human social interaction, it does not appear to observe a range of feminine or masculine qualities. Rather, the process of gendering typically assigns an object, a role, or a particular phenomenon as either male or female. The results of gendering affect the ways people think about a particular entity. The gendering of nature dates back to ancient Greece. The personification of the environment as Mother Nature, Mother Earth, or Earth Mother assigned feminine qualities to nature that have instilled universal and definitive conceptualizations about the earth and natural environments. Descriptions of land areas as fertile or barren are universally accepted terms that assign inherently feminine qualities to nature and reinforce the gendering of nature as female. Gendering the natural environment as female has led to society viewing women as being uniquely connected to nature.

In examining gendering in relation to exploitation and oppression, ecofeminist scholars concluded that the act of assigning a gender to nature, in addition to societal shifts in ideology, has contributed to designating a value to nature; nature became viewed in terms of its inherent benefits and worth. In *The Death of Nature: Women, Ecology, and the Scientific Revolution*, Carolyn Merchant examines the historical and symbolic connections between women and nature. Merchant (1993) argues that the Scientific Revolution caused a shift in ideology from regarding nature with respect to viewing nature as something to master and dominate, thus sanctioning its exploitation and degradation. In turn, exploitation of the environment is connected to the domination of women. Ynestra King (1995) argues that the central reason for women's oppression is her association with nature.

## Patriarchy and Hegemonic Masculinity

The history of ecofeminism began with a focus on patriarchy as the framework that "authorizes" forms of oppression (Gaard 1993). Ecofeminism recognized the "fundamental connection[s]" between Western, patriarchal cultures, and the domination of women and nature (Ruether 1995). Patriarchal cultures typically create a hierarchical structure based on male domination that not only gives power to men but also is the foundation for the exploitation of women and nature. According to Agarwal (1992), the exploitation of women and nature can be explained by the idea that in patriarchal paradigms, women are viewed as being closely linked with nature, while men are linked with culture. Since, in patriarchal paradigms, nature is regarded as inferior to culture, it follows that women are inferior to men. This view is grounded in the understanding that in patriarchal societies, masculine ideals are influential and feminine identification (based on a connection to nature) is seen as inconsequential in society. These social constructs lead to inequality and oppression on the basis of masculinity and patriarchy. Ecofeminist theory establishes that the ideologies that justify the exploitation and degradation of the environment are related to the ideologies that authorize injustices against women (Sturgeon 1997). Feminizing nature and animalizing women have become the justification for their domination and exploitation (Adams 1990).

The social constructs that lead to inequality on the basis of masculinity and patriarchy are important to exposing domination and oppression. In this sense, an examination of "hegemonic masculinity" can provide insights into ideological practices that are both overt and covert. Understanding hegemonic masculinity and tropes of domination expose the complex interconnection between nature and culture while portraying and recognizing the significance of ecofeminist values as ecological, non-binary, and non-linear.

The social construct of masculinity within a society founded on patriarchy is best understood in terms of "hegemonic masculinity." The concept of hegemonic masculinity evolved from the writings of Antonio Gramsci's "cultural hegemony" on the invisible or covert nature of power through "normalized" culture. The construct was then further developed and codified by scholars of masculinity (Connell and Messerschmidt, 2005) and identified as "patterns of behavior within a particular culture that permit and valorize men's dominance over women and over other types of masculinities." Embedded in the construct of hegemonic masculinity is the recognition of numerous forms of diverse masculinities. The existence of multiple masculinities within patriarchal societies generates a hierarchy producing a dominant group establishing dominance over women and men of less powerful masculinities (Connell, 1995).

Lemelle (1995) describes patriarchy as part of the hegemonic structures of domination in his study of Black Masculinity and Tropes of Domination. Men within this system not only dominate women; men dominate other men who may be viewed as less masculine by virtue of social status and the hegemonic structures. White male domination is legitimized through inherent systems of patriarchal cultures, which include various discursive systems that advocate and legitimize high-status male dominance (Rogers 1998). Discourse in patriarchal cultures serves to reinforce the patriarchy itself while providing the rationale for the subordination of women (Guillaumin 1995). Most provocative is discourse representing patriarchy, "as a fair and humane way of organizing social life" (Rogers 1998: 289). Rogers's (1998) study of the Clarence Thomas-Anita Hill hearings reiterates the ecofeminist conviction regarding the connection between men and culture (or, at the very least, it confirms the commandeering and management of culture by males). The dichotomous (either/or thinking) focus on the connections between male/culture and female/nature, with little room for a multiplicity of genders, masculinities, and natural environments. The limitations of dichotomous thinking leave no room for change and growth.

In contrast to a "sex-role" perspective of masculinity based on fixed, individual personality traits, hegemonic masculinity addresses the influence of power on behavior. Connell (1995) contends that masculinities are not equivalent to men but are defined by "patterns of practice" concerning power and position. Connell and Messerschmidt (2005) explain that hegemonic masculinity is founded on heterosexual power and that men engage in behaviors to position themselves into power over others. Hegemonic masculinity, therefore, is constructed upon the necessity to control and can be identified as a structure of domination. Within the framework of patriarchy, hegemonic masculinity justifies the exploitation of nature for profit (Connell, 1995). Ruether (1997) points out that hierarchical structures of patriarchy justify and create systems of "economic and legal domination of women, land, and animals" (35). Additionally, although these behaviors are predominately employed by men, both men and women engage in the patterns of conduct that define hegemonic masculinity (Connell and Messerschmidt, 2005).

Equally important to the construct of hegemonic masculinity is its connection to ecofeminism. Both ecofeminism and hegemonic masculinity are based on the connection between Western, patriarchal cultures and domination. Patriarchy creates the setting for hegemonic masculinity and legitimizes men's dominant position in society. Patriarchal cultures, embedded with dominant ideologies of capitalism, give power to men and perpetuate oppressive practices and behaviors toward women, the minoritized, and nature. The oppressive practices and behaviors are justified and "made to appear 'natural' and inevitable" (Ruether 1995: 35). The mutual conditioning of patriarchy and hegemonic masculinity creates patterns of behavior based on power and domination, which are justified, reproduced, and ingrained with intransigent opposition to ecofeminist values (Connell, 1995).

## Colonialism

Colonialism imposes ideologies from patriarchal cultures based on bestowing power to men and justifying oppression for capitalistic objectives.

Ecofeminism as a praxis must be situated within colonialism. In this sense, colonialism and Eurocentrism are founded on a form of speciesism within a human mindset. As colonial powers expanded and exploited lands, indigenous peoples were treated as a subspecies. The cultures of indigenous peoples throughout the colonized world were often described in dehumanizing terms that differentiated them from the colonialists. In the process, the lands of indigenous nations were usurped, exploited, and destroyed. Through colonialism, cultures were squelched as disdainful and uncivilized and subjected to genocidal practices such as the slave trade, relocation, and annihilation.

Language plays a significant role in oppressive practices. Terms like "tribe" or "tribal people," were used by colonialists not only to dehumanize indigenous people but to justify the murder of the indigenous and steal their land. Churchill (1992) breaks down the significance of language to oppress and dehumanize others. The use of the term "tribes" is similar to the ways groups of animals are named, such as a "gaggle of geese" or a "pack of wolves" (Jaimes*Guerrero 2003). Throughout Africa, Asia, and the Americas, European colonial powers invaded, occupied, divided, and destroyed indigenous people and their lands, while colonialism operated to systematically disempower enslaved or relocated indigenous peoples using patriarchal metaphors. Jaimes*Guerrero (2003) utilizes the phrase "patriarchal colonialism" to refer to the Eurocentric notions of the inferiority of other non-white or non-Western "races," and of all women in general, in contrast to the presumed superiority of the Anglicized, Euro-American male. Female-led resistance, Native Feminists, and Native Womanists have participated in activist and leadership roles to protect indigenous life and land (Jaimes*Guerrero 2003). For racial-ethnic women and indigenous women, the lived experiences of colonialism and the harm to life and land are personal. The attacks on people and their land have a long history that has continued and includes the pollution and poisoning of land where women live and take care of their families, causing significant health risks and deaths. Colonialism, the precursor to exploitative capitalism, is ideological in reproducing and growing racism, sexism, classism, and speciesism.

New insights and issues that are significant are brought about by the various lived experiences of people, the subjection to colonialism, patriarchy, sexism, and the exploitation of nature, including exposure to pollutants that contaminate the environment and are harmful to people. Ecofeminist scholars have incorporated lived experiences into the research focus of oppressions. Lived experiences have guided social transformation movements such as the food justice movement, climate change, and environmental justice. Ecofeminism joins together lived experiences and actions, sharing the knowledge that is created and discovered and positioning ecofeminist knowledge within the stories of our lived experiences.

## THEORY OF INTERSECTIONALITY AND ECOFEMINISM

As ecofeminism evolved as an area of study, there was the recognition that limiting the focus to patriarchy as the primary domination from which all other dominations emanated denied the role that oppression, such as racism, played as the primary domination in the experiences of many. The call for deeper analysis led ecofeminism to focus on the structure of domination and examine the ways all forms of oppression are linked. Ecofeminism had already established the connections between nature/culture and exploitation/oppression but began to focus on the unjustified domination that results from racism, sexism, classism, and other "-isms of domination" (Warren 2000) that exist within social systems.

These "-isms" of domination often intersect and produce multiple forms of discrimination (Warren 2000). Further, the interaction of multiple and intersecting identities such as race, gender, and class, results in experiences of exclusion and oppression that are unique to women of color. The emergence of the Theory of Intersectionality provides a theoretical framework that explains oppression and domination experienced by women of color (Crenshaw 1991; Deckha 2012; Collins and Bilge 2020), is utilized to critique and dismantle power, and is recognized as a valuable contribution for feminist scholarship. Collins and Bilge describe intersectionality as

> a way of understanding and analyzing the complexity in the world, in people, and human experiences. The events and conditions of social and political life and the self can seldom be understood as shaped by one factor. They are generally shaped by many factors in diverse and mutually influencing ways. (2020: 2)

In this sense, intersectionality is a theory and methodology that examines the "integrative nature of social identities as well as the power relations and the structures and hierarchies of difference to which they give rise" (Deckha 2012). Fort Collins and Bilge (2020), intersectionality is a tool to eliminate oppression and domination. Intersectionality, as a tool, brings understanding to the interconnected nature of identities such as gender, race, and class that creates interdependent systems of discrimination and experiences of oppression that are unique to women of color (Collins and Bilge 2020).

Although gender, race, and class are often addressed in intersectionality theory, this framework recognizes all integrated identities that are used by dominant groups to minoritize and discriminate against, such as sexuality, disability, religion, or physical appearance (Collins and Bilge 2020). While the term intersectionality has recently become a "buzzword" in popular culture for recognizing the various identities of women and supporting these women, intersectionality's origins and intellectual history must not be lost or obscured.

The necessity for intersectionality theory can be traced back to the first wave of feminism, demonstrating the ways that feminism neglected women of color (Collins and Bilge 2020). Before the suffrage movement began, Sojourner Truth spoke about the unique experience of discrimination by being a woman and being Black. Despite the involvement and leadership of Black women in the suffrage movement, most Black women were denied the right to vote and were excluded and subordinated by white feminists (e.g., being asked to walk at the back of the women's parade in 1913). The feminist agenda established by Elizabeth Cady Stanton focused on issues that affected white middle-class women, again excluding women of color. In the 1970s, a group of Black feminist scholars, many of whom identified as LGBTQ+, began developing theoretical frameworks to broaden the scope of feminism, address issues affecting women of color, and examine racism and classism within the feminist movement.

Black feminist scholar Bonnie Thornton Dill (1979), in *The Dialectics of Black Womanhood*, demonstrated how women's work roles in African American culture generated an alternative notion of womanhood and emphasized differences in culture and class based on the experiences of racism and racialization. Dill described and reframed what it meant to be Black in a white world in terms of Black women and the strengths and strategies Black women developed through workforce participation, especially within terms of working and managing family and raising children. These practices were in direct opposition to patriarchy (Dill 1979).

In 1981, Angela Davis examined the history of the feminist movement in *Women, Race, and Class*, describing the racist and classist discriminations that have existed from the beginnings of feminism. Davis's powerful analysis of US history and the women's liberation movement examines the impact of class and race on capitalism and demonstrates the ways Black women and other women of color have been excluded by feminism.

By the 1980s, scholars were exploring the negative effects of living with multiple statuses perceived by the dominant culture. For example, the gerontology literature took the term "double jeopardy" to describe the combined effect of being female and old (Chappell and Haven 1980).

Collins (1990), in *Black Feminist Thought: Knowledge, Consciousness, and the Politics of Empowerment*, emphasized the interconnections between race, class, and gender in the development of a Black feminist standpoint. Collins explains how the diversity among Black women—historical era, age, social class, sexual orientation, or ethnicity—produces different concrete experiences that in turn shape various reactions to the core themes of struggle against racism, poverty, sexism, and sexual violence. Collins examines the interplay between oppression and activism, among individual empowerment and collective action in making change. The interconnectedness is key in Collins's call for action.

The term "intersectionality" is attributed to the work of Kimberle Crenshaw (1989; 1991; Collins and Bilge 2020), highlighting the multidimensionality of Black women's experience. The peer-reviewed literature now uses the term intersectionality as non-negotiable. While people may still experience marginality, this "dialectic," or "interconnectedness," is now characterized as intersectional. One's unique status set (race, class, gender, sexuality, work, education, health, and ability), one's sense of identity, and the struggle for that identity (identity politics) are part of the ecofeminist movement.

## CRITIQUE OF ECOFEMINISM: ESSENTIALISM

As ecofeminist ideology and activism progressed, it was not without its detractors. The most vocal and prevalent criticisms came from feminists' denouncements aimed at ecofeminism. One of the exact criticisms leveled at feminism was the accusation that the movement was based on essentialism. The major problem with essentialism is the notion that if an entity or construct (such as gender) is identified as having a fixed set of characteristics that define its identity, the consequences are the invalidation of differences and the escalation of stereotyping. Essentialism is rooted in biology and disregards social and cultural construction. The idea that all entities have an innate "essence" has contributed to scientific racism and modern notions of race. The anti-ecofeminism backlash within the feminist movement resulted in resistance from researchers. A major outcome was researchers distancing themselves from the term "ecofeminism" and labeling their work as "ecological feminism" (Warren, 1991) or "critical feminist eco-socialism" (Plumwood, 2002).

The foundation of ecofeminism is a praxis to identify and root out the exploitation of women, people of color, and nature in patriarchal societies. The hierarchical infrastructure of society (institutions, norms, values, beliefs) is based on patriarchy where male domination and power reproduce the exploitation of women and nature; oftentimes, both are devalued in society, treated as secondary insignificance, and subservient to men.

Critics of ecofeminism argue that its essentialist bias construes the identity of women as grounded in biology based on shared universal traits such as women's closeness with nature (Twine 2001; Fuss 1989).

The presumption that women and men possess innate and immutable qualities (such as men's connection to culture and women's connection to nature) creates a reductionism that limits and regresses views about women, resulting in an inescapable future based on biological determinism. At the heart of the essentialist critique against ecofeminism is the charge that suggesting a universal connection between women and nature only reinforces patriarchal stereotypes, misrepresents women and people that identify as female, and limits the efficacy of ecofeminism.

The rejection of essentialism is a charge to reject the dichotomous focus because it reinforces patriarchal stereotypes and limits social movements striving for change.

Ecofeminism is not only a philosophy but also an active social movement. In this sense, ecofeminism and the ecological model are too dynamic to be consistent with essentialism. The essentialist claim based on women's connection to nature is invalid since an essence "is not in itself pansocial or presocial or a determinant of social structure" (Carlassare 1994). Ecofeminists maintain that although women and nature have been historically connected in a Western, patriarchal culture in their oppression and exploitation, neither entity possesses "innate essences" nor "an essential connection" (Carlassare 1994). Further, despite patriarchy's manipulation of the women and nature association, as a means for oppression, it does not diminish the powerful relationship between people and the earth.

## CRITIQUE OF FEMINISM: INCLUSION

While the primary goal of this chapter was to provide an overview of ecofeminism, beginning with its historical origins, this chapter raises important issues for feminists and ecofeminists. The re-articulation of the four waves of feminism reveals some of the significant and valuable contributions made by Black women activists that have been previously omitted from feminist history. This chapter exposes the moral and ethical iniquities in feminism's past, specifically racism. History provides insight into the present. Many women of color feel disenfranchised from the feminist movement.

As ecofeminists, the wrongs of the past and those who have suffered because of those wrongs must be addressed. It is not enough to have the knowledge of racism within feminism's history; it must be acknowledged. Acknowledgment is an official public declaration, an admission of wrongdoing that becomes a statement of established truth and fact. While actual history cannot be changed, the public acknowledgment of racism within the feminist movement can potentially provide the healing needed among all feminists. The acknowledgment of racism within feminism's history can give a voice to those who have been dismissed, providing a platform for the stories that have been omitted from feminism's history. Acknowledgment does not excuse past behavior but demands conscientious diligence moving forward, mindful not to repeat the past.

Ecofeminism demands action that leads to a social transformation from oppressive behaviors, even if those behaviors exist within the education of feminism. The retelling of a feminist history that disregards the role of Black women in the emergence of the feminist movement calls into question our role in continued oppression. Feminist pedagogy must be reexamined. It is essential that feminist history be updated to reflect the acknowledgment of racism within feminism, and more importantly, a commitment to accuracy. Perhaps we should question the continued use of the "four waves" metaphor altogether, knowing that it is a perspective that divides the history of women's activism based on the outcomes of white women.

## RESISTANCE TO FEMINISM AND ENVIRONMENTALISM

The idea that supporting feminist ideology would increase political participation is inherent even if difficult to measure. Kay (1985) attempted to measure the relationship between holding feminist ideals and political participation by comparing whites and Blacks in two different time frames using structured, dominant methods and data; she seemed to end up describing an outcome that went against her lived experiences, intuition, and knowledge. The structured data that she had explored did not allow for the flexibility and consistency in defining feminism and did not include the breath of political participation that goes beyond merely participating in an electoral election. (i.e., contacting officials, joining issue-oriented groups, signing petitions, canvassing, reaching out, protesting, and now engagement with social media). It is not surprising that when ideological knowledge bases, like feminism and environmentalism, increase political participation, there would be resistance to such ideologies. The ideological stance that seeks to position the protection of nature and our planet at the expense of the status quo, or attempts to change the status quo, increases the likelihood of resistance and detractors.

This resistance is not monolithic and merely external to those that hold both feminist and environmental values. Rather, such resistance may be considered organic and diversified—sometimes taking the form of discourse by those that support gender equality and protection of natural environments. Other times there are strategic responses to counter feminist and environmentalist ideals with blatant disregard for the conditions of others and nature. Resistance can take the form of showing up for a mass demonstration like the 2017 Women's March. In some circles, resistance to feminism has been called "antifeminism" and can come from people of different genders, classes, and races. Protection of our natural environment results in a plethora of suggestions and strategies for action and knowledge building. Power and power struggles are key in terms of which ideas and strategies are disseminated. In today's balkanized media ecosystem (Rose and Bartoli 2020), both suppression and subversion of disseminated ideas are based on the influence of norms and values. For example, Bernstein (2017), in her essay "On Mother Earth and Earth Mothers: Why Environmentalism Has a Gender Problem," there is a prime example of someone that is clearly a feminist and an environmentalist and articulates a problem within lived experiences. In particular, she articulates how expectations of supporting nature and naturalism through the support of organic, homemade, natural foods (lifestyle environmentalism) are done in a manner that reifies traditional gendered domestic labor of feeding and caring for one's people (partners, offspring, and other household members). Bernstein (2017) argues that "lifestyle environmentalism" romanticizes wholesome, farm-based, home-cooked foods without seriously challenging traditional arrangements of domesticity. However, she also recognizes that there is a limited number of households that have the necessary time, skills, and stability to live this lifestyle (Bernstein 2007). Environmentalism is complex in that it includes way more elements than any one of us can be an expert on. Bernstein harshly critiques Vandana Shiva, one of the major feminist activists to articulate ecofeminism (Mies and Shiva 1993/2014) as "rhapsodizing" rural life and the connection of the feminine with nature and natural environments. Bernstein argues that modernization, urbanization, and work outside the home are a means to escape discrimination through the opportunity to participate in education, health care, and the public sphere.

The peace and tranquility experienced when tending a garden are in opposition to the stress and anxiety experienced in working outside of the home, being in school, and dealing with health management systems. Additionally, the stress, anxiety, and anger experienced when insects, small animals, and disease destroy one's garden is in opposition to the satisfaction found in doing meaningful work, learning new things, and having access to healthcare. In this sense, addressing resistance is not about what's good, bad, right, or wrong. Rather it provides a more all-inclusive socio-ecological model that has room for multiple ecological systems to understand resistance to feminism and environmentalism.

Weiss (1987), in her essay, "Rousseau, Antifeminism, and Woman's Nature," concludes that the benefits of having separate spheres for the sexes do not necessarily require a rigid division of the sexes and that, in fact, the so-called "goods" or benefits may not actually be necessary. It seems this conclusion can be used to apply an understanding of resistance in general. Resistance does not need to be thought of as only direct opposition or a zero-sum with winners and losers. Rather, there are a multiplicity of possible solutions in which there is a minimal detriment in supporting feminist or environmentalist agendas.

A strategy in dealing with resistance and increasing political participation benefits from strategies like "horizontalism." In her essay "Feminism: Then and Now," Alcoff (2012) describes the protests in Argentina and the use of "horizontalidad." The organizational structure of this strategy takes place in a participatory manner among workgroups and is organized on a horizontal model. This model provides equitable treatment for all members and is based on a policy of openness and exposure of every faction of the organization. In contrast to the horizontal organizational structure, Western hierarchies establish vertical levels within the organization. Members of higher levels not only have more power than those of lower levels but operate in ways that are covert and disassociated from members of lower levels.

Alcoff (2012) describes the process of horizontalism to be organized with agreed-upon statements, but no one person is in charge that can be eliminated or co-opted. In trying to understand why activists might adopt horizontalism as an organizational pattern, Ancelovici (2016) found that it was not purposeful or based on past experiences but was a political process that participants developed organically by improvising and using what seemed to work and modifying practices that did not. In this sense, Ancelovici described this process as "open-ended."

The development of this strategy has its roots in feminist strategies from the 1960s and 1970s. Alcoff (2012) attributes the development of this strategy to the earlier feminists who focused on "issues of process." In other words, early feminists early worked to develop strategies and new knowledge without experts. Work was accomplished through the use of "affinity groups." These groups provide a means in which direct action or civil disobedience could bring about knowledge and political participation. Alcoff (2012) states that early feminists' affinity groups were a "way to intensify mutual support through emotional engagement." The 2017 Women's March is a clear example of multiple groups, mostly women, who attended demonstrations around the world in protest of the current president's offensive, sexist, racist, and ableist statements.

In understanding the role of resistance and constructions of political participation, one can find inspiration by Alcoff (2012: 274–275) when she reminds her readers that "Foucault is quite useful. He asks us to notice: Who is speaking? Who has authority? Who is reduced to the role of the listener?" She also adds another question, "Whose claims get discredited before they are out of the gate?" Asking these questions when examining resistance to feminism, ecofeminism and environmentalism may help us to look at hidden agendas regarding encouraging, limiting, or discouraging political participation in said resistance. Ideological stances (such as feminism, ecofeminism, and environmentalism) include a mismatch of beliefs and the means by which political participation is measured in the dominant political spectrum (Herrera 1992). The steps to instigate social change (beliefs and practices) begin with articulation and action. Feminism, ecofeminism, and environmentalism are non-centralized ideologies that position gendering within the discourse regarding constructions of the natural environment.

## CONCLUSION

Ecofeminism is the challenge to view the world through the eyes of an activist and ask: What are the problems on this planet, and how can the world be healed? Poverty, homelessness, inequalities in healthcare, food insecurity, sexual and gendered violence, unemployment, human rights violations, legal discrimination, and the degradation of the environment are the symptoms of the larger primary problem: the disconnection from each other and from nature.

Humanity's separation from the natural world was influenced by the Scientific Revolution and a shift in an ideology where the natural environment was no longer viewed as sacred. The separation has resulted in a world where patriarchy embraces capitalism and reduces humans to consumers, and treats the natural environment and non-human animals as products to be used and exploited for profit. The justifications used to dominate nature and non-human animals are the same justifications that permit domination over women. At the same time, the devastating and toxic consequences of environmental exploitation are not limited to the planet's land, water, or air but are disproportionately experienced by women, minoritized groups, and most profoundly by women who identify with multiple minoritized groups.

Many women are inflicted with multiple social, economic, and political injustices, and with greater severity, depending on the woman's race, sexual orientation, and economic status. The linked oppressions of women, LGBTQ+ individuals, immigrants, and other minoritized individuals are the result of human systems of domination, such as racism, sexism, and classism, where distorted conceptual frameworks are used to force an unjustified hierarchy to determine human worth and treatment. Ecofeminism is dedicated to ending all oppressions, recognizing that all oppressions are linked.

Ecofeminists know that humans are not separate from the natural world and recognize the interdependence between humans and between humans and nature. Whereas human domination is based on competition, the natural world is based on cooperation. Ecofeminism promotes the integrity of all living things and seeks to end oppression. Ecofeminist scholars dedicate themselves to achieving equality in social systems by exposing the "logic of domination" and replacing this destructive manner of relating to each other and to nature.

This chapter traces the development of ecofeminism and provides a quick glance of scholarship about women, by women, women's status, and women's work in developing and articulating knowledge and scholarship as feminism. The inclusion of ecofeminism's critique as "essentialist" provides an explanation for the multiplicity of ecological systems that emphasizes a dynamic element beyond dichotomous, linear, and binary thinking that leads some feminist scholars and researchers to shy away from or reject ecofeminism. Significant in this chapter was the description of the impact of gendering on society while focusing on the links between race, class, and gender. This chapter establishes the theoretical foundation for the analysis of the changes in social and political ideology discussed in the following chapters, that is, changes that became the impetus for the historical increase in women's political activism.

# *Chapter 3*

# The Denigration of Women and Minoritized Groups

The current surge in women's political activism was a direct response to the dramatic shift in the dominant social and political ideology toward the denigration of women, minoritized groups, and the environment. The shift in ideology, ignited by the presidential campaign of Donald Trump in 2016, became the catalyst for the current surge in women's political activism. The unconventional presidential campaign that began with racist comments about immigrants would continue to promote an ideology grounded in racism and sexism. The Trump campaign manifested into a presidency, marking the beginning of the most anti-progressive time period in recent US history. The Trump presidency began with the expeditious dismantling and elimination of established rights of those in society whom he had denigrated throughout the campaign. Trump disrupted the social-ecological system (economy, politics, culture) with "isms of domination" (Warren 2000), specifically racism, sexism, and classism. Under attack was equality of women, women's protection from gendered violence, protections for members of the LGBTQ+ community, protections for immigrants, affordable healthcare, and protections for the environment. The views, policies, and actions that promoted Trump's denigration of women, minoritized groups, and the environment are not only worthy of examination but are important considerations in the analysis of the current surge of women's political activism, unprecedented since the civil rights era of the 1960s. This chapter presents an ecofeminist analysis of the dramatic social and political shift through an examination of four distinct components of Trump's politics: (1) Mainstreaming hate; (2) Sexual and gendered violence against women; (3) Eliminating the rights of women and minoritized groups; and (4) Violating human rights.

## MAINSTREAMING HATE: WHITE MALE SUPREMACY

The 2016 presidential election marked a drastic and dramatic shift in American politics toward public displays of hate. A thorough examination of Trump's narratives exposes rhetoric of hate that permeated and intensely altered the political discourse in the United States. This was done by "mainstreaming hate" and shifting ideology and federal policies toward the denigration of minoritized groups and the elimination of established rights. An ecofeminist analysis of Donald Trump's presidential campaign, and the subsequent years as president, reveals an agenda grounded in white male supremacy and gendered violence.

White male supremacy, along with its inherent gendered violence and terrorism, is rooted in racial dominance and linked to the history of organized hatred and violence both within and outside of governing entities. Promoting both the ideology of white male supremacy and the violence and terror needed for subjugation, leaders often utilize "hate speech" to embolden racist behavior through indirect implication or explicit suggestion. The preponderance of evidence not only confirms Donald Trump's white supremacist political agenda but also traces Trump's narratives to an intensified emergence of a "contemporary" white supremacy.

### Non-Binary Gendered Violence

Inherent in white male supremacy and domestic terrorism is non-binary gendered violence. Pain (2014) describes gendered violence as characterized by three conditions: (1) violence that is part of a larger complex of harm and control, (2) exists within racialized hierarchies, and (3) achieves "its work by the control of emotions, particularly fear" (Pain 2014:352). Anthony Lemelle (2010), in his book *Black Masculinity and Sexual Politics*, explains the gendering of marginalized groups, including non-white men, as a form of oppression. Sociopolitical forces throughout history have feminized "Black males" as a process of subjugation (Lemelle 2010). In an effort to reestablish white male dominance, the Ku Klux Klan (KKK) carried out horrific assaults of severe, sexualized violence known as "lynching" to impart fear and insurmountable trauma on individuals with the power to extend and deliver extraordinary trauma to the families and the communities of the victims (Cardyn 2002). Lynching is an intimate, racialized, and sexualized violent crime primarily specific to black males and includes disrobing, humiliation, mutilation of the body, castrations, and the instilling of fear (Carter 2012).

Black men were not the only victims of lynching; both black women and white women were lynched. Feimster (2009), in her book *Southern Horrors: Women and the Politics of Rape and Lynching*, emphasizes how the lynching of women was used to establish a low value of womanhood, especially black womanhood. Lynch mobs inflicted "torture, mutilation, tarred and feathered, shot, burned, stabbed, dragged, whipped, or raped" those that opposed or challenged white male supremacy (Feimster 2009:159). The Ku Klux Klan, with "design and deliberation," used the systematic deployment of gendered sexualized violence as a means of instilling terror to achieve their social and political goals "precisely because of its effectiveness in accomplishing their ends" (Cardyn 2002: 679). The gendered violence of lynching has been characterized as "state-sanctioned" terror (Ore 2019: 86).

For almost 40 years since the 1970s, there has been progressive weakening in the Klan's organization, resulting in the declined public presence and activity of the Klan (Vinas-Nelson 2017), until the 2016 presidential campaign when Donald Trump stepped into the political arena, inspiring and revitalizing white supremacy (Hershenov 2019; Begley 2018). White supremacists enthusiastically supported Donald Trump (Cook 2016), causing a resurgence of white supremacist membership, activity, and violence in the United States and around the world (Hershenov 2019; Stack 2019; Southern Poverty Law Center 2019). The 30 percent increase of hate groups in the United States "coincides with Donald Trump's campaign and presidency" (Martinez 2019). Numerous experts from global and national anti-hate organizations attribute Donald Trump's behavior and hate rhetoric to the newly energized and emboldened radical alt-right (Hershenov 2019; Martinez 2019).

## Trump and the Emergence of "Contemporary" White Supremacy

The analysis of Trump's presidential campaign and that of the Trump administration demonstrates an agenda that mainstreams hate and is grounded in white male supremacy and gendered violence. Further examination has revealed that Trump's narratives have intensified the emergence of a "contemporary white supremacy" (CWS). White supremacist ideology, traditionally promoted covertly through norms, values, and practices, is embedded within the dominant culture and then reinforced with violence and terror as a means for subjugation. However, CWS seeks control overtly through political and economic social systems. Trump's role in the emergence of CWS, and his control over political and economic social systems, has resulted in a shift in the dominant ideology where white supremacy and the subjugation of others are openly promoted and achieved through mainstream political dialogue and federal policies.

Violence from individuals involved with traditional white male supremacist groups continues to exist and has been encouraged by the president on many occasions. The election of Donald Trump has shown that CWS has significantly more power to achieve dominance by elite white men of power while subjugating women, people of color, and non-human nature through political and economic policy mechanisms within social systems. Such policies are legitimized, thereby securing and reinforcing white male dominance in the United States. Berbrier (2000) describes the difference between the "traditional white supremacy," which is based on violence as a tool for subjugation, and a "contemporary white supremacy" that is based on social interaction that promotes a "new racist" discourse. Through social interactions, individuals intentionally conduct themselves in ways that portray appearances and identity (Goffman 1959). In an endeavor to present themselves as socially acceptable and completely dissimilar to traditional white supremacists that engage in explicit protests and violence, contemporary white supremacists attempt to "present an intellectualized version of themselves" (Berbrier 1999: 412). Contemporary white supremacists are aligned with right-wing populism and claim that they speak for "the people"; they believe that their concerns have been dismissed by arrogant elites resulting in a threat to America (Canovan 1999).

Central to contemporary white supremacy (CWS) is the social construction of victim status and the promotion of the narrative that white males are victims of discrimination. Berbrier (2000) describes how the concepts of "male" and "white" privileges are inseparable. This is evident in the number of white women that support and work to reproduce white male privilege using Trump's tactics of lies and misleading information. The battle to control the rhetoric of "antiracism" is a site of contestation. This rhetoric has been appropriated by CWS to claim that white males are the ones in need of protection (Gordon and Klug 1986) and suggest that their rights have been overridden by imposing policies such as affirmative action. This rhetoric also includes claims that their freedom to support their beliefs has been denied by "political correctness" (Berbrier 2000). Dobratz and Shanks-Meile (1997) identified the predominant goal of contemporary white supremacists as becoming politically mainstream and seeking domination of the political and social systems that control and maintain the power hierarchy in society. Donald Trump's presidency has been a prime example of CWS.

Through a succession of MAGA rallies that continued throughout his presidency, the rhetoric of hate espoused by Trump has supported and promoted violence while demonizing and subjugating non-white people and presenting white males as a group that needs defending. Donald Trump's usurpation of the American political system has denounced political leaders, the American political system, and the US Constitution. Consistent with CWS, Trump has attempted to take control of political and economic social systems with policies that reinforce white male supremacist ideology.

An ecofeminist analysis of Trump's white supremacist agenda reveals an effort to reinstate racial hierarchy. The racist statements made by Trump during the presidential election and his presidency indicate a conceptual framework, or way of thinking, that designates a higher value to white men. Grounded in this ideology of white supremacy is the idea of the "other." Collins (1986) explains that a common feature of racist ideology is the tendency for dominant groups to treat other groups as the "others." Characterizing minoritized groups as "the others" not only creates a distinction from the dominant group but objectifies people as "objects lacking full human subjectivity" (Collins 1986; p. S18).

Trump's rhetoric regarding immigrants embraces the racist ideology that negates minoritized others as being fully human and, in consequence, allows for unjustified domination and oppression. Trump's political agenda is in complete contrast to an important tenet of ecofeminism that embraces biological and cultural diversity and recognizes such diversity as valuable and necessary for social transformation toward peaceful coexistence and the elimination of unjustified oppressions.

## THE POLITICS OF SEXUAL AND GENDERED VIOLENCE AGAINST WOMEN

Considering that women as a demographic comprise a significant portion of the voting population, candidates running for political office, in an effort to invoke support, will generally address issues important to women. Among the many relevant social issues, sexual and gendered violence against women might be the most serious and far-reaching issue that affects women of all ages. However, the 2016 presidential campaign season was not a typical campaign season, and the dramatic cultural shift that would alter the dominant social and political ideology was beginning to take hold. As the unprecedented presidential campaign of Donald Trump dominated American culture, the United States was confronted with a Republican candidate who frequently and overtly demonstrated extreme misogyny. Throughout the presidential campaign, Donald Trump inundated the US mainstream culture with misogynistic verbal attacks about and directed to women, with the use of vulgar and derogatory language. In addition, Trump's behavior with women was made clear by revelations of Trump's multiple sexual misconduct and abuse allegations, made public during the presidential campaign. The extensive misogynistic rhetoric and behavior of Donald Trump are significant in that the role of the US president generally establishes the tone for acceptable behavior. This section analyzes Trump's rhetoric and behavior regarding women in an effort to bring an understanding of the ways the mainstream political dialogue and social ideology was shifted toward a "new normal," overflowing with public misogyny and includes the Trump administration's political efforts to abolish protections for victims of gendered violence.

## SEXUAL AND GENDERED VIOLENCE AGAINST WOMEN

Violence directed at individuals on the basis of gender is known as gendered violence and targets women and other feminized groups. The risk of gender-based violence increases for those who are not male (Wathen 2019). Gendered violence contributes to maintaining structural gender inequalities within patriarchal societies (Erturk 2009) and includes rape, sexual assault, intimate partner violence/domestic violence, and sexual harassment. Sexual violence and rape are common in the United States. According to Breiding et al. (2014) 19.3 percent of all women are raped at some point in their lives, while 43.9 percent experienced sexual violence other than rape. Every year, there are at least 10 million incidents of domestic violence in the United States, according to the National Coalition Against Domestic Violence (Lee 2018). Dr. Courtney Cogburn, from Columbia School of Social Work, put the statistics in perspective when she tweeted: "Every woman you know has been assaulted, narrowly avoided assault, had to calculate the possibility of being assaulted or has held the hand of another woman who was assaulted" (2018).

Violence against women is a violation of human rights (Fried 2003) and, while it manifests in many places and in many forms, notably high rates of gendered violence are found at college campuses and in the military (Wathen 2019). Although sexual assault often goes unreported, the US Department of Health and Human Services concluded that sexual assault is common at college campuses where women experience rape or sexual assault through physical force, violence, or incapacitation (Cantor, Fisher, Chibnall, Townsend, et al. 2015). Females in their first and second semesters of college have the highest risk of sexual assault (Kimble, Neacsiu, et al. 2008). Other gendered females who identify as lesbian, bisexual, or gay have a higher risk of sexual assault on college campuses than heterosexual women (Krebs, Lindquist, Berzofsky, Shook-Sa, and Peterson 2016).

### The Misogyny of Trump and Sexual Harassment

Presidential candidates are historically evaluated by their actions that occur during the campaign, as well as behavior that ensued long before becoming a candidate. Donald Trump came into the presidential arena with a lengthy history of degrading women that included accusations of sexual harassment and sexual assault. He ran a campaign that exhibited persistent hostility toward women, especially those in positions of authority and/or power, and demonstrated attitudes toward sexual assault that appeared to condone violence toward women.

Trump's attitudes toward women and sexual assault were made clear during the presidential campaign. Trump suggested that the underlying cause of sexual assault in the military was the decision to integrate women into the armed forces. Trump defended an earlier statement in which he questioned, "What did these geniuses expect when they put men and women together?" (Steinhauer and Rosenberg 2016). Trump's remarks were condemned by lawmakers and military experts who stated that Trump's statements about sexual assault in the military demonstrate ignorance about the subject, victim-blaming, and lack of awareness about the historical role of women in the military, working alongside servicemen since the Revolutionary War (Steinhauer and Rosenberg 2016). Trump's attitudes toward women and sexual assault prompted more than 50 retired generals and military leaders to sign a letter denouncing Trump's candidacy to become commander-in-chief and declared him unfit to be president. The primary concern was that Trump's election could compromise progress in the efforts to eradicate sexual assault in the US military. Trump's election did have a negative impact on women in the military. According to a Pentagon study (2016–2018), sexual assaults and sexual harassment within the military had a dramatic 38 percent increase after Trump's election (VandenBrook 2019).

An ecofeminist analysis of Trump's attitudes regarding sexual assault in the military reveals an adherence to patriarchy where power is given to men and women have no place in the system. Trump's statement appears to justify sexual assault as the natural result of men working together with women; Trump's position was both ignorant and dangerous while providing evidence for patriarchy as an unhealthy social system.

Trump's views about women were made public through speeches and compulsive use of Twitter (Buncombe 2018). Donald Trump did not limit his disdain for women; Trump verbally attacked hundreds of individuals, communities, countries, and institutions. His attacks have been tracked and documented by various news outlets, including the *New York Times* (Lee and Quealy 2019), *Washington Post*, and CNN. Trump's most vile and vulgar insults, however, have been reserved for women. Donald Trump has demeaned women through denigrations that belittle, sexualize, stereotype, objectify, and compare women to animals (Shear and Sullivan 2018).

The Republican candidate's history in regards to his statements about women became the subject of the Republican Primary Debate when political moderator Megyn Kelly questioned Trump on his views about women. He was asked about his disparaging and misogynistic comments, including his referring to women as animals. The Republican candidate did not deny referring to women in degrading terms but dismissed his behavior by stating, "the big problem this country has, is being politically correct" (Berenson 2015). One day later, Donald Trump tweeted vulgar insults directed at journalist Megyn Kelly that included mocking female bodily functions with "You could see there was blood coming out of her eyes, blood coming out of her wherever. In my opinion, she was off base" (Rucker 2015). It was not the first time Trump mocked female bodily functions (Diamond 2015).

Trump's misogynistic public conduct through the years has been documented and has often involved the degradation of women. He has regularly reduced women to their body parts and objectified women, including his wives and daughters (Filipovic, 2017). Sexual objectification is a powerful form of gender oppression and a contributing factor for other types of oppression experienced by women: employment discrimination, the trivializing of women's work and accomplishments, and sexual violence (Fredrickson and Roberts 1997). Researchers have examined the reinforcement of overt forms of inequality by Donald Trump through his misogynistic attitude, hostile rhetoric, and propaganda against women and concluded that the actions of this president are moving the country into an "endemic misogynist normal" (Rothe and Collins 2019: 965).

Many of Trump's attacks were directed at women of power, specifically women who were presidential candidates in the primaries. During the final presidential debate, Hillary Clinton, the Democratic nominee for president, was in the middle of answering a question when Trump called Clinton "such a nasty woman" (Diaz 2016). While Trump, the presidential candidate, was preoccupied with hurling insults at women and about women, revelations of his background exposed violence toward women.

Sixteen women have accused Donald Trump of inappropriate behavior, sexual harassment, or sexual assault before and during the 2016 presidential election. The *New York Times*' 2016 expose, based on interviews with over 50 individuals, revealed Donald Trump's private behavior with women as being misogynistic and involving sexual harassment. The harassment of women by Donald Trump included aggressive, non-consensual kissing and groping (Keneally 2019).

During the 2016 presidential campaign, allegations of rape by Donald Trump surfaced and were made public. Trump has been legally accused of raping a wife, a child, and a business associate. In a 1990 deposition, Ivana Trump gave sworn testimony of a vicious rape by her husband that was chronicled in a book about Donald Trump. Lawyers for Trump pressured the publisher to paste a statement by Ivana Trump inside the book stating that she did not want the rape to be interpreted in "a literal or criminal sense" (Mayer 2016). When the story made headlines during the 2016 campaign,

Trump's advisor and personal lawyer, Michael Cohen, stated, "you cannot rape a spouse" (Santucci 2015). This statement by Trump's lawyer is legally inaccurate yet consistent with Trump's views on sexual abuse.

According to a lawsuit filed in a US District Court in New York, Donald Trump was accused of the rape of a 13-year-old girl at a party hosted by billionaire and registered sex offender, Jeffrey Epstein. According to the legal documents, a witness corroborated the events, claiming that Trump was advised that the child was a minor (Riotta 2017). Days before the 2016 presidential election, the victim's attorney, Lisa Bloom, announced that the case would be dropped due to the numerous death threats to the victim (Ahmed 2019).

In addition, writer and columnist E. Jean Carroll publicly described her experience of sexual assault/rape by President Trump (Carroll 2019). Trump was apparently unaware of Carroll's proof of the sexual assault (Orden 2020; Klasfeld 2020) and responded to Carroll's allegations by calling Carroll a liar. Trump defended himself against Carroll's rape allegations by telling reporters that he would have never raped Carroll because "she's not my type" (Ransom 2019). Trump stated that he had "never met this person" and accused Carroll of lying in an attempt "to get publicity" and "sell a book" (Mangan 2019). Carroll sued Trump for defamation, and in a highly unusual move, the US Justice Department, under the direction of William Barr, replaced Trump's private legal team with government lawyers, paid by taxpayer money, to defend Trump (Feuer 2020).

Aside from allegations of his abusive behavior with women, Donald Trump has gone out of his way to consistently defend men accused of sexual misconduct, including himself (Fortin, 2018). In defense of Republican Senate candidate Roy Moore, who was accused of preying and sexually assaulting teenage girls, Trump made a public statement declaring, "He totally denies it, He says it didn't happen." Long after it was made public that five women received financial settlements paid by 21st Century Fox due to sexual harassment claims against Fox News host Bill O'Reilly, President Trump decided to make a public statement in defense of O'Reilly announcing, "I don't think Bill did anything wrong. . . . He is a good person." When the overwhelming amount of evidence of sexual harassment forced Roger Ailes, the founder of Fox News, to step down from his position as chairman and CEO, Trump again made a public statement in defense of a prominent man accused of sexual harassment. Trump defended Ailes stating: "I can tell you that some of the women that are complaining, I know how much he's helped them" (Berenson 2016).

Trump's views about women were made clear by his misogynistic rhetoric to and about women, as well as the revelations of his behavior with women that included accusations of sexual misconduct and sexual assault. The misogyny of Trump permeated through mainstream society throughout the 2016 presidential campaign, and yet, weeks before the election, a new level of intense misogyny would dominate and alter mainstream political dialogue throughout the United States. An audiotape surfaced of the Republican nominee for president, describing his behavior with women. Trump boasted about being in a position of power and engaging in acts consistent with violence, aggression, and sexual assault of women. Trump's infamous comment, "You can do anything. . . . Grab 'em by the pussy" was repeatedly broadcast on social media, mainstream news outlets, television news, and radio. Trump's denigration of women was dehumanizing, reducing women to their body parts. Trump dismissed his "pussy" comment (Barbaro and Twohey 2016) and defended his vile descriptions and personal admissions of sexual harassment as merely "locker room banter" (Fahrenthold 2016).

## Abolishing Protections for Victims of Gendered Violence

Aside from Donald Trump's misogynistic rhetoric, the revelations of sexual abuse and harassment of women, the Trump administration began taking legal measures that subverted the rights and safety of women. Donald Trump and his administration cut the budgets of federal agencies serving women, dismantled legal safeguards designed to protect women, and diminished protections against gender-based violence (O'Hara 2017). Furthermore, key positions in women's leadership posts were left vacant. For over a year after Trump took office, the Violence Against Women office at the US Justice Department was left without a director (Hohmann 2018).

Before even taking office, the Trump team advocated drastic budget cuts to the federal Violence Against Women program at the Department of Justice (Westcott 2017). According to The National Coalition Against Domestic Violence (NCADV), Trump's budget request for the Fiscal Year 2019 cut many critical programs for victims of domestic abuse. NCADV maintains that the Violence Against Women Act (VAWA) is funded at $100 million below the level authorized by Congress, despite the false claims made by the Trump administration that the VAWA is fully funded (NCADV 2018).

Aside from budget cuts to the federal Violence Against Women program, legal safeguards protecting women were dismantled. Within two months after taking office, Donald Trump signed an executive order revoking the Fair Pay and Safe Workplaces Act. One important part of the FPSW Act served to protect women in the workplace by ensuring that companies with federal contracts complied with 14 labor and civil rights laws and included a ban on forced arbitration clauses for sexual harassment, sexual assault, or discrimination claims (O'Hara 2017). The Trump administration's dismantling of the Fair Pay and Safe Workplaces Act now makes it easier for men to sexually harass women and keep it out of court and public records. Revoking the Fair Pay and Safe Workplaces Act allows federal contractors with chronic violations of sex discrimination to continue receiving federal funding.

As President Trump and his administration attacked programs designed to address violence against women and sexual assault in the workplace, protections against gender-based violence diminished. Without public announcement, the Department of Justice's Office on Violence Against Women quietly and significantly changed the definition of domestic violence. The definition change limits domestic violence to only include physical harm that constitutes a felony or misdemeanor (Nugent 2019). According to Oppenheim (2019), the change in definition can affect "millions of victims of gender-based violence." Forms of domestic violence that include psychological abuse and coercive control are no longer recognized as domestic violence. The Trump administration's campaign to eliminate rights is not limited to abolishing the protections of women who are victimized by sexual and gendered violence.

In addition, the Trump administration rescinded several sexual harassment protections for college students under Title IX. The Trump administration's new rules governing sexual assault on colleges created new barriers for victims to come forward and report sexual assault and "for most victims, eliminates the possibility altogether" (Bedera 2020). The changes not only create barriers to reporting, but the Trump administration also changed the definition of sexual harassment on college campuses to a narrow range of actions that must meet the criteria of being "severe, pervasive, and objectively offensive." The new definition reduces the number of cases universities can investigate and is putting students at greater risk of sexual harassment and assault (Bedera 2020). The Trump administration changes also allow educational institutions to require a greater burden of proof from victims when investigating cases. The Trump administration claims the changes will save money due to the reduction in the number of Title IX investigations. Weakening Title IX will only increase the problem with reporting sexual harassment or sexual assault on college campuses, especially for women who are reluctant to notify university officials because they fear they will not be believed.

## THE POLITICS OF ELIMINATING RIGHTS OF WOMEN AND MARGINALIZED GROUPS

As the Trump administration began scaling back regulations and protections for women victimized by sexual and gendered violence, federal policies designed to ensure and safeguard the rights of women and marginalized groups were systematically abolished through executive orders signed by Donald Trump. As a democracy, the United States protects the rights of its citizens by relying on a constitution and the establishment of three separate, yet equally powerful, branches of government. The Legislative Branch, consisting of both houses of Congress (the Senate and the House of Representatives), has the duty of making laws. The Judicial Branch, consisting of the Supreme Court, federal courts, and judges, has the duty of interpreting the constitutionality of laws. The Executive Branch, consisting of the president and cabinet members, has the duty of enforcing the law.

There is a small, yet precarious, area of ambiguity within Article II of the US Constitution. It comes in the form of "implied powers" that are entrusted to the president. The Constitution requires that presidents "take care that the laws be faithfully executed" and authorizes unspecific and ambiguous "executive power" to achieve the goal. Through the years, "executive power" has manifested through executive orders, signed directives from the president for the purpose of managing the administrative operations of the many departments in the federal government. The "implied powers" entrusted to a US president can provide a way for a president to autonomously bypass Congress and change federal policies (Blake 2017). Executive orders have the power of law, yet they are not classified as "legislation," which means that executive orders do not require approval from Congress, and Congress is basically powerless to overturn them (American Bar Association 2018). It is within this ambiguous area of "implied powers" that Donald Trump operates.

Within three months of his presidency, Donald Trump autonomously eliminated dozens of existing federal laws and policies with a signature. Nearly every executive order signed by Trump in his first year was designed to abolish existing rules and regulations put in place to protect individuals within society (Bump 2017). Seventy-seven executive actions were signed by Trump, including 29 executive orders (Cillizza and Petulla 2017; Freking 2019). With conduct described as "obsessed" (Blow 2017; Sinclair 2017; Wolf 2018), Trump dedicated himself to undoing the work of his predecessor (Sinclair 2017). As each executive order was systematically signed, protections for women and marginalized groups were rescinded, resulting in diminished rights and freedoms for women, members of the LGBTQ+ community, and young people with DACA (Deferred Action for Childhood Arrivals) status.

## Eliminating Rights of Women

In his first year in office, Donald Trump and his administration managed to destroy years of progress for women's rights and basic freedoms. Existing policies that were put in place to guard against gender inequality were eliminated while actions taken by the Trump administration imposed federal rules that further diminished the rights of women. Executive orders were signed, and policies aimed at protecting the rights of women were revoked, making it easier to discriminate based on gender, limit women's economic opportunities, eliminate women's access to basic health care, and diminish the reproductive rights of women. The politics of Trump were made very clear and resulted in a regression of a multitude of rights for women in just one year after taking office.

One of the first policies to be abolished by the Trump administration was the Fair Pay and Safe Workplaces Act. The Act protected women's economic opportunities in the workplace by requiring wage transparency. Trump eliminated the EEOC rule requiring large companies to disclose what they pay employees by sex, race, and ethnicity. The EEOC rule was intended to remedy unequal pay by ensuring that companies with federal contracts complied with the 14 established labor and civil rights laws. The labor and civil rights laws cannot be changed by Trump, but without the Fair Pay and Safe Workplaces Act, compliance by large companies is unchecked. With his signature, Trump made it easier for employers to discriminate based on gender, resulting in limiting the economic potential of women in the workplace (O'Hara 2017).

In a move that has negative impacts on women's health as well as women's finances, the Trump administration has undermined the Affordable Care Act's existing birth control benefit. Trump's new rules allow employers to opt out of contraception coverage, a basic health care need for women that was explicitly mandated by the Affordable Care Act. Daniels and Mosher (2013) have compiled extensive data to determine that "virtually all women" who had ever had sexual intercourse have used at least one contraceptive in their lifetime (99 percent). Contraceptives are among the most widely used medical services in the United States and provide the ability for women to plan their pregnancies (Jones et al. 2012). Numerous studies have determined that the access and use of contraceptives have had significant positive outcomes for women and their families. Access to contraception has been associated with higher wages for women (Bailey et al. 2012) and with lower rates of poverty, particularly in households headed by single women (Browne and LaLumia 2014). The Trump administration's new rules permit employers to legally discriminate against women and eliminate a basic health care need for women that not only has repercussions to women's health but to women's finances.

## Eliminating Rights of Young People with DACA Status

One of the most complicated issues involving immigration involves young adults who were brought into the United States as infants and young children without proper documentation. Raised as Americans and integrated into schools and communities, many of these young people were unaware that they did not have legal documents to work, go to college, or stay in the United States. In 2012, an immigration program called DACA, Deferred Action for Childhood Arrivals, was initiated to address the immigration situation of individuals who arrived as minors, were raised as Americans, and identify as Americans. The program allowed these young people to apply for DACA, which did not grant citizenship, but officially recognized these individuals within the United States, offered protection from deportation, the ability to work, and eventually provided a pathway to citizenship through several possibilities, including military service. DACA recipients were vetted; no one with either a felony or "significant misdemeanor" was eligible to apply for DACA. As of June 2019, there were 652,880 active DACA recipients, with more than 80 percent born in Mexico and entered the United States as infants or small children (MPI 2019).

Throughout Donald Trump's presidential campaign, his prejudice and antagonistic views of Mexicans were publicly proclaimed in countless racist and xenophobic remarks. Using Mexican immigrants as scapegoats, Trump consistently attacked Mexicans with false and fabricated evidence, referring to Mexicans in crude, degrading, and offensive terms, and blamed them for America's crime and economic problems. Not surprising was Trump's focus on illegal immigration and promises of "deporting all of them" (Park and Griggs 2017).

Once in office, Trump ordered aggressive enforcement of immigration laws, including legally defining immigrants as "criminals" (Shear and Nixon 2017), and proposed "migrants to be immediately deported without a trial" (Silva 2018). Trump's extreme policies regarding illegal immigration were predictable based on racist statements made during his presidential campaign. Trump's determination to eradicate DACA, an existing and fully functional immigration program, resulted in "an unprecedented act in U.S. history" where a generation of young people, who were part of the DACA program and have only known the United States as their home, were stripped of their official recognition and deported to a country where many had little or no familiarity.

In September of 2017, Trump's Justice Department announced the end of DACA and began deporting DACA recipients, many of whom had never been to Mexico, did not speak Spanish, nor have any family members in Mexico. The average age when DACA recipients entered the United States was three years old. In June of 2020, the US Supreme Court blocked the Trump administration from immediately terminating DACA (Montoya-Galvez 2020). On November 16, 2020, Montoya-Galvez (2020) reported:

> Judge Nicholas Garaufis of the U.S. District Court in Brooklyn found that Wolf was "not lawfully serving" as acting secretary of the Department of Homeland

> Security (DHS) when he issued a memo limiting the protections of more than 640,000 current Deferred Action for Childhood Arrivals (DACA) beneficiaries and indefinitely closing the program to new applicants.

The November 2020 decision was a win for those individuals that have aged into adulthood during the Trump presidency and have been waiting years to apply for DACA status.

## Eliminating Rights of LGBTQ+ Individuals

While it is difficult to compare the anguish and substantial harms resulting from the discriminatory elimination of legal rights and protections, perhaps no other group was more blindsided by Trump's attacks than members of the LGBTQ+ community. Supporters of Trump within the LGBTQ+ community were encouraged by his repeated messages of allegiance. The community witnessed, along with the rest of America, the explicit pledges to protect LGBTQ+ individuals made by Donald Trump throughout the presidential campaign. In fact, Trump was seen as "embracing" the LGBTQ+ community in ways that were not only "loud and proud," but historic for a Republican candidate (Grenell 2016). In a grand move, to very publicly demonstrate his devotion to the LGBTQ+ community, Donald Trump did something at the 2016 Republican National Convention that no other Republican presidential nominee had ever done in the history of the party. "Donald Trump made history with an explicit pledge to protect LGBTQ+ people during his speech accepting the GOP presidential nomination" (Johnson 2016; Beckwith 2016). It was the first time in history that a Republican presidential nominee included and addressed the LGBTQ+ community in a positive way while accepting the nomination. It was not surprising then, to see Donald Trump in the presidential campaign holding up a rainbow flag with the words: "LGBTs for Trump," and proudly parading around the stage in front of thousands at a Colorado rally just days before the election (Gutierrez-Morfin 2016).

And then came the betrayal. With an inconceivable swiftness, Donald Trump denounced the LGBTQ+ community with attacks that began moments after being sworn into the presidency. Despite all his displays of rainbow flags and repeated pronouncements declaring himself a "pro-LGBT" candidate during the 2016 campaign, Donald Trump has secured his position as the most overtly anti-LGBTQ+ president in the history of the United States.

Through executive orders and covert policy changes within government agencies, the Trump administration began a campaign against LGTBQ+ Americans. Official mention of the LGBTQ+ community was eliminated throughout the federal government (Capatides 2017). Trump himself initiated a ban that discriminated against these individuals (Hirschfeld and Cooper

2017), while the administration began systematically eliminating established rights from the LGBTQ+ community. The elimination of established legal rights not only endangered the lives of people but created and permitted the ability for anyone to legally discriminate against individuals within the community. Most disturbing, however, through pernicious actions that extend far beyond discrimination, the Trump administration is attempting to legally deny the existence of the transgender community in the United States (Woodstock 2018).

The first attack came quietly and without publicity. On the day of Donald Trump's inauguration, in an unprecedented move, the acknowledgment of an entire demographic of US citizens was eliminated from US government websites. "Moments" after Donald Trump took the oath of office, the entire page devoted to LGBT rights disappeared from the White House website (Capatides 2017). The Department of Labor removed a report on LGBT workers' rights from its website (Itkowitz 2017). This was only the beginning of the Trump administration's attack on the LGBTQ+ community.

The second major attack on the LGBTQ+ community came on the morning of July 26, 2017. The attack was startlingly brazen and came in the form of three "tweets" from Donald Trump, who autonomously decided to ban transgender individuals from serving in the military (Hirschfeld and Cooper 2017). Trump claimed that he made the decision "after consultation with my Generals and military experts" (Phillip, Gibbons-Neff and DeBonis 2017). However, the Joint Chiefs of Staff and Chairman General Joseph Dunford had no idea that the president would make such a decision on his own. The ban blindsided the Pentagon (Starr, Cohen, and Sciutto 2017). Former US Navy secretary Raymond Mabus, Jr., criticized Trump's autonomous reversal of a policy that was developed with consensus at the highest levels of military leadership and stated, "It's a bigoted policy. It has not one shred of evidence behind it" (Gaouette 2019). Republican senator John McCain, who was serving as the chairman of the Senate Armed Services Committee at the time, formally criticized Trump's decision and the manner in which it was done (Phillip, Gibbons-Neff and DeBonis 2017). Defense Secretary Jim Mattis was on vacation when Trump's tweet went viral. Mattis was "appalled" by Trump's behavior in announcing his ban by tweet, with complete disregard for transgender active-duty service members, including those deployed overseas (Hirschfeld and Cooper 2017).

The third attack on the LGBTQ+ community has been an extensive and methodic endeavor to abolish established rights from individuals. Systematically, the Trump administration began eliminating federal policies that protected the civil rights of individuals in the transgender community. In a move described as "reckless and cruel," Trump abolished protections for transgender students, denying them the right to use the bathroom that corresponds with their gender (Peters, Becker, Davis 2017). Established research has confirmed that "restrictive policies draw unwanted negative attention to trans and gender-nonbinary teens" (Bracho-Sanchez 2019). Murchison, Agenor, Reisner, and Watson (2019) found that transgender and gender-non-binary teens with restricted bathroom or locker room access are at a greater risk of sexual assault in schools. Among the transgender and gender-non-binary teens with restricted bathroom or locker room access, 35 percent reported being sexually assaulted within a 12-month period (Fitzsimons 2019; Murchison et al. 2019).

The next attack on the LGBTQ+ community might be the most disturbing and extend beyond discrimination as the Trump administration attempted to legally deny the existence of the transgender community. In October of 2018, the Trump administration began efforts to legally change the definition of "gender" to a biological and unchangeable condition determined at birth, a definition with absolutely no basis in science (Woodstock 2018). The acknowledgment that biological characteristics differentiate from the social or psychological distinctions has been an accepted principle throughout the scientific community for decades. Since the 1960s, the term "sex" has been employed to exemplify biological traits, and "gender" has been used to distinguish the amount of femininity and masculinity exhibited by a person (Robert Stoller 1968). However, gender is now recognized as an identity construct independent of biology (Torgrimson and Minson 2005). Trump's attempts to redefine the scientific definition of gender contradicts all scientific evidence prompting over 1,600 scientists, including nine Nobel Prize winners, 700 biologists, and over 100 geneticists, to sign a letter condemning Trump's definition of gender as being "in no way 'grounded in science' as the administration claims" (BBC News 2018).

In a memo dispersed among the Departments of Education, Justice, Health and Human Services and Labor, the government agencies were requested to adopt the new definition of "gender" since it would "establish uniformity in the government and increase the likelihood that courts will accept it" (Green, Benner, Pear 2018). The Trump administration's contrived definition of "gender" essentially excludes and disregards an entire population of people, permitting the federal government to eliminate the legal, economic, and social rights of transgender Americans.

The elimination of rights through policy changes enacted by Trump and his administration served as a major attack on the LGBTQ+ community based on discrimination. The disturbing efforts of the Trump administration to legally deny the existence of transgender individuals is not only a contradiction of Trump's campaign promises, but it is also antithetical to the US Constitution. The Trump agenda regarding LGBTQ+ individuals is grounded in efforts that seek to remove acknowledgment of the community from the attention of the US government, resulting in the harmful elimination of rights.

An ecofeminist analysis of Trump's policies regarding the LGBTQ+ community reveals an oppressive conceptual framework that authorizes a "logic of domination" (Warren 2000). The oppression that justifies domination has its roots in the rationalism of hierarchically organized value dualisms (Plumwood 1991). Trump's federal policy changes to the definition of gender attempt to redefine what it means to be "fully and authentically human" by imposing an either/or dualism of sex/gender. Similar to dualisms such as woman/man or human/nature, the dualisms of sex/gender exist to create a hierarchical structure that is in opposition to each other and where one is valued higher over the other (Warren 2000). "A dualistically construed dichotomy typically polarizes difference and minimizes shared characteristics, construes difference along lines of superiority/inferiority, and views the inferior side as a means to the higher ends of the superior side" (Plumwood 1991: 17). Plumwood (1991) suggests that an effective strategy for challenging dualisms involves recognition of the excluded qualities, those qualities that are denied or "construed as alien" (17) by the dominant oppressor as justification for domination.

## HUMAN RIGHTS VIOLATIONS OF THE TRUMP ADMINISTRATION

One of the most famous pronouncements of human rights can be found in the United States' Declaration of Independence. The conviction that all men are created equal and endowed with "unalienable rights" was articulated by the founders and has become the measure by which we evaluate American freedoms. The United Nations defines human rights as: "rights inherent to all human beings, regardless of race, sex, nationality, ethnicity, language, religion, or any other status" and affirms the obligation of all governments to promote and protect the human rights of all individuals, without discrimination. From the time he took office, Donald Trump and his administration have taken extensive and pernicious actions that violate human rights and enacted policies that are illegal under international human rights law.

With innumerable executive orders, Trump has implemented federal policy changes that target individuals from non-white countries are based on discrimination of nationality and religion and feed into Trump's xenophobic rhetoric while reinforcing his false narrative of immigrants and refugees as criminals and terrorists. In the process, Trump and his administration have violated human rights through the persecution of immigrants and their children, racist policies based on religion, and causing further victimization of refugees.

## The Persecution of Immigrants and their Children

Human rights were not at the forefront as Donald Trump announced his bid for the presidency with a series of shocking and racist comments about immigrants from the Mexican border (Reilly 2016). Immigration policy became the primary issue in Trump's presidential campaign, despite a continuous ten-year decline of undocumented immigrants in the United States with the lowest level in over a decade (Markon 2016; Passel and Cohn 2018). The Trump administration manifested his racist dogmatism in an aggressive and inhumane policy designed to control the immigration of Mexican and Latinx American migrants by forcibly seizing their children as a deterrent.

In April 2018, the Trump administration issued a policy that branded immigrants without proper documentation as "criminals" (Kates 2018) and imposed mandatory criminal detention for all, despite outcries from human rights advocates and proclamations from the United Nations Human Rights spokeswoman Ravina Shamdasani, who maintained that the United States "should not be criminalizing what is an administrative offense of irregular entry or stay" (Nebehay 2018; Rizzo 2018 ).

Consistent with the conceptualization of gendered violence inherent in white male supremacy (discussed earlier in this chapter), the Trump administration's "zero tolerance" immigration policy was based on inflicting terror onto parents and trauma to their children. Fueled by Donald Trump's numerous episodes of racists "hate speech" directed at Mexican migrants (Reilly 2016), the Trump administration designed a plan to control migrants by causing severe emotional harm that they believed would be effective in accomplishing their goals in reducing immigration to the United States (Carranza and Gonzalez 2018). Acting Secretary of Homeland Security, John Kelly, confirmed reports almost immediately after Trump was elected that the administration was planning to seize and forcibly separate immigrant children from their parents as a way to deter illegal immigration (Diaz 2017). Kelly defended the policy of separating children from their parents, stating, "The children will be taken care of—put into foster care or whatever" (NPR 2018).

Attorney General Jeff Sessions directed federal prosecutors, along the US border from Texas to California, to make immigration cases a higher priority. In turn, Kelly was urged to refer "one hundred percent" of all detained immigrants to federal prosecutors, "including those initially arriving or apprehended with minors" (Sacchetti 2018). The administration completely disregarded the fact that many migrants from the southern border are families with young children who travel together seeking asylum (Bump 2019) from the increasing violence in Central America (Nebehay 2018). This goes against the international law that was ratified by the United States in 1968

(United Nations 1968) that protects the rights of asylum seekers and prohibits punishment based on illegal entry.

Immigrants were branded as "criminals" and were sent to federal US attorneys for prosecution. Sessions instructed each US attorney to seek "felony charges," even suggesting charging immigrants with "aggravated identity theft, which carries a mandatory two-year prison sentence" (Zapotosky and Horwitz 2017). As adult immigrants entering the United States without proper documents were immediately arrested and jailed, the children of the immigrants, who had traveled to the United States with their parents, were then officially (and unethically) designated as "unaccompanied minors," allowing government officials to forcibly seize their children, toddlers, and infants (Almukhtar, Patel, Watkins and Yourish 2018).

The children were placed in detention centers at the border under the federal custody of the Office of Refugee Resettlement, a program within the Department of Health and Human Services. According to legal court documents, the children were kept in caged sections in detention centers with filthy conditions and poor treatment (Taxin 2018) before being sent thousands of miles away to various shelters across the United States (Almukhtar et al. 2018). This practice was in violation of federal guidelines limiting the detention of children to 72 hours—based on studies linking child and parent separation to severe, long-lasting trauma (Almukhtar et al. 2018). The Trump administration's immigration policy from 2017 to 2018 resulted in an estimate of more than 5,400 children being forcibly separated from their parents (DaSilva 2019).

The exact number of immigrant children seized from their parents is unknown since the Department of Homeland Security never had a database nor a proper tracking system with information for both parents and their children, indicating that reuniting the children with their parents was never planned (Soboroff 2019). The Trump immigration policy at the southern border shocked the United Nations as they described the policy as "unconscionable" and "government-sanctioned child abuse"(Cumming-Brice 2018).

As part of a United Nations global update, the Trump policy was reported as a "cruel practice" of deterring immigrating parents by inflicting abuse on their children, producing "irreparable harm" and "lifelong consequences" (United Nations 2018). The United Nations condemned the Trump immigration policy and declared that the policy of separating immigrant children from their parents is a violation of human rights and international law (Cumming-Bruce 2018). The Trump administration was responsible for inflicting "known trauma and lasting negative effects" (Caty 2019) on thousands of children, the majority of whom were under the age of ten (Robbins 2018).

Human rights advocates fought to reunite parents with their children. On June 26, 2018, a nationwide injunction ordered the end of family separation and ordered reunification (Campbell and Gage 2018; Dickerson 2018). Because of the covert nature of the family separation policy (Dickerson 2020), reunification was intensely problematic, if not impossible. As of October 21, 2020, the parents of 545 children had not been reached (Dickerson 2020). Trump's term in office would end with hundreds of immigrant children lost in the system.

## Racist Policies Based on Religion

Donald Trump's violations of human rights have not been limited to immigrants at the southern border. Similar to Trump's "criminal narrative" used to enact a racist immigration policy, Trump espoused a "terrorist narrative" toward Muslim people in the United States and abroad and used this narrative to justify another racist policy. From the beginning of Donald Trump's presidential campaign, he advocated for a "total and complete shutdown of Muslims entering the United States" (Johnson 2015). Promoting racist views and fabricated evidence, Trump suggested surveillance on mosques and establishing a database for all Muslims living in the United States.

On January 27, 2017, Trump signed an executive order that violated the basic rights of individuals and implemented a ban on travelers based on their religion. Individuals from seven Muslim-majority countries (Iran, Iraq, Libya, Somalia, Sudan, and Yemen) were immediately banned from entering the United States. Consistent with his racist views, Trump named the executive order, "Protecting the Nation from Foreign Terrorist Entry into the United States." The ban immediately had detrimental effects not only on people who had a legal right to enter the United States but on all people who practice Islam. The wording of the ban served to promote Islamophobia and feed into Trump's false narratives describing all immigrants from Muslim countries as terrorists, despite the evidence that not one individual from any of the banned countries was involved in a terrorist attack on US soil in more than 18 years.

In fact, none of the 13 terrorists engaged in the fatal attacks in America on 9/11 were from any of the countries listed on the ban (Martinovich 2017; Ravesz 2017). The executive order excluded all three countries connected with the 9/11 attacks. Saudi Arabia, the United Arab Emirates, and Egypt, the countries of origin for every one of the nineteen al-Qaeda members, are countries where Trump has strong "long-standing" ties to his personal business (Fahrenthold and O'Connell 2018; Geewax and Martin 2017). A panel of human rights experts from the United Nations has described Trump's Muslim ban as a violation of international human rights obligations (Berman 2017).

## Victimizing Refugees

Throughout his campaign and into his presidency, Trump has consistently and publicly made offensive and racist comments about non-white immigrants. The Trump administration's policies have not only violated human rights but have further victimized refugees. In January of 2018, a group of bipartisan lawmakers met in the Oval Office to discuss protecting immigrants from Haiti, El Salvador, and African countries, to which Trump responded, "Why are we having all the people from s***hole countries come here?" (Scott 2018). This was not the only racist comment made at that meeting as Trump suggested that the United States should "bring more people from countries such as Norway" and that he would consider having more immigrants from Asian countries since "he felt that they help the United States economically" (Scott 2018). Although lawmakers in the room were "taken aback" by the president's racist and offensive comments, the White House never renounced Trump's remarks. Trump's racist views were defended by a White House spokesman in a statement claiming that "Trump will always fight for the American people" and that Trump is "fighting for permanent solutions that make our country stronger by welcoming those who can contribute to our society, grow our economy and assimilate into our great nation" (Dawsey 2018).

Months earlier, Trump had already revoked protections for Haitians from an existing humanitarian program. In 1990, George H.W. Bush signed into law "The Temporary Protected Status program." When in 2010, a devastating earthquake destroyed much of the country in Haiti, 60,000 Haitians were granted Temporary Protected Status, allowing them to live and work in the United States. Trump revoked their status and protections, and Haitians were told to leave or face deportation (Dawsey 2018).

Trump further victimized Syrian refugees with an executive order implemented to ban them. Trump justified the ban on Syrian refugees with his terrorist narrative, despite the fact that "no Syrian refugee had even been charged with the intent to carry out an attack on US soil in more than four decades" (Ravesz 2017). Trump continued his banning of certain people from entry to the United States by suspending all US refugee programs. Based on US law, refugees are people who have been forced to flee their country due to the violence of war or persecution and are of special humanitarian concern to the United States. They are protected under international law. To reject refugees who cannot return to their countries violates human rights. Historically, the United States led the world in accepting refugees and assisting with their resettlement until Trump was elected.

## CONCLUSION

The anti-ecofeminist views, policies, and actions of Donald Trump and his administration have resulted in the denigration of women and minoritized groups. This ecofeminist analysis examined the various multidimensional social ecosystems in which race, class, gender, immigration status, national origin, and place/displacement are intertwined. The dramatic social and political shift that culminated with the election of Donald Trump in 2016 reveals the disruptions caused by mainstreaming hate, "normalizing" misogyny, eliminating protections for victims of sexual and gendered violence, eliminating the rights of women and marginalized groups and the violation of human rights. The harm that Trump and his administration have caused to global social ecosystems is only matched by the harm that has taken place to environmental ecosystems. In the Trump administration, the denigration of women and marginalized groups extended to the denigration of the environment. The next chapter continues with an ecofeminist analysis of environmental justice and the exploitation of the environment.

## *Chapter 4*

# Environmental Justice and the Exploitation of the Environment

Women have often been at the forefront in striving to protect the environment and understanding the negative impacts of environmental degradation (Mies and Shiva 1993/2014). Environmental activist work has been initiated and accomplished by Black women, indigenous women, and women of color, who many times live and work in communities overly burdened by toxic industries and environmental hazards (Gomez, Shafiei, and Johnson 2011). The capitalistic drive toward the exploitation of natural resources is intimately connected to the degradation of nature, women, minoritized groups, and people of color. Ecofeminist scholars have established the link between the oppression of the environment and the oppression of women. Numerous ecofeminist studies have provided overwhelming evidence that environmental hazards resulting from the exploitation of the environment disproportionately affect "the health of women and children, particularly in poor communities of color" (Warren 2000: 10).

Sociologist Dorceta Taylor (1997) maintains that the intersectionality of racism and sexism has left women of color disproportionately carrying the burden of environmental hazards. An analysis of the oppression experienced by minoritized groups, in regard to the negative impacts of environmental degradation, focuses on intersectionality and the links to interrelated "isms of domination" (Warren 2000). These systems of oppression—racism, sexism, classism, and colonialism—serve to mutually reinforce other oppressions, resulting in the current and ongoing global environmental crisis (Gaard and Gruen 1993).

The shift in the dominant social and political ideology toward unrestrained and unregulated exploitation of the environment contributed to the surge in women's political activism. Environmental issues were a major focus at the 2017 Women's March. Climate change, environmental degradation, and environmental justice were identified as key issues calling women to get politically involved. Additionally, all of the successful women candidates new to Congress and elected in the 2018 Midterm elections presented a platform addressing many of the environmental concerns emphasized at the march.

The actions and the policies of the Trump administration have resulted in substantial environmental damage, an increase in toxic pollution, and an increase in human health risks and death. This chapter documents the strategies used by the Trump administration to undermine the EPA and the established protections for the environment and humans from hazardous environmental pollution. This chapter also examines the ways racism, sexism, and colonialism have left minoritized groups struggling for environmental justice. The chapter begins with a review of human domination over the environment, examining human impacts on nature, the effect of capitalism, and the attempts to change course through the environmental movement and the creation of the Environmental Protection Agency. The second section examines the Trump administration's politics of environmental exploitation and the strategies used to achieve unrestrained and unregulated environmental exploitation. This section examines Trump's anti-environmental propaganda based on a war against science, the tactics used to take control of the EPA, and the executive orders that permitted an escalation of damage to land, water, and air. In the final section, attention is given to the significant harms suffered by individuals and communities from environmental degradation and pollution caused by the policies of the Trump administration and the struggle for environmental justice facing people of color and indigenous people. The final section also documents the Standing Rock Protests that began in 2016, focusing on indigenous women that serve as water protectors. The gathering of thousands of protestors and the police brutality that was experienced by indigenous protestors will be presented as a foreshadowing of the showdown between Black Lives protestors in Portland and Minneapolis and police forces during Black Lives Matter movements in 2020.

## DOMINATION OF THE ENVIRONMENT: HUMAN IMPACTS, CAPITALISM, AND THE ENVIRONMENTAL MOVEMENT

No animal on earth has harmed the planet the way humans have. The pollution caused by human activity continues to have devastating consequences to the animal kingdom, the ecosystems that keep the planet healthy, and to humans themselves. The most destructive human impacts on the environment have been motivated and justified by capitalism. The exploitation of the environment for capitalistic goals has resulted in the unethical destruction of nature and toxic harm to humans and animals. This section examines the human impacts on the environment and the ways capitalism has increased and intensified human domination over the environment. This section also includes the attempts to protect the environment and humans from the deadly hazards of pollution through the environmental movement and the creation of the Environmental Protection Agency. The analysis provides a background of the dominant social and political ideology toward the environment before Trump, and his administration ignited an extreme shift in ideology toward increased exploitation, prompting women, indigenous people, people of color, and other minoritized groups to become political activists seeking social change and protection of the environment.

## Human Impacts on the Environment

The human impact of control over earth's "biological, chemical, and geological processes" and the depletion of earth's natural resources has been "unofficially" called the "Anthropocene" epoch (Crutzen 2006; Crutzen and Schwägerl 2011). That is, human activity in the last two hundred years has changed the climate and nature of our planet in significant and detrimental ways. The Anthropocene era is characterized by human activity focused on controlling nature through technological advancement, land use/abuse, deforestation, mountain top blasting, fracking, burning fossil fuels, biotechnological manipulation, and limiting biodiversity through monoculture agriculture. These human activities have endangered our ecosystems within natural environments and within built environments and societies. The human impacts on the environment have negatively affected the existence of animals and plants. A profound number of animal species, including birds and bees, and vegetation, have gone extinct or are identified as endangered. Additionally, many species that have yet to be identified may likely become endangered or extinct.

The increase in frequency and intensity of natural disasters have been linked to human impacts on the environment. Pollution caused by human activity has resulted in global climate change. The change in global climate over the past twenty years has steadily escalated the yearly number of hurricanes, tornados, droughts, and wildfires. The increased intensity of natural disasters in recent years has generated some of the most destructive and deadliest disasters in history. The resulting aftermath of extreme and unprecedented weather events caused by climate change has left natural environments and built environments destroyed and include the unimaginable and massive loss of human life. In 2018, the American Meteorological Society identified 15 extreme weather events in 2017 that were directly due to human-caused climate change.

## Capitalism and the Domination of Nature

One of the most popular television commercials ever created addressed the issue of environmental pollution. An anti-litter organization, Keep America Beautiful, produced the 1971 advertisement and is ranked as one of the best commercials of all time (Dunaway 2017). The ad was so popular that it was replayed throughout the 1970s and replicated on billboards and print ads. The commercial featured an Italian-American actor, dressed in traditional Native American attire (Dunaway 2017). The character encounters a polluted lake and landscape before ending up with trash on his moccasins when a paper bag and fast-food wrappers are thrown out of the window of a passing car. As the actor looks into the camera, a single tear falls gently down his face, while the narrator admonishes the viewer: "People start pollution. People can stop it." The ad became a symbol of environmental idealism for many Americans. In reality, the commercial was a deceptive scheme orchestrated by capitalistic industry polluters. Keep America Beautiful was a front organization created and controlled by leading beverage and packaging corporations that actively fought against environmental legislation. The commercial served as a form of capitalistic propaganda to shift the responsibility of environmental pollution from corporations, placing it entirely on individual actions.

The 1971 award-winning commercial is just one example of the ways corporations have dominated environment policy. The strategy of the "anti-pollution" advertisement was clear: control public perceptions about environmental issues while working to obstruct the ability to protect the environment behind the scenes. The successful strategy used in 1971 is indistinguishable from Trump's 2016 approach to dominating the environment. This section analyzes capitalism's domination of the environment for profit, providing a brief historical background of capitalistic exploitation that would become the hallmark of the Trump administration.

The environmental impacts of capitalism are the result of human domination of the environment. Ecofeminist researchers Shiva and Mies (1993) explain that patriarchal societies have an inherent compulsion to dominate. The domination of nature in pursuit of capitalistic goals includes plundering natural resources for unequally distributed economic gain. Human dominance over the environment has resulted in significant and detrimental harms to our planet and to individuals belonging to minoritized groups. A brief historical background on capitalism's interaction with the environment reveals the influence of the scientific revolution and the industrial revolution on capitalism's drive toward human control and oppression of the environment.

The scientific revolution was a period of drastic change in scientific thought. Abstract reasoning and developments in physics, chemistry, mathematics, and biology transformed the ways people understood and viewed the world. Carolyn Merchant (1993) explains that the scientific revolution changed society's understanding of the natural environment and how humans regarded nature. Once viewed with reverence and respect, nature became perceived as an entity that could be mastered and dominated.

The realization of human domination over the environment began in the late 1700s with the industrial revolution. Advances in manufacturing transformed societies and economies while producing significant impacts on the environment. American society became structured on multiple industries' capitalistic goals as the development of the steam engine led to the mechanized production of goods in mass quantities. Rural agricultural communities with economies based on handmade goods and agriculture were abandoned for life in urban cities with large factories based on an economy of industrialized manufacturing. Innovations in the production of textiles, iron, and steel provided increased profits to private companies. Simultaneously, those industries exerted authority over the environment and began dumping hazardous by-products in public lands and waterways. As capitalism drove the domination over the environment, the results have led to devastating negative impacts on nature, animals, and humans.

The impact of capitalism and its dominance over the environment is toxic pollution that has denigrated the environment, caused health risks and death. American culture based on constant consumption has resulted in environmental waste from multiple industries, most notably the fast fashion industry, petroleum industry, and the agricultural industry: clothes, plastics, and animal waste from mass agricultural production litter the planet. The over-consumption of chicken and beef is responsible for significant health issues such as obesity, diabetes, and heart disease. Further, the consumption of animals generates a tremendous amount of water, land, and air pollution. Animals destined for slaughter are regularly given antibiotics and hormones that eventually enter and pollute water and soil environments, which are also polluted by fertilizers and pesticides used in forage production, the plants eaten by livestock that remove more nutrients from the soil than other crops. In addition to the excessive amount of water and land pollution, hundreds of harmful gases, including 80 percent of ammonia emissions, have polluted the air and are caused by animal excreta from the production of animals for consumption. While household garbage has contributed to the pollution of land, water, and air, the preponderance of harmful pollution is the result of corporations and their industrial waste.

## The Emergence of the Environmental Movement

In 1962, scientist and feminist Rachel Carson's *Silent Spring* became a worldwide bestseller, igniting a global environmental movement. Carson addressed the detrimental effects that humans have had on the natural world, explicitly focusing on the production and use of hazardous and toxic pesticides. In combination with an abundance of scientific evidence, Carson's engaging writing style provided the public with a heightened awareness of environmental pollution and its detrimental effects, including the dangerous health risks to humans and animals and the environmental damage caused by chemical manufacturers in the United States. Carson called into question the authority of scientific experts tied to chemical manufacturers' private interests and profits.

The impact of Rachel Carson's *Silent Spring* not only resulted in greater awareness of environmental issues, but Rachel Carson and her detailed research affected government policy. In 1963, Carson appeared before a Senate subcommittee to share her research on toxic chemicals used in the United States and their impact on humans and the environment. Carson not only reported the data but presented her recommendations for policy changes that she had been working on for the previous five years (Griswold 2012). Due to *Silent Spring* and the efforts of Rachel Carson, DDT and every toxic chemical named in her book were banned or severely restricted (Griswold 2012). *Silent Spring* ignited a global environmental movement that caused individuals throughout the United States to become increasingly more attentive to their surroundings, particularly polluted areas.

By 1970, the environmental movement started vigorously addressing pollution issues and the depletion of non-renewable resources. At the time, no legal or regulatory policies existed in the United States to prevent or limit industries' unrestrained dumping of hazardous pollution into the environment. The lack of a national environmental, political agenda motivated US Senator Gaylord Nelson to create Earth Day to educate the public about the environment and position ecological issues on the national agenda. The first global Earth Day, April 22, 1970, initiated a movement of global activism. The awareness of environmental issues that began with *Silent Spring* would eventually result in the creation of an independent government agency dedicated to protecting the environment and humans from environmental pollution.

## The Environmental Protection Agency

The Environmental Protection Agency (EPA) was created in response to heightened public concern for environmental pollution addressed in *Silent Spring* and an almost unbelievable environmental disaster in 1969: a major river running through the middle of Cleveland caught on fire and exploded into flames. Environmental pollution became an issue that could no longer be ignored. The Cuyahoga River was polluted for years with sewage, oil-soaked debris, and industrial waste. The Cuyahoga was known to have absolutely no visible signs of life, not even sludge worms. While it was not the first time an industrial river had exploded into flames, the 1969 burning of the Cuyahoga brought attention to unregulated dumping that contaminated nearly every river in major metropolitan areas throughout the United States (Latson 2015).

The Environmental Protection Agency was established in December of 1970 "in the wake of elevated concern about environmental pollution" (EPA.gov). The Environmental Protection Agency was entrusted with the crucial purpose of protecting both the environment and the health of the public from environmental hazards. The EPA is responsible for maintaining and enforcing national standards in regard to pollution levels. The most significant tool used by the EPA is the creation of regulations that are based on scientific research conducted by EPA scientists establishing links between pollution and human health risks. The EPA oversees standard-setting, monitoring, and the enforcement of regulations. The EPA is also charged with enforcing federal laws passed by Congress that deal with protecting the environment, including the Clean Air Act, the Clean Water Act, the Endangered Species Act, Pollution Prevention Act, Occupational Safety & Health Act (OSHA), and the Safe Drinking Water Act. In 1972, regulatory authority over the nation's water bodies was granted to the EPA and the Army Corps of Engineers.

The year 2020 marked the 50th anniversary of the EPA and the first Earth Day, celebrated each year globally on April 22. The environmental movement has continued to advocate for environmental protections, encourage environmental awareness, support recycling, and promote green technologies and renewable energy sources. The EPA, in turn, prevented the unregulated dumping of hazardous toxic waste into the environment until the election of Donald Trump.

According to past directors of the EPA, representing both Republican and Democratic administrations, the EPA's mission and core duties have been undermined by Donald Trump. Christine Todd Whitman, former Republican EPA director during the George W. Bush administration, testified to Congress, "I'm deeply concerned that five decades of environmental progress are at risk because of the attitude and approach of the current administration" (Grandoni and Dennis 2019). The attitude of the Trump administration is clearly grounded in the exploitation of the environment for capitalistic gain; the approach of the administration focused on restricting the EPA's ability to protect the environment and public health. Since the standards set by the EPA are based strictly on evidence from scientific research, Trump's strategy began with attacks on scientific evidence.

## THE POLITICS OF ENVIRONMENTAL EXPLOITATION

When Donald Trump famously tweeted that climate change was a "hoax" created by the Chinese (Wong 2016), it was a precursor to his role in perpetuating racism against Asians and producing a clear shift in the political and social ideology regarding environmental issues. The 2016 presidential campaign and presidency of Donald Trump resulted in a drastic adjustment of environmental priorities in the United States. Environmental concerns were pushed aside for the potential capital gains that could be reaped from exploiting the environment (e.g., the fracking industry and the plans for the Dakota pipeline). The Trump administration promoted federal environmental policy with rhetoric and priorities grounded in the rejection of existing and overwhelming scientific evidence about serious environmental problems and the dire consequences those policies had on humans, animals, and the planet. As the new dominant perspective toward environmental destruction began to take hold, the progression from ideology to federal policy faced an obstacle: the Environmental Protection Agency.

As an independent federal agency, the EPA operates outside of the Executive Office of the President in order to monitor and enforce regulations that restrict the amount and types of pollution that companies discharge into the environment. The EPA operates with congressional authority to create legal regulations that are based strictly on standards established by scientific research findings, not politics. While Trump did not have the authority to abolish the EPA, the tactics employed by Trump and his administration effectively stripped the federal agency of its ability to protect the environment and the public from environmental hazards. Without oversight from the EPA, executive orders authorized the use of public lands and lands belonging to indigenous people to pursue projects that resulted in extensive environmental destruction, an escalation of toxic pollution, and a significant and increase of human health risks and deaths. The extreme shift toward the politics of environmental exploitation is examined through Trump's war on science, the takeover of the EPA, and the resulting and drastic changes to environmental protection policies. The increased levels of pollution in the land, water, and air due to the Trump administration's dominance over the environment resulted in vast human costs. The final section examines the increase of human health risks and the death toll resulting from the Trump administration's policies on air pollution.

### The War on Science

Donald Trump's war on science became evident during the course of the 2016 presidential campaign. Trump directly propagated falsehoods about environmental issues in campaign speeches and through Twitter. Acknowledged for fabricating and disseminating thousands of completely false or misleading claims since taking the oath of office, Trump's attacks on the environment have transformed into attacks on verified facts and scientific evidence (Rose and Bartoli 2019). Trump's behavior has been characterized by the scientific community as a "War on Science" (Krauss 2016; Chen 2017; Green 2017; Benen 2018; Merritt Johns and Levy 2019; Relman 2019) and "scientific oppression" (Tonko and Schatz 2019). Terms such as "alternative facts" have been consistently used by Trump and have come to be recognized as "claims that do not conform to objective reality" (Cummings 2018).

An example of Trump's war on science is his stance on global warming. Despite the fact that 97 percent of the worldwide scientific community is in consensus about the existence of global warming, that it is caused by humans and will have devastating consequences on the human population (Cook et al. 2016; Union of Concerned Scientists 2018), Trump has posted 115 tweets denying climate change (DiChristopher 2017). Trump has frequently promoted the false narrative that bouts of cold weather prove that global warming does not exist (DiChristopher 2017).

Trump's contradictions with science are more than a rejection of data and facts. Evidence confirms that the strategies employed by the president demonstrate an effort to eliminate the existence and application of established facts supported by scientific research. While continuing to propagate doubt about scientific evidence regarding the hazards of environmental pollution, Trump enacted federal policies that affected public knowledge of existing scientific evidence. Based on alarming statements made by Trump during the presidential campaign, a large group of volunteers representing scientists, researchers, and academics, began archiving essential federal government scientific data used to create environmental regulations in an attempt to protect vital environmental data from political interference (Dennis 2016). Trump would eventually seek restrictions on the EPA's use of scientific data.

Understanding the extreme nature of Trump's war on science and his efforts to restrict public knowledge of scientific evidence requires a brief glimpse of the EPA's interaction with the public before Trump was elected. Public awareness of EPA research and scientific evidence linking pollutants to health risks has traditionally been achieved through the EPA's interaction with the news media. Journalists would often contact the EPA in regards to scientific findings of vital importance to the public. In addition, the EPA utilized social media to increase public awareness of vital information. The standard practice at the EPA involved the sharing of information with the public regarding the agency and important environmental research data generated by EPA scientists and used to create environmental policy. EPA websites and EPA social media accounts were dedicated to the public awareness of scientific, environmental data, and the EPA would routinely dispatch several new posts a day. The election of Trump and his war on science restricted public knowledge of existing environmental hazards and of scientific evidence of health risks due to industrial pollution.

Moments after Trump's inauguration, nearly all mentions of climate change were deleted from the official White House website, with the exception of his intention to eliminate the previous administration's policies on climate change (Davenport 2017). Trump then ordered the EPA to remove the entire climate change page from the EPA website (Volcovici 2017). Within weeks, access to EPA information of public importance was blocked. Trump ordered a complete "media blackout" at the EPA. The Trump administration instituted similar "media blackouts" at several other federal agencies. (Biesecker and Flesher, 2017). Journalists were instantly forbidden access to the agency or any data and findings resulting from scientific research at the EPA. In addition to the "media blackout" restricting public access through the banning of journalists, Trump further suppressed public access to the EPA's environmental research data by issuing a "gag order" that banned EPA scientists from communicating with the public. The communication lockdown at the Environmental Protection Agency prevented the staff from distributing public press releases, updates, and prohibited agents from posting any information on the EPA's social media accounts (Marsh and Merica 2017). Public access to critical EPA research findings was effectively restricted, as was the public's awareness of scientific evidence about environmental concerns and specific health risks from various environmental pollutants.

While the strategies employed by the president demonstrate a clear effort to eliminate public awareness of established scientific facts about environmental hazards, Trump's war on science would be further exemplified by attempts to actually eliminate the existence of those established, evidence-based facts. Trump's efforts became aimed at eliminating scientific evidence about environmental pollution by preventing the application of research data. The EPA's ability to use scientific data was restricted as the Trump administration proposed new rules at the EPA. The new rules restrict the use of scientific and medical research that the EPA would be permitted to use in setting standards for public health regulations. Without access to scientific research data, the EPA is unable to enact regulations.

Under the guise of "strengthening transparency in regulatory science," the Trump administration seeks to forbid the use of any scientific and medical research by the EPA unless scientists hand over and make public all of their raw data, revealing explicit information about each individual in the entire study "including confidential medical records" (Friedman 2019). The Trump guidelines for scientific and medical research not only lack a legitimate rationale but are a violation of the code of ethics adhered to by medical researchers in maintaining the confidentiality of research subjects (American Medical Association 2019). Since ethical researchers would naturally adhere to the Code of Medical Ethics, the Trump guidelines only serve to exclude the use of crucial scientific studies that are essential to EPA health and safety regulations (Wernick 2019). The new guidelines would prohibit the EPA from using groundbreaking public health research and studies that have established the link between air pollution and health conditions such as asthma, increased risk of stroke, heart disease, lung cancer, and diabetes. Further, the new restrictions are retroactive and permit the elimination of current EPA regulations since the new rules would be applied to previous research. Scientific research data deemed unusable by the Trump administration's new guidelines would result in invalidating the established findings of previous research.

Boston College's Dr. Philip Landrigan, one of the world's leading advocates for children's health, has confirmed the danger of Trump's new EPA rule regarding scientific research (Wernick 2019). "This proposal has nothing to do with transparency and regulation. It has everything to do with dismantling regulations that have been in place for many years, that have been very effective at reducing pollution in the United States, and very effective in preventing disease that is caused by pollution" (Wernick 2019). Landrigan has called the new guidelines "dangerous," as it allows the administration to retroactively disregard established research findings from groundbreaking scientific studies that confirm known health hazards and allows the administration to abolish existing regulations that have protected the health of the public (Wernick 2019).

Trump's war on science has propagated doubt about existing scientific evidence about environmental issues and restricted public access to scientific research regarding serious environmental problems, including established health risks from exposure to pollutants. The Trump administration's proposed guidelines restricting the use of scientific data eliminate the EPA's ability to protect the environment and public health. The restrictions placed on the EPA reinforced the shift toward the politics of environmental exploitation, but Trump's ability to take control of the EPA from within the agency demonstrates the extreme nature of the changes to environmental priorities in the United States.

## Expropriating the EPA

This section examines the Trump administration's ability to eliminate any barriers to the Trump mission of increased environmental degradation by taking possession and control over the EPA. Trump's control over the EPA is demonstrated through a review of EPA directors and administrators appointed by Trump and his administration. A further indication of Trump's control of the EPA is examined through evidence confirming that environmental guidelines at the EPA were dictated by the coal industry.

Despite its designation as an independent federal agency, the Environmental Protection Agency was expropriated by Donald Trump and his administration. The EPA was breached by positioning individuals who have direct connections to industrial polluters as federal directors, administrators, and agents within the EPA. Control of the agency, and its mission to protect the environment and the health of the public from hazardous industrial pollution, was handed to individuals with known associations to the fossil fuel and chemical industries, the very industries the EPA is charged with regulating. Public records, including documents filed with the US Office of Government Ethics, confirm that nearly half of the political appointees hired at the EPA under the Trump administration are ex-lobbyists and corporate lawyers of energy industries.

From the time between Trump's inauguration and the 2018 Midterm Election, all key positions at the EPA were filled by former opponents of the EPA who have spent years involved with blocking EPA public health and environmental protection regulations on behalf of energy industries. The obvious conflict of interest in appointing lawyers and lobbyists of industrial polluters to key positions within the Environmental Protection Agency was legally excused through the dispensing of "ethics waivers" to the former fossil fuel representatives. Trump's leading attorney, White House counsel, Don McGahn, has issued "at least 37 ethics waivers to key administration officials at the White House and executive branch agencies" (Biesecker 2018). Trump's EPA directors, deputies, and administrators, with financial ties to fossil fuel and chemical industries, have been instrumental in the shift away from the EPA's mission and core duties and have led to the reversal of more than 60 environmental regulations.

In December of 2016, Donald Trump nominated Scott Pruitt, the self-described "leading advocate against the EPA," to become the director of the EPA. Before becoming the director of the EPA, Pruitt had become one of the most outspoken critics of environmental protections and of the EPA. Pruitt consistently challenged federal environmental regulations with lawsuits aimed at blocking regulations that attempted to limit industrial pollution. Throughout the years, Pruitt has sued the Environmental Protection Agency fourteen times (Lipton and Davenport 2017). "In 13 of those cases, the co-parties included companies that had contributed money to Mr. Pruitt or to Pruitt-affiliated political campaign committees" (Lipton and Davenport 2017). Despite obvious ethical issues with his known "close" connections to the fossil fuel industry (Lipton and Davenport 2017), Pruitt was confirmed by the Republican-led Senate.

Scott Pruitt became the director of the very agency that he fought in multiple lawsuits. Pruitt's control of the EPA began with abolishing EPA regulations designed to protect the environment and public safety. In emails that were made public, it was revealed that top officials of a major oil and gas company would often assist in the drafting of Pruitt's letters to federal officials in order to reduce enforcement of environmental regulations (Dennis and Mufson 2017).

One of the most important environmental legislation passed by Congress held polluters accountable for the environmental damage they caused. In 1980, Congress created a "Superfund" for the EPA through the Comprehensive Environmental Response, Compensation and Liability Act (CERCLA). The Act addresses the problem of uncontrolled and abandoned hazardous waste sites, accidents, spills, and other emergency releases of pollutants and contaminants, many of which currently exist in populated communities where companies have previously dumped and buried dangerous waste material. Through CERCLA, Congress entrusted the EPA with the Superfund for the explicit purpose of cleaning, containing, or removing pollutants and hazardous materials when the responsible party cannot be immediately found. Under this Act, the EPA is authorized with the power to track down the parties responsible for the most dangerous abandonment, spill, or release of hazardous waste at sites assigned "Superfund" status and demand participation of the responsible party in the clean-up efforts. The Act also grants the EPA power to recover costs from the responsible companies involved. Each EPA regulation, rule, and federal act provide the means for the EPA to achieve its mission of protecting the environment and the health of the public.

In addition to Pruitt's active dismantling of regulations, The EPA director's control of the Superfund designated by Congress for the clean-up of the nation's most toxic and uncontrolled or abandoned waste sites raises serious questions. The Superfund's rules, procedures, and manner of use were explicitly established by CERCLA. Despite clear guidelines established for the use of the Superfund, Pruitt created a "Superfund Task Force" and hired a powerful chemical industry lawyer and ex-lobbyist as the EPA's Deputy Assistant Administrator and chair of the newly created task force. Steven Cook was the former senior attorney for one of the world's largest chemical, plastics, and refining companies, LyondellBasell Industries. EPA records reveal LyondellBasell Industries as being suspected of polluting at least three dozen sites that are now designated as "Superfund polluted sites" and under the jurisdiction of Steven Cook (Biesecker 2018). According to the EPA, the former representative of LyondellBasell Industries, Steven Cook, will provide EPA recommendations for expediting and restructuring the clean-up process of the country's most toxic and contaminated sites, many of which were caused by LyondellBasell Industries. In addition, per the recommendation by Cook and his Superfund Task Force, the EPA will be obligated to reduce the burden on cooperating parties and provide incentives for responsible parties (EPA.gov 2017).

The dramatic shift in environmental priorities at the EPA continued as Scott Pruitt, the EPA director, continued to advocate on behalf of Cheniere Energy, "the only exporter of liquefied natural gas (LNG) from the continental United States" (Bleseker 2018). Using EPA funds, Scott Pruitt began traveling extensively in first-class foreign trips spending $40,000 in taxpayer funds traveling to Morocco to promote "the potential benefit of liquefied natural gas (LNG) imports on Morocco's economy," despite the fact that the Department of Energy, and not the EPA, has jurisdiction over natural gas imports (Santucci, Mosk, Ebbs 2018). It was later revealed that Pruitt had been living in a luxurious Capitol Hill condo co-owned by the wife of J. Steven Hart, a lobbyist for Cheniere Energy.

While Scott Pruitt's conflict of interest did not prevent him from becoming the director of the EPA, multiple investigations into his spending caused Pruitt to resign in the summer of 2018. Trump immediately nominated coal lobbyist Andrew Wheeler to replace Pruitt as the director of the EPA (Schwartz 2018). For nearly a decade, Wheeler had been lobbying against pollution limits and EPA regulations on behalf of Robert E. Murray. Records show that from 2009, up until his nomination as EPA director, Andrew Wheeler was paid $300,000 and more annually by Murray Energy (Mufson 2018).

Robert E. Murray is the owner of the largest privately owned coal mining company in the United States. Through numerous lawsuits, Murray has successfully prevented federal regulations that address climate change by limiting pollution (Drabold 2016). Murray has also funded climate denial groups to cast public doubt on human-created climate change, donating one million dollars in 2019 alone (Friedman 2019). While these descriptions of Robert E. Murray's attacks on the environment are significant, Murray's greatest role in altering the US environmental policy would be found in his relationship with Donald Trump. Murray was one of Trump's largest campaign donors and played a key role in Trump's campaign fundraising (Drabold 2016). Murray also donated an additional $300,000 to Trump's inauguration (Pramuk 2017). Two months after Trump's inauguration, Andrew Wheeler arranged and attended a private meeting with Energy Secretary Rick Perry and Robert E. Murray to discuss specific changes for the EPA (Biesecker 2018; Mufson 2017; Mufson 2018). Andrew Wheeler was then confirmed as the EPA director by the Republican-led Senate, despite his close involvement with the coal industry, and more specifically, with Robert E. Murray and Murray Energy.

It would later be discovered that Andrew Wheeler's nomination to the EPA was on a list of requests made by Robert E. Murray and arranged at the private meeting attended by Energy Secretary Rick Perry, Wheeler, and Murray. In a PBS Frontline interview, Robert E. Murray boasted that he provided

Trump with an "action plan" for the EPA described as a "three-and-half-page long wish list" detailing everything that the coal executive wanted and expected from the Trump administration (Einbinder 2018). In the interview, Murray confirmed that everything on the first page was completed. A copy of the document was later uncovered and made public. The document confirms that all of the changes initiated by the Trump administration correspond to an entry on the coal executive's wish list, including a request for Energy Secretary Rick Perry to propose government subsidies for coal and nuclear plants (Friedman 2018). The discovery of the coal baron's wish list confirmed that the EPA's core mission was transformed into one that supported the coal industry.

Domination and control of the Environmental Protection Agency were achieved and maintained by positioning individuals connected with some of the world's largest industrial polluters in prominent positions throughout the EPA. Individuals in key EPA positions include: (1) EPA Senior Advisor for Agriculture, Jeffrey Sands, the former leading lobbyist for one of the world's largest pesticide manufacturers, Syngenta; (2) EPA Deputy Assistant Administrator for Water, Dennis Lee Forsgren, the former attorney for oil and gas lobbying firm, HBW Resources, which manages Consumer Energy Alliance, the prominent advocacy group promoting the controversial Keystone XL pipeline (Grandoni 2018); (3) EPA Lawyer, Erik Baptist, the former senior lawyer and registered federal lobbyist for the American Petroleum Institute; (4) EPA Deputy Head of Science Policy, David Dunlap, a former chemical engineer for petroleum and chemical conglomerate Koch Industries; (5) EPA Deputy Head of Chemical Safety David Fischer, the attorney and advisor for chemical companies associated with the American Chemistry Council; and (6) Associate Administrator for the EPA Office of Public Engagement and Environmental Education, Elizabeth Bennett, a former lobbyist for the National Rural Electric Cooperative Association, who lobbied against EPA regulations regarding carbon dioxide pollution. The numerous EPA administrators and directors from fossil fuel and chemical industries expose Trump's control over the EPA and his ability to drastically alter environmental priorities toward environmental destruction.

## Dismantling Environmental Protections

Over the course of four years, the Trump administration has completely dismantled the established protections for the environment, for human life, and for non-human life. The Trump-controlled Environmental Protection Agency has eliminated regulations designed to protect the health of Americans that served to limit industry pollution released into the air and into water sources. According to research conducted by Harvard Law School and Columbia

Law School, the EPA has "officially reversed, revoked, or otherwise rolled back" more than environmental rules and regulations (Popovich et al. 2020). Regulations regarding toxic substances, air pollution and emissions, drilling and extraction, and water pollution have been eliminated.

There are some toxic pollutants, identified as extremely detrimental to humans, that the EPA did not dare fully eliminate regulations tied to these toxins. The EPA's drastic elimination of regulations was merged with clever adjustments in the way toxins are regarded. One example of the EPA's clever adjustments under Trump is found in the EPA's change in regards to mercury and restricting mercury emissions from oil and coal-fired power plants. Mercury is a heavy metal that is linked to brain damage. While Trump's EPA did not eliminate restrictions on the release of toxic metals such as mercury, the EPA restructured the mercury pollution rule, creating a new method of calculating "the costs and benefits of curbing mercury pollution" (Friedman and Davenport 2020). According to environmental lawyers, the EPA's new restructured mercury pollution rule essentially abolishes the legal justification to control and limit the release of mercury into the environment. The drastic change in the way the federal government calculates the costs and benefits of dangerous pollutants could restrict the ability of regulators to control toxins in the future (Dennis and Eilperin 2020).

The Trump administration's agenda towards environmental destruction was not limited to the United States; Trump proclaimed globally that the United States would disregard its contribution to global pollution and its impact on climate change. Trump formally notified the United Nations that the United States would withdraw from the Paris Agreement on climate change, supported by nearly 200 nations committed to reducing greenhouse emissions and assisting poor countries already disproportionately affected by natural disasters caused by climate change (Friedman 2020).

The Trump-controlled EPA has made changes to environmental policy that are vast, involve a wide range of toxic substances that affect land, water, and air, and have dire consequences for the environment and the health of thousands of individuals now and in the future. The environmental degradation by the Trump administration has resulted in significant detrimental harms to individuals and communities. The next section examines the results of Trump's politics of environmental destruction.

## Air Pollution and the Human Cost of Environmental Exploitation

The Trump administration's shift in federal policies toward increased environmental exploitation for capitalistic gains disregards the substantial cost to human health and to the human death toll resulting from environmental pollution and destruction. The overwhelming amount of environmental damage caused by the Trump administration has affected land, water, and air. In each of these cases, there is a human toll. This section will examine the cost of environmental destruction to the air.

There is broad scientific consensus that air pollution is detrimental to human health. Numerous epidemiological studies have well-established the link between fine particulate matter pollution and dangerous human health impacts. More than 100,000 Americans die each year from health complications due to air pollution (Neuhauser 2019). Many of these studies are based on emissions data gathered by the EPA, and yet, the most powerful members of the Trump-controlled EPA have dismissed all scientific evidence linking air pollution to human health complications and death, with "some stating they did not even agree inhaling air pollution—including soot—could lead to an early death" (Neuhauser 2019).

Researchers have found that air pollution has significantly increased since Trump took office, and the data show that more people are dying due to health complications from air pollution since Trump took office. The increase in air pollution has resulted in multiple regions and counties being out of attainment with National Ambient Air Quality Standards (NAAQS). Before Trump's presidency, small-particle pollution had reached a 20-year low (Clay and Muller 2019). In 2018, EPA director Andrew Wheeler disbanded the academic panel of expert scientists that reviewed scientific data for the purpose of advising the EPA on standards for small-particle air pollution (Goldman 2019). In its place, Wheeler hired consultants from fossil fuel, pharmaceutical, and tobacco industries to advise the EPA on air pollution standards (Ingraham 2019). The Trump administration's control over the EPA has resulted in a significant and dangerous increase in air pollution. A 2019 study found that after a 24.2 percent decline in fine particulate matter (PM2.5) from 2009 to 2016, fine particulate matter in the United States had increased by 5.5 percent between 2016 and 2018, with many communities not meeting the NAAQS minimum air quality standards (Clay and Muller 2019). In 2018 alone, the increased air pollution in the United States was linked to nearly 10,000 additional deaths (Ingraham 2019).

The Trump environmental agenda has eliminated restrictions on the amount of chemicals and pollution that industries are permitted to release into the environment, increasing public exposure to toxic hazards that are directly linked to health complications and premature death. Research published in *The Journal of the American Medical Association* conservatively projected 80,000 additional air pollution-related deaths in the United States due to the elimination of landmark environmental policies and regulations by the Trump-controlled Environmental Protection Agency (Cutler and Dominici 2018).

## RACISM, SEXISM, COLONIALISM, AND THE STRUGGLE FOR ENVIRONMENTAL JUSTICE

The deadly human health risks, due to toxic pollution created and dumped in the environment by private corporations and industry polluters, do not affect all humans equally. Ecofeminist theory has established that the capitalistic drive to dominate nature and exploit natural resources is intimately connected to the oppression of women and other members of Black, Indigenous, and Latinx communities. Minoritized communities are disproportionately exposed and affected by deadly environmental hazards. As researchers investigated the correlation between toxic environmental waste and the disproportionate health risks to minoritized groups, inequities regarding environmental pollution were exposed. The need for environmental justice became clear. This section examines the role of racism, sexism, and colonialism in the struggle for environmental justice.

Robert Bullard, often described as the father of environmental justice, has been instrumental in bringing environmental justice issues to the forefront. In *Dumping in Dixie: Race, Class and Environmental Quality* (2000), Bullard established the standards for environmental justice based on the premise that Americans have a basic right to live in a healthy environment and links environmentalism to issues of social justice. In 1994, Executive Order 12898, "Federal Actions to Address Environmental Justice in Minority Populations and Low-Income Populations," was signed by then-president William J. Clinton to address the disproportionate environmental and health effects to minoritized and low-income groups. Environmental justice issues have emerged in each election since that time and were addressed at the 2017 Women's March.

### Disproportionate Harms to People of Color

The burdens of pollution are not shared among populations evenly. Racial disparities in exposure to pollution are well documented (Tessum et al. 2019). People of color are disproportionately affected by the pollution resulting from environmental exploitation. The disparities bring to light an important fact about environmental destruction and race: racial issues are embedded in environmental justice issues.

Bullard (1983) conducted extensive research investigating polluted environments around the country and found that toxic waste sites were most likely to be located in predominantly Black neighborhoods across the United States. Bullard's groundbreaking research exposed massive disparities in the burden of environmental degradation. Bullard's findings are confirmed by the fact that the most polluted environments in the United States are communities where people of color live and work. Communities of color are consistently targeted by private corporations and industry polluters to be recipients of hazardous waste materials through landfills, mining, and manufacturing plants.

Numerous ecofeminist studies have provided overwhelming evidence confirming that the environmental hazards resulting from the exploitation of the environment disproportionately affect "the health of women and children, particularly in poor communities of color" (Warren 2000: 10), revealing the role of racism, sexism, and colonialism in the struggle for environmental justice. Racism, sexism, and colonialism are recognized as "isms of domination" (Warren 2000) and serve as systems of oppression. Gaard and Gruen (1993) explain that racism, sexism, classism, and colonialism mutually reinforce other systems of oppression, resulting in the current and ongoing global environmental crisis and environmental injustice. An analysis of the oppression experienced by minoritized groups, in regards to the negative impacts of environmental degradation, focuses on intersectionality and the links to interrelated -isms of domination. Dorceta Taylor (1997), points out that the intersectionality of racism and sexism has left women of color carrying the burden of environmental hazards disproportionately.

Research from the American Lung Association found "startling racial disparities" in exposure to air pollution (Varanasi 2020). Indigenous people, Asians, Latinx, and, most significantly, Black Americans are disproportionately subjected to dangerous particle pollution and ozone pollution. Over 14 million people of color live in countries where they are exposed to short-term and year-long air pollution (Varanasi 2020). In addition, women of color suffer the consequences of pollution at an even higher rate. Exposure to higher temperatures caused by climate change or air pollution has been found to have detrimental consequences to women's health and, for pregnant women, creating a higher risk of underweight or stillborn babies. Bruce Bekkar and his research team (Bekkar et al. 2020) examined 32 million births in the United States and found that pregnant women exposed to higher temperatures or air pollution were more likely to have babies that were premature, underweight, or stillborn. The research confirmed that Black American mothers and their babies were harmed by the negative effects of climate change (higher temperatures) and air pollution at a much higher rate than the population at large (Bekkar et al. 2020).

## Disproportionate Harms to Indigenous People and the "Water Protectors"

The exploitation of land belonging to indigenous people in pursuit of capitalist goals has a long history in the United States. In 2014, the proposed Dakota pipeline was moved from Bismark, a 90 percent white community, to the border of the Sioux reservations. The Sioux Tribes opposed the proposed pipeline in and near the tribal lands. In April 2016, construction of the Dakota pipeline began. LaDonna Brave Bull Allard opened her property and founded the resistance camp sending a call to all tribes to stand with Standing Rock to protect the water. Within a month, neighboring tribes showed up. In August 2016, a young mother, Bobbi Jean Three Legs, organized a 2,000-mile youth relay run, "Rezpect our Water," from South Dakota to Washington, D.C., to protest the pipeline and deliver the message, "water is life," to the Obama administration. At the protests, the youth chant, "What do we do when our Water's under attack? Stand up! Fight Back! What do we do when our people are under attack? Stand up! Fight Back!"

In a testimonial, Chase Iron Eyes, a Native American activist/lawyer/politician, describes what happened on August 14, 15, and 16th (Iron Eyes 2020). He states that a group of protestors wanted to chain themselves to the gate where Energy Transfer Partners wanted to build an access road to build the pipeline. A group of mounted women and men came on the scene. The horses led the group to oppose the line of police officers and backed up the police unit (Iron Eyes 2020). While that was happening, four indigenous women decided to go up on the hill and crossed the fence line. "The women led us into unknown territory—territory they have not known since 1889" (Iron Eyes 2020). About 80 people rushed and followed. The women used their bodies to go between the heavy equipment, to protest "Financial Extractive Genocide and Eco-cide" for the protection of their families. When the Energy Transfer Partners (ETP) found out where the sacred lands were, they moved their heavy equipment more than 20 miles to the sacred site to destroy the land. ETP hired mercenary-style, private security. About 100 protestors (men, women, and children) began to protest, putting themselves in harm's way. The private security force, along with employees of the energy company, presented deadly attack dogs creating a major, credible threat to unarmed, peaceful protestors. With that thread, the warriors present on that day took it upon themselves to drive the equipment operators and the security forces out of the area (Iron Eyes 2020).

After the dog attacks, 1000s of natives across the nation started showing up. The security forces used Backwater Bridge to stop the forward movement of the protestors began brutally, inflicting pain and maiming unarmed protestors with the use of weaponry, including mace/pepper spray, tasers, non-lethal bullets, and flashbangs (Iron Eyes 2020). On November 21, 2016, over 300 water protectors (protestors) were hurt and injured (bone fractures, internal injuries, eye injuries, and hyperthermia) when North Dakota law enforcement officers used water cannons in 20-degree weather (Wong 2016; Iron Eyes 2020). Water that was sprayed on to the people in below-freezing weather creating a "mass casualty incident."

On December 4, 2017, two thousand to three thousand veterans came to the Standing Rock resistance camp to protect the water protectors and serve as a barrier between law enforcement and the water protectors, to "assemble as a peaceful, unarmed militia at the Standing Rock Indian Reservation." The Governor of North Dakota had signed an order for the protestors to leave the site by Monday, December 4. However, on December 5, 2017, President Obama and the US Army Corps of Engineers denied the permit to continue building the pipeline. There was a celebration on the news, and tens of thousands of people showed up to drive by the resistance camp to honor the win (Iron Eyes 2020). However, Trump had already been elected, and the news that Trump had personal investments in Energy Transfer Partners and other big oil companies, so it was known then that it was a temporary win.

Only a few days after the 2017 Women's March, a few days after Trump's inauguration as US president, Trump signed an executive order granting permission for the construction of the pipeline. Even though the pipeline was opposed by environmental and American Native groups, Trump signed an order approving the construction of the Keystone XL pipeline (Wolfe and Ries 2019). The Dakota Access Pipeline runs through Sioux Tribe territory; Trump's authorization for the pipeline violates an 1851 federal treaty.

Oil pipelines are notorious for leaking and spilling toxic pollutants into the soil, waterways, and air, causing destruction to the environment, contaminating water sources, and resulting in serious health risks, injury, and death for people, animals, insects, and flora that live near pipelines. Since 2010, nearly nine million gallons of crude oil have spilled from pipelines across the United States, amounting to a pipeline leak every other day (Harrington 2016).

Indigenous activists have led and organized the protests against the Dakota Access Pipeline and found an ally in the American Civil Liberties Union (ACLU), who brought lawsuits against the US government, arguing that the pipeline violated a federal treaty and unfairly exposed the community to significant health risks. United States District Judge James Boasberg deemed Trump's executive order for the Dakota pipeline as "highly controversial" since it provided permits for the construction of the pipeline without conducting the mandatory environmental impact analysis (Wamsley 2020). The federal judge further stated that the Energy Transfer Company should have never been allowed to build a portion of the pipeline under South Dakota's Lake Oahe, which serves as a drinking water source for the Standing Rock Sioux Tribe (Moore 2020). The federal court ordered the Dakota Access Pipeline to be shut down immediately until a full and complete environmental impact review is conducted, which takes approximately 13 months (Wamsley 2020).

Trump's lawyers went back to court, and within days, a federal appeals court decided that the Energy Transfer Company would be allowed to continue operating the Dakota Access Pipeline and given time for any further legal proceedings (Moore 2020). In October 2019, the Keystone 1 Pipeline leaked about 380,000 gallons of oil into wetlands (Wolfe and Ries 2019). Damage to the wetland ecosystem is unknown and won't be known for years to come. The kind of oil that comes through that pipeline is very thick, and a toxic dilutant is added to help the oil flow through the pipeline. The toxicity of the dilutant is unknown.

The exploitation of the environment and the oppression of indigenous people for capitalistic goals is an important ecofeminist issue that affects all living beings, as well as the health of the planet. The Trump administration's domination over the environment and indigenous people exposes the complex interconnections of capitalism, patriarchy, and colonialism as practices that oppress women, minoritized others, and nature while highlighting the linked oppressions of racism, sexism, and classism. Water protectors like Chas Jewett (Red Morning Star Woman), La Donna Brave Bull, BobbiJean Three legs are continuing to protest the pipeline. The message being sent around the world that "water is life." You can't drink oil. Chas Jewett (2017) has shared the message in her talks around the world on the importance of giving water the same status that corporations get, the status of people. Jewett cites the New Zealand river that was granted the legal rights of a human. The indigenous people, the Maori, see the waterway as a sacred ancestor.

## CONCLUSION

Trump's attacks on science and his ability to allocate EPA jobs and key positions in the EPA to individuals connected with the fossil fuel industry were instrumental in creating a drastic change toward environmental destruction, while women, black women, and indigenous women continue to be at the forefront of environmental protection and activism. The Standing Rock protest was the precursor to the 2017 women's social movements, which led to the overwhelming number of women to run and win elected offices. Chas Jewett, an indigenous organizer and activist, has said that the election of Trump has pulled back the curtain for all to see the ugliness of American exploitation.

This chapter described the expropriation, the takeover of the EPA, the raw, predatory exploitation of the earth's natural resources, the disregard for indigenous nations (including treaties, sacred lands, and waterways), and the harm to Black communities and Black Americans in general. The resistance has always been present, but with the unabashed "financial extractive genocide and eco-genocide" of Trump and his administration, there is a strong call to resist, stand up, and fight back. What the indigenous people started with the

Standing Rock resistance was just the beginning and served as a model for women and many others around the world.

An ecofeminist analysis of the Trump administration's engagement with environmental issues reveals Trump's domination mindset, devoted to expanding his power and establishing his influence and control in areas of government that are independent of the presidency. Trump's domination over the environment through the EPA has resulted in the oppression of the environment, women, indigenous groups, and people of color. Ruether (1995) maintains that there is a basic and intrinsic connection between Western, patriarchal cultures and the domination of women and nature. In a patriarchal society based on male domination, Trump's election to the presidency not only appeared to elevate his overall sense of power but became the justification for the exploitation of women, nature, and minoritized groups for capitalistic gains.

## *Chapter 5*

# The Battle Cry

## *Resistance and a Surge in Women's Political Activism*

The current women's movement began immediately following the 2016 presidential election (Eldeib 2016; Cauterucci 2016; Kearney 2016). The expectation, for many, was that the 2016 presidential election would result in the first woman president of the United States. Many believed that former secretary of state, Hillary Rodham Clinton, who was highly educated and experienced in law and policy development with significant experience in public service, would become the next president of the United States; the election was to be a celebration of breaking the glass ceiling in this country. The unexpected election results left many in complete disbelief, experiencing heartache, anger, and outrage when the most divisive candidate was elected. Trump was a candidate with little knowledge of the Constitution, minimal knowledge of US and International law, and almost no knowledge on how to develop public policy. Trump's presidential campaign promoted ideas and policies overtly grounded in racism, sexism, misogyny, Islamophobia, xenophobia, and the exploitation of the environment.

Trump's statements permeated society with hate rhetoric and crude terms directed at women. The tension was turned into shock for many when Trump was announced as the next president of the United States. His election was evidence that the dominant social and political ideology in the United States had indeed shifted, launching an era where racism, sexism, homophobia, and xenophobia emerged, taking front stage in the White House and dividing American society in those that supported Trump and those that did not. The dramatic shift in dominant social and political ideology compelled people from all walks of life to become politically active in ways that would become historic. The battle cry for resistance and political action began as women around the country turned to friends, family, and social media to vent, get answers, and ultimately, begin a movement that resulted in the 2017 Women's

**Figure 5.1 The 2017 Women's March in Washington D.C.** *Source*: Photo by Teresa Bartoli.

March, uniting over seven million people (Chenoweth and Pressman 2017) in the United States and worldwide in an inclusive and wide-ranging cause against hate and harm. The current women's movement would maintain its momentum by becoming a force in American politics through continued protests. Activism came in the form of fundraising, registering voters, and a national and unprecedented surge of first-time female political candidates seeking local, state, and national political offices. The surge of women who won elected offices changed the demographic of Congress in 2018 with the most diverse group ever elected.

This chapter will use an ecofeminist lens to examine and describe the current women's movement and the surge of political activism of women through an analysis of the Women's March and its impact on the 2018 Midterm Election. The first section in this chapter identifies the 2017 Women's March as a grassroots event that went global, an event providing energy and activism to two other grassroots movements: the Pussy Hat Project and the #MeToo movement. The second section is an analysis of the white privilege present on the day of the march and how the collective power of white women resulted in a spirit of inclusiveness with a representation of minoritized groups. The third section focuses on the significance of the "call to get politically active" at the march that resulted in activism to last well beyond 2017. The fourth section of this chapter reviews the data and analysis of the 2018 Midterm Election.

## GRASSROOTS: THE 2017 WOMEN'S MARCH

One day after Trump was elected, Teresa Shook created a Facebook event titled "Million Women March," calling for a march on Washington, D.C., on the inaugural weekend, Saturday, January 21, 2017. While she started this as a private invite, it was shared by others, and within days, over 300,000 women responded that they were interested (Kearney 2016). The genesis of the current women's movement, as an online grassroots movement, owes much of its success in outreach to the 2013 #BlackLivesMatter, which highlighted the significant role that social media plays in opening spaces for thinking through new possibilities for resistance (Cohen, Forbis, and Misri 2018). The Women's March was not merely a feminist march; it was an ecofeminist march. The march and its protesters rallied against the unjustified domination of the environment, minoritized groups, and the disadvantaged others: women, people of color, LGBTQ+ persons, children, the poor, and others.

In the analysis of the Women's March, the goals and issues addressed by protesters will be examined. The objective of march organizers to be inclusive will be explored through the leadership and challenges in selecting an official name for the march. In addition, an explanation of the significance and controversy regarding the knitted pink hats worn by protesters is addressed as well as assessing the impact of the Women's March, including its influence in the resurgence of the #MeToo movement.

## NAMING THE MARCH

There were many controversies that attempted to devalue/deflect the success of the Women's March—naming the march was one of the most significant. The name "Million Women March," raised issues of exclusion and overlooked the historical significance of using the word "Million." These issues took root in the comment section of the Facebook invite. While some comments were merely inquiries, many more were heated statements regarding "inclusion," focusing on the exclusion of others—husbands, men, children, and people of different genders and races. In fact, many women nationwide began planning marches in different Facebook groups. Less than a week later, the link to the original march was replaced with a new one titled the "Women's March." All the different marches that had been organized began to coalesce into one large women's movement under this link.

Nearly twenty years ago, in 1997, the "Million Woman March" in Philadelphia (Jones 2008) was designed by and for African American women to improve their communities and organize to address structural racism. The 1997 march, and the United States' racialized history, was the foundational rationale for changing the 2017 event name from the "Million Women March" to the "Women's March." This was a significant step in becoming an inclusive event. The consistent and historical contention within feminism has always been the predominance of white, upper-class, and middle-class women that appeared oblivious to intersectional issues of race, class, gender, age, and sexuality. The use of the word "million" revived the issue of racism in feminism and appeared to be an appropriation of significant and historic Black/African American social movements such as the historic 1995 Million Man March in Washington, D.C., and the historic 1997 Million Woman March in Philadelphia. These social movements were historic Black American/African American movements that were directed at bringing structural racism to the forefront as well as calling for a change in American society and the US criminal justice system.

The Million Man March was a massive social movement organized and promoted by prominent Black American civil rights leaders and faith-based leaders (NOI 2020). Black women were key organizers and worked behind the scenes, had a limited presence on the podium, and participated in a "Day of Absence" to stay home to care for children (Smooth and Tucker 1999). The phenomenal, historic march was designed to affirm the positive and unite Black men in America from all social classes and faiths to inspire self-help and self-defense against economic and social injustices rooted in systemic racism and violence. The theme of the march was "atonement," and those that could not attend in person stayed home for a "day of atonement." It was clear from the footage that more than a million black men attended the march (A.P. Archive 2015; Chandler 2019). The success of the march, the message of affirmation of Black communities, and the hope that was instilled in Black men and their families were ignored by mainstream media. In addition, the mainstream media underrated the march with claims that the march did not have a million Black men in attendance. Threatened with a lawsuit for underestimating the count of marchers, Congress embedded language in the 1997 appropriations bill to prohibit the National Park Service from estimating crowds in an attempt to avoid politicized statements regarding attendance (Smith and Milillo 1996).

Two years after the Million Man March, the Million Woman March took place in Philadelphia. The gathering included over two million women of African (Campbell 1997). Informal networks were used to spread the word of the march (Campbell 1997). The theme focused on the struggle against exploitation and the social decay of Black communities in the United States and around the world. Reproductive health, family, education, the criminal justice system, and the war on drugs were the important issues addressed. The main concern was the structural nature of human rights violations of African American women and communities. The global assault on women of African descent and their families was made front and center with the keynote speaker, Winnie Madikizela-Mandela, a South African anti-apartheid activist and politician. Both the Million Man March and the Million Woman March were organized by and for Black and African Americans. The focus on the intersectionality of race and gender was central in both of these marches, although the messages were very different.

For the Million Man March, the message was a conservative "reclaim your place in your family and community"; for the Million Woman March, the message was a radical focus on eliminating racism as the root cause of exploitation and oppression of Blacks in the United States and globally. The call was to root out structural racism in social institutions (particularly the prison systems and education systems) and eliminate racist policies and laws that furthered the exploitation, oppression, and murder of people of African descent, especially in American urban areas (Campbell 1997). The Million Women March focused on policies, laws, and policing. The information that the war on drugs was a deliberate attack on Black and African American communities was spread at the march (Webb 1996). Black Americans were finding out that crack cocaine was being spread throughout Black communities by the CIA (Campbell 1997). Following the march, contention arose against white feminist scholars and upper-middle-class black scholars in regards to their lack of support and attendance at the Million Woman March. Campbell (1997) writes:

> What was significant was the lack of sisterhood from privileged white women for the march. The silence of the white feminists and middle-class African American academics and gender technicians was deafening. This silence and lack of support for the march reflects the lack of support on a daily basis for the issues which confront oppressed Africans and other people of color in the U.S. (Campbell 1997:88)

The renaming of the 2017 march from "Million Women's March" to "Women's March" came from an understanding of the history of racial appropriation and in acknowledgment of the erasure of intersectional concerns related to race, class, gender, age, and sexuality. Women who had experience organizing national marches stepped up to organize this march. Additionally, women all over the world began to step up and organize various elements of the march for local areas. Different state and city sister marches were organized to accommodate those that could not travel. The movement began to take shape with a focus on making the march inclusive—antithetical to what the election of Donald Trump represented. The plans involved quickly with obtaining permits, the logistics of getting people to the marches, and having the resources available for the march, began to develop. The goal of the march was to send a bold message and stand united for human rights, social justice, and the protection of the environment.

## THE PUSSYHAT PROJECT: RECLAIMING OUR PUSSY AND SPOTLIGHTING SEXUAL VIOLENCE

On October 7, 2016, about a month before the presidential election, a 2005 *Access Hollywood* taped conversation was leaked and made public (Victor 2017). In this tape, Trump describes his encounters with women and states to Billy Bush, "You know I'm automatically attracted to beautiful—I just start kissing them. It's like a magnet. Just kiss. I don't even wait. And when you're a star, they let you do it. You can do anything. Grab them by the pussy. You can do anything" (Bullock 2016). The vile nature of describing one's sexual assault against women was disturbing. From this tape, the word "pussy" entered the everyday language of American culture. Within five days, the term "pussy" was being discussed broadly in the media. Brooks (2016) wrote an article titled "Where the Hell Does the Word 'P***y' Come From, Anyway?" Like many mainstream media outlets, her title does not spell out the profane word "pussy" but instead uses asterisks. Brooks (2016) traces the use of the term and writes, "Pussy is primarily used to talk about sex—whether it's the sexual organ or the woman attached to it, or some conflated and generalized combination of the two. Perhaps worse, the word can be used as a slur against effeminate or cowardly men." The use of the term "pussy" is considered vulgar and used to dehumanize women by serving as a euphemism for the vulva or vagina.

Trump used "pussy" in this sexualized sense to reduce women to sexual objects. Prior to the release of this tape, "pussy" was a form of colloquial profanity. It is a term commonly used in pornography that typically objectifies women's bodies for sex and sexual encounters (Engle 2017). Pussy has also been used as a form of affection to refer to kittens, kitty cats, and pussycats. Terms referring to cats often have sexual overtones when used on women. While many people were disgusted and outraged, the casual and unapologetic nature of Trump's response to the leaked tape as being locker room talk brought to the forefront the objectification of women's bodies and the pervasiveness of unwanted touching, sexual assault, and sexual violence that many women have experienced (Haberman 2016).

Krista Suh, like many women, "mourned Hillary's loss" (Suh 2020). Within days, Suh had committed to going to the Washington march on the inaugural weekend. On November 12, 2016, Suh thought of the idea to have everyone wear a pink hat as a show of solidarity and power. She contacted Kat Coyle, her knitting instructor, and owner of a small knit shop. On November 16, Suh's friend, Jayna Zweiman, joined Suh and Coyle at The Little Knittery in Los Angeles; they developed the Pussyhat pattern for knitting a hat. On November 18, Aurora Lady illustrated the manifesto for the pink hat project. Molly McKnight, of northern Virginia, agreed to collect the hats and distribute them at the Women's March (Lenghi 2017; Suh 2020). An organizer and P.R. person joined their team; the social movement to have every woman wear a pink Pussyhat in a show of solidarity took off and was shared via the website Pussyhatproject.com (Suh and Zweiman 2016).

Social media was used to spread the word (e.g., Just Saying 2016), share the knitting pattern, and organize knitting groups to begin knitting hats for women marchers (Wetli 2016). By December, the knitting campaign went national with the Pussyhat Project showcased in various media outlets. One news article described the knitting project: "The idea, launched by two women in Los Angeles and the owner of their local yarn store, for the Pussyhat Project is a big "F . . . you" of sorts to Trump and the values he espouses. They are hoping that the 200,000 marchers all wear the pink hats and send a strong message of resistance" (Dinkelspiel 2016).

In the Pussyhat manifesto (Suh and Zweiman 2016), the four women involved in starting the movement wrote about power: Power in numbers, power of pink, power of individuality within large groups, power of the handmade, and the power of pussy. The vulgar term used by Trump to degrade, objectify, and describe his sexual assaults against women would be co-opted by women, taken over, and turned into a symbol of power. The goal was to show solidarity among the marchers while still honoring individuality. The Pussyhats were designed to be more than a symbol of solidarity; they represented the power of women. The selection of pink had nothing to do with the color of one's pussy for these women. Rather, they write in their manifesto,

> Pink is considered a very female color representing caring, compassion, and love—all qualities that have been derided as weak but are actually STRONG. Wearing pink together is a powerful statement that we are unapologetically feminine and we unapologetically stand for women's rights. (Suh 2016)

The power of individuality and diversity is central to the Pussyhat project. The official Pussyhat pattern was developed to accommodate all knitting levels. Within the manifesto, it was recognized that individuality was important. They write,

> We created this hat pattern to be easily made no matter where you live or what your level of knitting is. Worsted weight is easily available at any knitting store or craft store. Please choose any shade of pink that delights you. At the march, with everyone wearing hats in different shades of pink, the overall effect will be beautiful. Please make any warm hat—you can knit it, crochet it, it can have cat ears, it can have a pom-pom, etc. We include the official "Pussy Power Hat" knit pattern to inspire you and help you. (Suh and Zweiman 2016)

Within the Pussyhat manifesto, the power of the handmade and the link of handmade goods to women was recognized as an important tradition in the history of feminist protests. They were not wrong. The creation and production of crafts such as knitting, needlepoint, and quilting have been used and worn by women as acts of protest. For example, "During the French Revolution, market women, who had led their own successful protest against the establishment in 1789, famously sat by the guillotine and knitted red 'liberty caps' worn by revolutionaries" (Age of Revolution 2017).

On the day of the Women's March 2017, thousands and thousands of women showed up to various marches with backpacks, huge bags, and large boxes filled with handmade Pussyhats. The hats represented hours and hours of work. Women from around the world knitted Pussyhats. Many women who were not going to attend the march spent the weeks beforehand knitting hats, and arrangements were made to get the hats to the march. The hats were generously passed out to every woman at the march. No woman paid for a hat. And so, just one day after the 2017 presidential inauguration, Washington, D.C., was flooded in a massive sea of pink. Immense rivers of pink flowed from coast to coast and on every continent in the world. The Pussyhats symbolized solidarity, defiance, and the power of women.

Trump's pussy comment drastically altered the American nomenclature. The social imagination was sexual and embraced by some but repulsive and vulgar to others. Some focused on the element of solidarity that wearing a similar hat has in a social movement. Some think of the pink Pussyhat as limiting representation with the notion of using pink to describe white women's pussy and claim that not all pussies are pink. Some worry about offending transgender women that have no pussy and called for the elimination of pink Pussyhats at future Women's Marches (Jagannathan 2018). Wearing or not wearing a pink Pussyhat is up to each individual woman. For many women who participated in the 2017 Women's March, attending the annual marches involved getting their pink Pussyhat out and making signs. Mandler (2019) wrote an article titled, "Please Stop Wearing Those Pussy Hats to Women's Marches: A Nonbinary Person's Thoughts on Trans Exclusion in Mainstream Social Movements." The point of her article written for *Seventeen* magazine is to emphasize the "pussy" by writing, "When it comes down to it, not all women have vaginas and not all people with vaginas are women." This argument inspires a discussion of "female parts."

In her book, *Womanhood: The Bare Reality*, photographer Laura Dodsworth does more than just show the diversity vulvas. Along with 100 photographs of different women's "private parts," Dodsworth shared stories these women had about their womanhood (Dodsworth 2019; Abernethy 2019). In an interview, Dodsworth is quoted as saying, "Lots of women were looking at themselves for the first time or they hadn't looked at themselves much. Some of them were very well acquainted with their vulva" (Abernethy 2019). "We tuck away many stories related to the vulva. I was blown away by the number of stories about sexual assault" (Abernethy 2019).

To some extent, Trump's vile and candid comments of sexual violation got many more women talking about sexual assault and violence. His contempt for women came out during his debate with Hillary Clinton when he called her a "nasty woman."

## 2017 WOMEN'S MARCH

Nearly two million people gathered in Washington, D.C., and about seven million others came together in city centers across the country; a total of 653 marches were recorded throughout the United States (W.M. 2017; Chenoweth and Pressman 2017). The Women's March was a historic protest, and a massive number of people marched in both the United States and around the world.

The march was inclusive, and the visual presence of women from all different races and backgrounds was awe-inspiring. Black women were there (Hill 2017); Latinx women were there (Puga, Armas, Alfaro, Nuño-Pérez, Gamboa, and Guadalupe 2017); Asian women were there (Fuch 2017); Native American Women were there (Belger 2017); White women were there (Bates 2017). In fact, the 2017 Women's March was the most diverse march for women's rights ever recorded (Bates 2017). Then senator (now vice president) Kamala Harris, along with Senator Tammy Duckworth, spoke at the march along with a diversity of speakers from many different walks of life—different racial, ethnic, religious backgrounds, people from the LGBTQ+ community, immigrants, refugees, wealthy, and poor. The march was criticized for being a white Women's March due to a large number of white women in attendance. However, we contend that the percentages were reflective of the racial make-up of the US population: 60 percent white, 18.5 percent Latinx, 13.4 percent Black, 5 percent Asian, 1.3 percent Native American, 2.8 percent mixed (US Census 2020).

The Women's March gave a voice to the millions of people who were opposed to the incoming presidential regime that promoted sexism, racism, and exploitation of the environment. Angela Davis delivered a powerful speech at the Women's March that puts the history of colonialism and slavery front and center. She started her speech with the following:

> At a challenging moment in our history, let us remind ourselves that we, the hundreds of thousands, the millions of women, trans people, men, and youth who are here at the Women's March, represent the powerful forces of change that are determined to prevent the dying cultures of racism, hetero-patriarchy from rising again. We recognize that we are collective agents of history and that history cannot be deleted like web pages. We know that we gather this afternoon on indigenous land, and we follow the lead of the first peoples who, despite massive genocidal violence, have never relinquished the struggle for land, water, culture, their people. We especially salute today the Standing Rock Sioux.
>
> The freedom struggles of black people that have shaped the very nature of this country's history cannot be deleted with the sweep of a hand. We cannot be made to forget that black lives do matter. This is a country anchored in slavery and colonialism, which means for better or for worse, the very history of the United States is a history of immigration and enslavement. Spreading xenophobia, hurling accusations of murder and rape, and building walls will not erase history. No human being is illegal. (Davis 2017)

Davis's speech is unifying and articulates the histories of different races, ethnicities, social classes, sexualities, and citizenship status. The organization of the Women's March, and the line-up of speakers, showed that the women who took the lead in organizing the march worked diligently to be sensitive to the myriad of diverse issues.

One of the many powerful moments, ideologically, during the 2017 Women's March in D.C. was when Ashley Judd came on stage. She began with, "I am Ashley Judd, and I am a feminist." The crowd went wild with cheers and clapping. Women had been made wary of calling themselves a feminist during the Backlash of the late 1980s, and each generation since had been taught to reject feminist labels. There was power in declaring oneself to be a feminist to a receptive crowd that went farther than the eye could see (Wallace and Parlapiano 2017).

Judd proceeded to recite a poem that she introduced as written by Nina Donovan, a 19-year-old from Franklin, Tennessee (Henry 2017). Donovan's poem starts with, "I am a nasty woman. I'm as nasty as a man who looks like he bathes in Cheetos dust. A man whose words are a distract to America." Her poem highlights and embraces the nastiness of womanhood as well as the nastiness of Trump and his ugly rhetoric. The last line of her poem, as read by Judd, was a powerful call to usurp and rearticulate what it means to be a nasty woman, "So if you a nasty woman, or you love one who is, let me hear you say, hell yeah." The crowd responded with "HELL YEAH!" Judd's recitation of Donovan's poem was powerful because the imagery of womanhood, which was once too vulgar for typical conversations, was now centered in the women's movement. Donovan's poem and Judd's reading of her poem embody a self-assured feminist that embraces womanhood, sexuality, and biology and is willing to take action by using their gifts and talents. To some extent, this exemplified feminism that utilizes a "raunch culture" to tap into female independence and emancipation (Genz and Brabon 2018). Seeing signs embracing the status of "nasty woman," and hearing Donovan's poem performed live where women could feel the power of taking and using the "nasty woman" designation served as a rallying cry of solidarity. Many women who took a road trip to D.C. wrote the phrase, "I'm a nasty woman!" on their car windows, indicating a major change in the culture of silence.

## #METOO

Since the women's movement, social media has played a significant role in opening up spaces for discussion possibilities on embodied resistance through protests (Cohen, Forbis, and Misri 2018). Ten months after the Women's March, Ashley Judd gave a first-person account of sexual harassment by Hollywood executive Harvey Weinstein in a news story published October 5, 2017 (Bahr 2017; CT 2020). Ten days later, actress Alyssa Milano popularized "Me Too" with the tweet, "If you've been sexually harassed or assaulted write 'me too' as a reply to this tweet" (Milano 2017). The #MeToo movement resonated with many women all over the world and became an international movement.

Although repopularized in 2017, the #MeToo movement actually began in 2006 by Tarana Burke, a Black American woman (Garcia 2017). The movement did not get national and international attention in 2006 like it did when it was used by a female celebrity. Prominent women began using the #MeToo to talking publicly about being sexually harassed, assaulted, or violated (CT 2020). It is not coincidental that #MeToo gained so much momentum after the 2017 Women's March. The wrongful behavior of Trump led to an outpouring of women finding their voice. The power of numbers leads to changes. This became evident when Harvey Weinstein, a former film producer, was sentenced to 23 years in prison for rape and sexual assault (CT 2020).

## ZERO-ARRESTS: WHITE PRIVILEGE AND THE COLLECTIVE POWER OF WOMEN

What made the Women's March unique was that despite the vast amounts of people marching in the streets, there were zero reported crimes or arrests. Jessica Watters (2017), in her article titled "Pink Hats and Black Fists," describes the "zero arrests" worldwide at the Women's March as being a measure of white privilege. White women have the power to garner widespread support of political platforms when they come out in masses. Many people were pleased with the peaceful nature of the protests and highlighted the fact that no arrests, damage, or riots occurred at the Women's March. While the national guard and police were very much present, they were not dressed and armed in riot gear. The ongoing helicopter presence was not a disruptive force at the Women's March like it was for the Million Man March and the Million Woman March. At both the African American Marches, the helicopters flew low over the crowds drowning out the speakers. This was reported by Dr. Anthony Lemelle in his description of the Million Man March (1995) and by Janofsky (1997) in his article on the Million Woman March. Watters (2017) describes how white women are typically given the benefit of the doubt and accorded judicial and protective rights with the exception of sexual assault. Women often turn to allies in their struggle against sexual violence; through the Women's March, it became evident that this allyship could be extended to Black women and their families who are subjected to state violence.

The power of the women's movement is significant on a personal level. Estes (2018) describes how the personal is political, especially for women in this era struggling against the conservative's war on womanhood, which comprises policies and legislation designed to limit women's rights and equality.

## ANSWERING THE CALL: THE HISTORIC ELECTION OF WOMEN TO CONGRESS

### 2018 Midterm Election—Ecofeminist Agendas

The overwhelming success of women seeking political office for the first time in 2018 transformed the House of Representatives with a diversity never before seen in Congress (Alter 2018). Sixty percent of the Congressional seats up for election were won by women. This resulted in a shift in power in the House of Representatives as the dominant political party was replaced; the Democrats gained control. The success of the political campaigns, based on intersectionality and inclusiveness, demonstrated ideals consistent with ecofeminism and contradictory to the dominant ideology of the anti-ecofeminist political agenda established in 2016 by the Trump administration.

An understanding of the historical magnitude of the 2018 Midterm Election results requires only a brief review of female representation in the US Congress. The concept of government "by the people and for the people" is ideally based on the concept of representation. As the legislative branch of government, Congress is composed of the Senate and the House of Representatives. The Senate is made up of 100 members who represent the interest of the states; The House of Representatives is made up of 435 members who represent the interest and popular will of the people. As a patriarchal society, the United States established and maintained a Congressional representation that was exclusive to men. For more than a century after the establishment of the United States, every representative in both the Senate and the House of Representatives were male.

In 1917, Jeannette Rankin became the first woman ever elected to serve in the US Congress. Rankin, a social worker and activist in the women's suffrage movement, was elected to represent Montana (Manning and Brudnick 2018). While Rankin's election to the House of Representatives was historical and considered a great achievement for women, female representation in elected government positions remained nominal.

Based on data from the US Congressional Research Service, 23 women served in the 97th Congress composed of 535 Congressional members. The year was 1981, and the 4.3 percent female representation was an achievement that took 64 years after Rankin. Women in the United States comprise 51 percent of the population, yet since 1917, Congress had averaged only 6.17 percent female representation with an average growth increase of 45 percent throughout the country's history (Manning and Brudnick 2018).

An explanation for low female representation in Congress can be found in the many obstacles that women who seek political office have encountered. A recent study revealed that although male and female candidates received similar amounts of attention, female candidates endured significantly more negative attacks on social media (Shah 2019). One of the many challenges facing female candidates is raising money for their campaigns. Newly elected Congresswoman Rashida Tlaib shared a story about receiving $1,000 from a proponent of Muslim candidates. She later discovered that the same man gave the maximum contribution of $2,700 to Keith Ellison, who became the first Muslim man in Congress. Tlaib was very grateful for the contribution made to her campaign but recognized the fact that the donor gave nearly three times as much money to a male Muslin candidate (Zernike 2018). The Cook Political report tracked political fundraising and revealed significant differences along gender lines (Overby 2018). An analysis of campaign finance records uncovered a "gender gap" in campaign fundraising where the women who ran for Congress averaged $500,000 less than male candidates (Overby 2018). Male candidates tend to be more connected to businesses and organizations, or they have the personal fortunes to fund their own campaign, while women rely on small donations from many individuals (Zernike 2018).

Despite all obstacles, the 2018 Midterm Election became a groundbreaking event for female candidates. The historic number of women elected to Congress reflected a solid 4 percent increase in one election (Desilver 2018). The increase of women representatives resulted in the largest percentage of female representation in the history of Congress at 23.40 percent.

Across the country, women whose previous political involvement was limited to voting transformed into serious political candidates with a resolute determination to transform Washington.

Campaigning for Congressional seats in the Senate and House of Representatives, as well as state legislatures, women stepped into the political arena in record-breaking numbers (Pramuk 2018). According to data from the Center of American Women and Politics at Rutgers University (2018, 2016), the historic surge of female candidates for the House of Representatives alone represented a 74.4 percent increase from the 2016 election. In what has been described as "the Pink Wave," "a revolution," and even "payback" (Alter 2018), there were more female candidates in the 2018 Midterm Election "than any other election in U.S. history" (Shalby 2018).

## DATA ANALYSIS AND RESULTS

Research presented at the 2019 Annual Meetings of the American Sociological Association in New York indicates that the increase in anti-ecofeminist policies is directly correlated with the historic number of women elected to Congress in 2018 (Bartoli and Rose 2019). Qualitative and quantitative data collected from the public campaign websites of women elected to the US House of Representatives and Senate in 2018 were examined. The campaign websites were a means to communicate with the public and provided information about their political platforms.

The conceptualization of ecofeminism was drawn from the established and developing scholarship. For this research, five ecofeminist platforms were identified as significant issues: health care, environmental justice, equality for women, protections for immigrants, and protections for LGBTQ+ individuals. This study examined the public websites of the incoming class of newly elected women to evaluate the presence of ecofeminist values. The Pink Wave created an opportunity to document opposition to patriarchy, exploitive

| | REPRESENTATIVE | CONGRESSIONAL OFFICE WON | CAMPAIGN WEBSITE |
|---|---|---|---|
| 1 | Cindy Axne | HR Iowa's 3rd District | Cindyaxneforcongress.com |
| 2 | Marsha Blackburn | SENATE Tennessee | Marshablackburn.com |
| 3 | Angie Craig | HR Minnesota's 2nd District | Angiecraig.com |
| 4 | Sharice Davids | HR Kansas's 3rd District | Shariceforcongress.com |
| 5 | Madeleine Dean | HR Pennsylvania's 4th District | Mad4pa.com |
| 6 | Veronica Escobar | HR Texas's 16th District | Veronicaescobar.com |
| 7 | Abby Finkenauer | HR Iowa's 1st District | Abbyfinkenauer.com |
| 8 | Lizzie Fletcher | HR Texas's 7th District | Lizziefletcher.com |
| 9 | Sylvia Garcia | HR Texas's 29th District | Sylviaforcongress.com |
| 10 | Deb Haaland | HR New Mexico's 1st District | Debforcongress.com |
| 11 | Jahana Hayes | HR Connecticut's 5th District | Jahanahayes.com |
| 12 | Katie Hill | HR California's 25th District | Katiehillforcongress.com |
| 13 | Kendra Horn | HR Oklahoma's 5th District | Kendrahornforcongress.com |
| 14 | Chrissy Houlahan | HR Pennsylvania's 6th District | Chrissyhoulahanforcongress.com |
| 15 | Cindy Hyde-Smith | SENATE Mississippi | Cindyhydesmith.com |
| 16 | Susie Lee | HR Nevada's 3rd District | Susieleeforcongress.com |
| 17 | Elaine Luria | HR Virginia's 2nd District | Elaineforcongress.com |
| 18 | Lucy McBath | HR Georgia's 6th District | Lucyforcongress.com |
| 19 | Carol Miller | HR West Virginia's 3rd District | Electcarolmiller.com |
| 20 | Debbie Mucarsel-Powell | HR Florida's 26th District | Debbiemucarselpowell.com |
| 21 | Alexandria Ocasio-Cortez | HR New York's 14th District | Ocasio2018.com |
| 22 | Ilhan Omar | HR Minnesota's 5th District | Ilhanomar.com |
| 23 | Katie Porter | HR California's 45th District | Katieporter.com |
| 24 | Ayanna Pressley | HR Massachusetts's 7th District | Ayannapressley.com |
| 25 | Jacky Rosen | SENATE Nevada | Rosenfornevada.com |
| 26 | Kim Schrier | HR Washington's 8th District | Drkimschrier.com |
| 27 | Donna Shalala | HR Florida's 27th District | Donnashalala.com |
| 28 | Kyrsten Sinema | SENATE Arizona | Kyrstensinema.com |
| 29 | Mikie Sherrill | HR New Jersey's 11th District | Mikiesherrill.com |
| 30 | Elissa Slotkin | HR Michigan's 8th District | Elissaforcongress.com |
| 31 | Tina Smith | SENATE Minnesota | Tinaforminnesota.com |
| 32 | Abigail Spanberger | HR Virginia's 7th District | Abigailspanberger.com |
| 33 | Haley Stevens | HR Michigan's 11th District | Haleystevensforcongress.com |
| 34 | Rashida Tlaib | HR Michigan's 13th District | Rashidaforcongress.com |
| 35 | Xochitl Torres Small | HR New Mexico's 2nd District | Xochforcongress.com |
| 36 | Lori Trahan | HR Massachusetts's 3rd District | Loritrahan.com |
| 37 | Lauren Underwood | HR Illinois's 14 District | Underwoodforcongress.com |
| 38 | Jennifer Wexton | HR Virginia's 10th District | Jenniferwexton.com |

**Figure 5.2 The Pink Wave. The surge of political activism resulted in a significant increase of women participating in the 2018 Midterm Elections as candidates for local, state, and national political leadership positions.** *Source*: Bartoli, Teresa and Lydia Rose (2019) "Ecofeminist Analysis of the 2018 Midterm Election of Women in the United States Congress." Paper presented at the 2019 American Sociological Association Meetings in New York.

capitalism, and colonialism through a reassertion of important issues that contribute to the overall well-being of people living in the United States.

The public websites of the 38 women newly elected to Congress were examined during the weeks of December 13, 2018 to January 9, 2019. Figure 5.2 is a list of each representative's name, the Congressional office they won, and their website.

| | Newly Elected Women/ First-Time Politicians of the 2018 Midterm Elections | HEALTH CARE | ENVIRONMENTAL JUSTICE | EQUALITY/ PROTECTING WOMENS RIGHTS | PROTECTIONS FOR IMMIGRANTS | PROTECTIONS FOR LGBTQ+ INDIVIDUALS | Total Score |
|---|---|---|---|---|---|---|---|
| 1 | Cindy Axne (D) | 1 | 1 | 1 | 0 | 0 | 3 |
| 2 | Marsha Blackburn (R) | 1 | 0 | 0 | 0 | 0 | 1 |
| 3 | Angie Craig (D) | 1 | 1 | 1 | 0 | 0 | 3 |
| 4 | Sharice Davids (D) | 1 | 0 | 0 | 0 | 0 | 1 |
| 5 | Madeleine Dean (D) | 1 | 1 | 0 | 1 | 1 | 4 |
| 6 | Veronica Escobar (D) | 1 | 1 | 0 | 1 | 0 | 3 |
| 7 | Abby Finkenauer (D) | 1 | 1 | 1 | 0 | 0 | 3 |
| 8 | Lizzie Fletcher (D) | 1 | 0 | 0 | 1 | 0 | 2 |
| 9 | Sylvia Garcia (D) | 1 | 0 | 1 | 1 | 1 | 4 |
| 10 | Deb Haaland (D) | 1 | 1 | 1 | 0 | 1 | 4 |
| 11 | Jahana Hayes (D) | 1 | 1 | 1 | 1 | 1 | 5 |
| 12 | Katie Hill (D) | 1 | 1 | 0 | 0 | 1 | 3 |
| 13 | Kendra Horn (D) | 1 | 1 | 1 | 0 | 0 | 3 |
| 14 | Chrissy Houlahan (D) | 1 | 1 | 0 | 0 | 1 | 3 |
| 15 | Cindy Hyde-Smith (R) | 1 | 0 | 0 | 0 | 0 | 1 |
| 16 | Susie Lee (D) | 1 | 1 | 1 | 1 | 0 | 4 |
| 17 | Elaine Luria (D) | 1 | 1 | 1 | 0 | 0 | 3 |
| 18 | Lucy McBath (D) | 1 | 1 | 1 | 0 | 0 | 3 |
| 19 | Carol Miller (R) | 0 | 0 | 0 | 0 | 0 | 0 |
| 20 | Debbie Mucarsel-Powell (D) | 1 | 1 | 1 | 1 | 0 | 4 |
| 21 | Alexandria Ocasio-Cortez (D) | 1 | 1 | 1 | 0 | 1 | 4 |
| 22 | Ilhan Omar (D) | 1 | 1 | 1 | 0 | 1 | 4 |
| 23 | Katie Porter (D) | 1 | 1 | 1 | 1 | 1 | 5 |
| 24 | Ayanna Pressley (D) | 1 | 1 | 1 | 1 | 1 | 5 |
| 25 | Jacky Rosen (D) | 1 | 1 | 1 | 1 | 0 | 4 |
| 26 | Kim Schrier (D) | 1 | 1 | 1 | 1 | 0 | 4 |
| 27 | Donna Shalala (D) | 1 | 1 | 1 | 1 | 0 | 4 |
| 28 | Kyrsten Sinema (D) | 1 | 0 | 1 | 1 | 0 | 3 |
| 29 | Mikie Sherrill (D) | 1 | 1 | 1 | 0 | 1 | 4 |
| 30 | Elissa Slotkin (D) | 1 | 1 | 1 | 0 | 1 | 4 |
| 31 | Tina Smith (D) | 1 | 1 | 1 | 1 | 1 | 5 |
| 32 | Abigail Spanberger (D) | 1 | 1 | 0 | 0 | 0 | 2 |
| 33 | Haley Stevens (D) | 1 | 1 | 1 | 1 | 1 | 5 |
| 34 | Rashida Tlaib (D) | 1 | 1 | 1 | 1 | 1 | 5 |
| 35 | Xochitl Torres Small (D) | 1 | 1 | 0 | 1 | 0 | 3 |
| 36 | Lori Trahan (D) | 1 | 1 | 1 | 1 | 0 | 4 |
| 37 | Lauren Underwood (D) | 1 | 1 | 1 | 1 | 0 | 4 |
| 38 | Jennifer Wexton (D) | 1 | 1 | 1 | 1 | 1 | 5 |
| | | | | | | | N=38 $\bar{x}$=3.45 |

**Figure 5.3 Ecofeminist Platforms of Women Elected to Congress in 2018.** An examination of the 2018 political platforms of newly elected women in the Senate and House of Representatives revealed a focus on five crucial issues that encompass ecofeminist values: equal access to healthcare, striving for environmental justice, equality and the protection of rights for women, protections for immigrants, and protections for LGBTQ+ individuals. *Source*: Bartoli, Teresa and Lydia Rose (2019) "Ecofeminist Analysis of the 2018 Midterm Election of Women in the United States Congress." Paper presented at the 2019 American Sociological Association Meetings in New York.

Figure 5.3 includes the scores each Congresswoman received for each of the five ecofeminist issues identified on their webpage. The five ecofeminist areas of interest (healthcare, environmental justice, equality for women, protections for immigrants, and protections for LGBTQ+ individuals) were selected because of their direct opposition to the Trump administration. If the platform was consistent with ecofeminist values, the Congresswomen received a score of 1 on that issue.

The review of issues was limited to the content on the campaign websites, so the candidates received a zero if no mention of the selected issue was found on the website. The overall mean of the 38 candidates' total scores is 3.45, with a standard deviation of 1.23. Nearly 20 percent of the newly elected candidates addressed all five issues on their webpages (18.42 percent). Of the candidates that did not address all five issues, over a third mentioned four of the five issues on their pages (36.84 percent), and nearly another third mentioned at least three of the ecofeminist values on their webpages (28. 95 percent). Overall, 84.21 percent of the newly elected candidates specifically mentioned three or more ecofeminist values.

## DISCUSSION OF RESULTS

The data reflects the notion that current Republican platforms disregard ecofeminists values such as the health of the masses (healthcare), the environment (environmental justice), women's issues (equality of women), immigrants and refugees, and the LBGTQ+ community. Where science has been "the most celebrated tool for the domination of the world by Western man" (Lemelle 1995), the Trump administration has overtly rejected science in favor of exploitative capitalism. Decisions that were once justified on the basis of scientific evidence and foundational documents such as the Constitution of the United States have been replaced by capitalistic goals and standards. Capitalism serves as the prevailing tool for domination and justification for the exploitation of peoples and land. The exaggerated use of tropes of domination, and the overly assertive valorization of hegemonic masculinity, has provided a disruption to a political system that resulted in a significant increase in women's political activism.

One of the political policies and actions that counters an ecofeminist agenda is the United State's withdrawal from the 2015 Paris Agreement on Climate Change despite overwhelming scientific data warning of disastrous harm to the planet Earth and its inhabitants. The direct support of capital enterprise over the protection of the environment in the United States (water, air, soil) is most evident by the budget/funding cuts for the Environmental Protection Agency (EPA); The Trump administration cut the EPA budget by 31 percent.

The constant attempts to repeal the Affordable Healthcare Act reinforce the values of capitalism over the health and well-being of people living in the United States. The signed Executive Orders that allow states to deny funding to Planned Parenthood is a direct attack on the reproductive health of women and youth. In addition, Executive Orders were signed revoking the 2014 Fair Pay and Safe Workplaces Order designed to ensure compliance with 14 labor and civil rights laws protecting women in the workplace. The Trump administration has also acted in a systematic effort to reverse protections for members of the LGBTQ+ community including, overturning an interpretation of the Civil Rights Act that provided protection to transgender workers.

Ecofeminism recognizes the value of all life. Carlassare (2000) observes that ecofeminists "call for social changes that foster egalitarian social relations and believe that such changes are a prerequisite for an ecologically healthy society." Additionally, the historic shift in women elected to the US Congress may be understood by the analysis of their political platforms that promoted the ecofeminist values that resulted in their election. Understanding the role of hegemonic masculinity and tropes of domination in society exposes the resistance displayed in the 2018 Midterm Elections. Elections were won on platforms that revealed the complex interconnection between nature and culture while portraying and recognizing the significance of ecofeminist values.

People from all over the world became vocal in opposing the reassertion of patriarchy, exploitative capitalism, and colonialism and advocated values consistent with ecofeminism. The advocation of values consistent with ecofeminism showcased how ecofeminist theory can quickly come to the foreground. The success of the political campaigns, based on intersectionality and inclusiveness, demonstrates the ideals consistent with ecofeminism and represented a clear rejection of the dominant ideology of the anti-ecofeminist political agenda established in 2016.

## CONCLUSION: THE GROWING INCREASE OF WOMEN RUNNING FOR POLITICAL OFFICE

The election of Donald Trump as president of the United States, despite his continuous undignified and sexist remarks, sparked political action around the world. There was a shared sense that more involvement in politics was necessary. This sentiment was the catalyst for the 2017 Women's March, a grassroots movement that grew from a single Facebook post to become a global event. As news of the event spread, people from all around the world joined in by organizing sister marches. This resulted in activists in every continent participating in the march, including Antarctica. The Pussyhat project exemplifies the solidarity and unity of women. Many women who could not attend the marches participated by knitting hats and sending them to the march. Although the pink hats served as a visible symbol of unity, they were not without controversy. Some people saw the pink hats as a representation of white women and exclusionary of minoritized groups (i.e., people of color, transgenders).

The state violence that emerges from systemic racism, when people of color gather in protest, is displayed through the use of riot gear, pepper spray, weapons, and mass arrests. These violent tactics have been used time and time as a means of control. White women are often granted privileges not afforded to Black Americans, indigenous peoples, and peoples of color. The white privilege at the march was evident by the fact that there were zero reported crimes or arrests, despite the fact that millions of women globally came out. When white women and women from minoritized groups join together, state violence is reduced. This march set a political agenda and reinvigorated other movements, particularly the #MeToo movement that brought the prevalence of sexual violence against women to the forefront.

One of the greatest outcomes of the 2017 Women's March was the significant number of women that won Congressional seats in the 2018 election. After the 2018 Midterm elections, there were 127 women that were elected to the US Congress; after the 2020 election, there are at least 141 women elected to Congress (eight races are still outstanding during the writing of this book). There was also an increase in the number of minoritized women; in 2018, there were 48 women of color serving in Congress. This number was increased to 51 in 2020 (again, that might increase depending on the outcomes of the outstanding races). Many of the women, who were new to Congress in 2018, sought a second term and won. However, there was also an upsurge in the number of female Republican candidates who ran for office and won a seat.

While all reports show that President-elect Joe Biden received the most votes in both the popular vote and the electoral college in the 2020 election, there was no "Blue Tsunami" in Congress as was expected. Although the number of women running for office in 2020 increased, about half of them represented the GOP. This was a significant difference in comparison to the 2018 election, where only one of the 38 newly elected women was a Republican. The power of pink stands.

# *Chapter 6*

# Pernicious Political Tactics

## *COVID-19 and Voter Suppression*

The COVID-19 global pandemic came at a time when major political divides in the United States peaked. To conduct an ecofeminist analysis of the increase of women involved politically is to recognize this polarization. Polarization of either/or thinking, binary thinking, is counter-ethical to an ecofeminist stance. The 2016 and 2020 presidential elections exhibited this binary thinking and are exemplified in support of Hillary R. Clinton in 2016, Joseph R. Biden, Jr., in 2020, or Trump in both 2016 and 2020. Ecofeminism is a theory and tool to reject this binary thinking by centering analysis and emphasize ecological systems that bring attention to the connections among natural environments, social environments, and the impact of patriarchal domination and oppression. In spite of a global pandemic and pernicious political tactics that were aimed to suppress voters, there has been a profound increase of women participating in politics, running for public office, and being elected to political offices. As of November 15, Biden has been called the winner of the 2020 presidential election with the largest voter turnout in history. However, more than half of white women voters supported Trump (Wolf et al. 2020).

In December 2019, with the identification and spread of a novel coronavirus with detrimental impacts on human lives, societies around the globe were required to radically shift the ways in which one participated in society. While many strategies were implemented to mitigate the spread of the virus, there was also a strong political response to the ensuing pandemic, including an array of resistance and counter-effective tactics. Voter suppression tactics began when state officials attempted to reschedule and "retool" the election process. Twenty-one states changed the voting process to mitigate the spread of the virus (NCSL 2020). In Ohio, it was announced the day before the primary vote that all voting polling places were going to be closed and that the deadline for voting through mail-in ballots would be extended (Rakich 2020). Most states encountered resistance to proposed changes. When Wisconsin attempted to institute similar processes as in Ohio, they were stopped by the courts. People were forced to make a choice between going in person to vote during the pandemic or not voting at all. In states like Wisconsin, where new voting protocols were rejected, the rapid spread of the virus is attributed to in-person voting (Rakich 2020).

COVID-19 had an unprecedented impact on democracy. This chapter is organized into four sections. The first section is documentation and examination of the social justice issues that emerged from the political polarization tactics of Trump, his administration, and his supporters during the pandemic, and their denial of the seriousness of the virus. The polarizing thought process has the effect of maintaining oppressive domination over marginalized groups. The second section will also describe the social-ecological disruptions caused by the pandemic to traditional social institutions—family, work, and education. Changes to these institutions highlight the social-ecological justice issues: moving social interactions to online spaces, expanding the use of home spaces, and socially constructing who are "essential" workers. The third section will discuss how Trump, his administration, and his supporters continued the practice of spreading misinformation and lies to attack American democracy. These lies resulted in the spread of COVID-19 and the mass loss of lives. The last section of this chapter will explore the environmental and ecological disruptions of the anthropocentric polluting practices that occurred during the early stages of the pandemic societal "shutdown." Understanding these disruptions can provide answers and strategies for dealing with expanded ecological issues such as climate change, animal well-being, and the well-being of the earth.

## COVID-19: A HISTORICAL RECORD AND TIMELINE

As of November 15, 2020, COVID-19 has taken the lives of over 251,268 people in the United States (Worldometers 2020). Globally, more than 54 million cases of COVID-19 have been reported, with over a million deaths worldwide (Worldometers 2020). This illness was first recognized on December 31, 2019—China reported a cluster of pneumonia in Wuhan, with the first death occurring on January 11 and was due to a novel coronavirus (Schumaker 2020). On January 20, the CDC confirmed the first case of the virus in the United States (Holshue et al. 2010). On January 30, images of a deceased Chinese man who fell dead on the streets of Wuhan were circulated worldwide (France-Presse 2020), indicating to many the seriousness of the disease.

On January 31, 2020, the US Department of Health and Human Services (HHS) declared the coronavirus a public health emergency, and the U.S. Centers for Disease Control and Prevention (CDC) issued a 14-day federal quarantine for American evacuees from Wuhan, China (Schumaker 2020). The last enforced large-scale isolation and quarantine instituted by the US government was during the influenza ("Spanish Flu") pandemic in 1918–1919 (CDC 2020).

On February 8, 28 days since the first reported death, China reported over 800 people had died from the coronavirus. Three days later, the World Health Organization (WHO) named this illness COVID-19 (COrona-VIrus-Disease, 2019). The name was chosen as a way to focus attention on the novel coronavirus while avoiding the stigmatizing effect of naming an illness by geographic location or by groups of people. This was a public health lesson learned from the AIDS epidemic; the initial name for the disease was "Gay-Related Immune Deficiency" and focused on a social identity rather than the spread of a virus (Rose 1993; Rose 1997).

On February 20, the first known local transmission of the virus in Italy took place. Within four days, two major provinces in Northern Italy were shut down, with the announcement that the rest of the country would soon follow, as a way to limit the spread of the virus. In less than a week, US students studying abroad in Italy (and around the world) were called back to the United States (Kano 2020).

The first US reported death occurred in Washington State on February 29, 2020 (Acevedo and Burke 2020). The WHO announced on March 11, 2020, that COVID-19 had become a global pandemic and that every nation should take steps to mitigate the spread of the virus (Branswell and Joseph 2020). On March 13, 2020, Trump declared a National Emergency. By March 30, the bodies in New York were piling up so fast that local morgues ran out of space. Refrigerated trucks were brought in to store the excessive amount of bodies (Musumeci 2020).

## Rejecting a Medical Response

The polarization of how to address and respond to this illness began with Trump refusing to develop a national medical response. In the United States, the president was unwilling to establish a unified national action plan to limit the spread of the virus. The responsibility of protecting the health and welfare of Americans fell to state governors, who began developing state-based policies and practices aimed at curtailing the pandemic within their own states. Trump used oppressive and biased rhetoric and action to create chaos in developing strategies to address COVID-19 issues by ridiculing and demonizing Democratic governors. State governors found themselves competing among each other for masks, gloves, and other protective gear for health care workers, along with ventilators and test kits (Subramanian 2020). As medical experts around the world recognized that this new virus had become a global pandemic, individuals were advised to wear masks and avoid social gatherings to protect themselves from COVID-19. However, the various state policies created to decrease the transmission and spread of the disease reinforced the pre-existing social divides among the privileged and those most susceptible to the virus. Conditions such as being immune-compromised, diabetes, obesity, asthma are the same kinds of conditions that are associated with certain social determinants such as social class status.

## Flattening the Curve

The lesson learned in Italy and New York was that any peak rise in the viral transmission would overwhelm hospitals and leave healthcare staff unable to care for the mass of individuals in need of critical care and ventilators. The goal for state governors was to "flatten the curve." Steps were taken to mitigate the spread of the illness, so as people got sick and needed medical attention, the hospitals would have the capacity to care for them. The major strategy was to create a social norm for both wearing face masks and maintaining a social distance of six feet. Public health service announcements and weekly addresses to constituents included messages on handwashing, disinfecting spaces, and doing one's part to flatten the curve.

## "Stay-in-Place" Orders

"Stay-at-home" measures and "social distancing" were instituted in early March by most US states. These measures were created after observing how the rapid spread of COVID-19 caused a major strain on the health care system. In both Italy and New York, the health care systems were unable to accommodate the massive number of people who required critical care. The major concern was to avoid overwhelming hospitals and ensure that there would be access to life-saving ventilators for anyone who needed one.

On March 15, Puerto Rico was the first territory to institute a "stay-at-home" order, closely followed by California (March 19). On March 20, 2020, the New York Governor Andrew Cuomo signed the "New York State on PAUSE" Executive Order, which included a 90-day moratorium on any residential or commercial evictions. Other states also put into place similar actions. Within four weeks of the first order, 42 states had "stay-at-home" orders in place. A few states, Oklahoma, Wyoming, and Utah, only recommended that people stay home but did not close businesses. In those states, the larger cities instituted stay-at-home orders. Five rural states had no orders in place (North Dakota, South Dakota, Nebraska, Iowa, and Arkansas).

Typically, in cities and states with "stay-at-home" orders, leaving home was limited to the following: (1) activities related to health and safety, (2) acquiring necessary supplies and services, (3) participating in outdoor activity, (4) going to essential jobs, and (5) taking care of others. The language of "stay-at-home" brought to the forefront the number of people who did not have homes, and the language was changed to "stay-in-place." During this time, many people lost their jobs due to the closing of businesses and were unable to pay their rent or mortgages. These housing issues, particularly the issue of housing insecurity and evictions, resulted in moratoriums on evictions. In September, as the 90-day moratoriums began to end and millions of renters and homeowners faced eviction, the CDC offered an additional 90-day moratorium on evictions. However, the financial obligation of rent was not relieved, resulting in a rise in debt. Landlords that rely on income from rents are no longer receiving income. In January 2021, many residents and landowners will be faced with trying to meet back rent payments or face evictions. This will result in a major housing crisis in the near future if no action is taken.

All businesses that were deemed "non-essential" were forced to close. Non-essential businesses included stores that sold clothing, entertainment goods, electronic goods, and luxury goods, as well as service shops such as hair salons, bars, clubs, entertainment venues, recreational centers (i.e., gyms, fitness centers, ice skating rinks, arcades), and movie theaters.

The goal was to limit social contact with others as a means of inhibiting the spread of the virus. The social distancing orders prohibited gatherings of 10 or more individuals. People were told to stay six feet in distance from each other and avoid handshaking, hugging, and other forms of physical contact. Public health messages, circulated via the internet, focused on ways to avoid spreading the virus by explaining the proper way to wash hands and use hand sanitizers. Lockdown concerns began circulating throughout the nation. The "stay-at-home" orders created a cascading effect culturally, economically, politically, and psychologically. The strain on residents created disproportionate outcomes for the poor, the disadvantaged, the racially minoritized, and working families. Thirty million people became unemployed due to the stay-at-home orders losing their source of income (Jones 2020).

## SOCIAL-ECOLOGICAL DISRUPTIONS TO TRADITIONAL SOCIAL INSTITUTIONS: FAMILY, WORK, EDUCATION, AND FOOD SYSTEMS

The stay-in-place orders to mitigate the spread of COVID-19 radically transformed traditional social institutions such as family, work, and school. Most social interactions were moved online, and home spaces were reconfigured for work and school. From an ecofeminist stance, disruptions in traditional social institutions are multidimensional and have serious life-transforming outcomes for families, workers, and students. The many different ways that families were impacted by the shutdown, highlighted the diversity of families. Families and households are described in many ways, including the following: elderly couples (living in residencies or in caretaking facilities); single-person households with or without pets; multi-person households (with one or more roommates); people who are married or partnered, with or without kids (kids can range from babies and toddlers to school-age children (ages 4–17), to adult (some in college, some not); and multi-generational or extended families (i.e., grandparents, grandchildren, aunts, uncles).

Parents who worked in offices found themselves having to convert home spaces into workspaces. The lines between "parent" and "employee" blurred. Housework, child-rearing, and home-teaching, overlapped with the responsibilities and duties of working from home. The disruptions to both work and parenting were layered in such a way that household stress, parenting stress, and work stress all became conflated. Parents with school-aged children who worked jobs defined as essential were required to work outside of the home and experienced extreme role strain and conflict; these parents were forced to find solutions for childcare and schooling when schools and daycare centers shut down. Essential workers also had to deal with the additional stress of possibly exposing their families to COVID-19.

The mass shutdown of non-essential economic activity resulted in large numbers of people, who work in precarious jobs, being laid-off, let go, or furloughed. This created financial stress, instability, and insecurity in the home. This significant increase in household stress is likely to magnify violence in the home. Traditional ways to manage and mitigate violence in the home were disrupted—almost 20 percent of reported child abuse cases come from teachers. Additionally, people who are abused tend to wait for opportunities to seek help when the abuser is outside of the home. Prior to the COVID-19 pandemic, the CDC reported that one in four women and one in ten men experience intimate partner violence, which can be physical, emotional, sexual, or psychological in nature (Smith, Zhang, et al. 2018).

The traditional support from teachers, counselors, social workers, mental health care professionals, and health centers was initially shut down, and families were cut off from much-needed services. As these services were moved to online environments, the digital divide became even more apparent than before COVID-19. The mass and immediate transition to home-based online environments for work and education revealed major holes in the infrastructure of connectivity to the internet. Disadvantages in the US telecommunications infrastructure included access to high-speed internet and access to adequate devices (phones, tablets, computers) that could accommodate the various online applications, platforms, and software needed to successfully access and complete online work, online school/learning activities, and telehealth activities.

## Food Supply Ecosystems

The most basic function of the family is to provide food and shelter. As the functions of the family expanded during the pandemic, the ecosystems surrounding food and sustenance experienced major disruptions. As news came of the upcoming societal shutdown, panic buying ensued. Rushing to the stores, people cleared out the shelves, causing massive alarm and stressing the food and supply systems. People began mass purchasing household items such as toilet paper, cleaning supplies, disinfectant wipes, and hand sanitizers, as well as processed food supplies such as pasta, packaged foods, cereals, spaghetti sauces, ramen noodles, mac n' cheese, canned goods, frozen food products, baby food, and baby formula; those who had ample financial resources purchased needed items in large bulk. Shopping increased at large box stores (such as Walmart and Target supercenters) and warehouse club stores like Costco and Sam's Club. People and families started to feel the strain on their budgets in trying to buy more than they usually do, and those with no financial cushion, or limited credit, were unable to purchase the additional items. Families that live from check to check were unable to purchase food and supplies during this panic buying phase. Inventories in grocery stores and box stores were cleaned out in early March, with very limited restocking well into April.

With limited supplies, stores put limits on the number of items people could buy and reduced shopping hours so clerks would have more time to restock shelves (Kassraie 2020). Concerns regarding the food supply chain, and the massive need to employ essential workers to stock shelves, created more concerns about the spread of COVID-19 among clerks and the people shopping. New concerns also arose that the virus could be on your groceries. Videos were shared on how to disinfect your groceries and how to limit contact with others while shopping. Along with family food insecurity was the impact of family members who worked in the food industry.

## Grocery Workers: Essential Workers and Economic Disadvantage

During this time of panic buying, grocery stores became understaffed as they struggled with trying to keep shelves fully stocked. When store shelves were cleared out, job postings for grocery workers jumped 60 percent (Richardson 2020). When looking for new employees, managers hired disadvantaged people (who had lost their job during the pandemic but did not qualify for

**Figure 6.1 Empty shelves at a grocery store during the early days of the pandemic.** Photo by Lydia Rose.

unemployment payments). Although people who worked in grocery stores were recognized as essential, the jobs remained low wages with little benefits. Many of the grocery workers were also working without, or with limited, protective gear (Richardson 2020). Such essential workers were at risk of contracting and spreading the virus. In early April, approximately 40 grocery worker deaths were attributed to COVID-19, and around 1,500 workers tested positive (Richardson 2020).

New protocols were instituted to mitigate the spread of COVID-19. Disinfecting strategies and protocols (in one door, out another door, one-way aisles) were initiated within stores. With mandatory "social distancing," shopping for groceries online with curbside-pick-up increased as a way to limit contact between grocery clerks and the public (Herships and Garcia 2019). A limited number of grocery stores closed to the public completely and only offered online shopping with curbside pickup (Bona 2020). Protective gear like Plexi guards at registers, face masks, and gloves became mandatory. People were asked to limit shopping to once a week and to send only one family member to the store. Certain store hours were set aside for elderly and immuno-compromised people to shop.

"Dozens of [essential] workers, including meat cutters, supermarket greeters, airport screeners and bus drivers have died as the disease has spread" (Grabell, Yeung, and Jameel 2020). A major outbreak of COVID-19 occurred in the meat-packing industry (Bagenstose, Chadde, and Wynn 2020), and a number of large plants had to close.

> A bill introduced in the U.S. House of Representatives on Tuesday [April 19] would require OSHA to issue enforceable safety standards to protect workers from COVID-19. A day earlier, 32 Democratic and two independent U.S. senators sent their concerns in a letter to the Trump administration asking what was being done to protect food workers and the supply chain. (Bagenstose, Chadde, and Wynn 2020)

On April 28, President Trump signed an executive order using the Defense Production Act (DPA) to force meat processing plants to stay open; he designated them as critical infrastructure (Gangitano 2020). Trump told reporters that the order would address "liability problems" related to the food supply chain and specifically mentioned Tyson Foods (Gangitano 2020). This order did nothing to stop the spread of COVID-19 among workers in the meat-packing industry.

> High rates of absenteeism, whether from sickened workers or fearful employees staying home to avoid infection, have for weeks plagued the meat-packing industry, where workers often labor in close quarters. A Center for Disease Control and Prevention study released on Friday showed more than 4,900 workers in meat and poultry processing facilities have tested positive for Covid-19, and at least 20 have died [as of May 1]. (Westwood 2020)

## Food Insecurity

Many who lost their jobs no longer had an income or a financial buffer. Food banks became responsible for providing food for the new surge of people who lost their income. With the fear of spreading the virus, volunteers and donations of food fell way below average. While an average food bank or food distribution center might only see 50–100 people, suddenly eight to ten times that amount of families were showing up nationwide (Kulish 2020), indicating a major breakdown in the food system. Governors called the National Guard to work at food banks to ensure food was distributed safely and smoothly (Ruwitch 2020; Lakhani 2020). COVID-19 revealed that major food insecurity issues are a national crisis in the United States. The disruption in food systems became a global issue, and widespread human starvation emerged throughout the world (Klare 2020).

## Educational Institutions

Just before the World Health Organization (WHO) declared the global pandemic and requested nations to take measures to mitigate the spread of the virus, different groups and states within the United States began taking action. The shutdown started with educational institutions. Colleges and universities, with students in study abroad programs in Italy and South Korea, recalled students at the end of February (Kano 2020). Beginning March 4, colleges and universities began closing their buildings and sending students home to engage in remote learning (Baker, Hartocollis, and Weise 2020). On March 12, Ohio governor, Mike DeWine, was the first to order the closing of public and private schools, followed by seven other states and large school districts (Meckler 2020). The governor of Kentucky was not initially willing to take strong steps but did recommend that schools cease in-person classes (Meckler 2020). With the death toll growing substantially in New York, states around the country started taking actions that indicated the pandemic was serious. By April 4, 2020, all states in the United States mandated school closings (Nagel 2020).

Classes and teachers began using video conferencing, and students with little or no access to the internet were left out. Technological divides became evident. Prior to the pandemic, many disadvantaged students in urban and rural areas relied on public libraries or local fast food or business establishments to access the internet. With stay-at-home measures, these places were no longer available (Diallo 2020). Some teachers started using email and phones to reach their students, and schools started looking for ways to get technology and internet hotspots out to their students. Although schools were closed, administrators marked the distance in which the internet could still be accessed from outside the buildings. Students with no internet at home were informed that there were places in the parking lots around the schools in which the internet could be accessed—but it was an inefficient strategy. Local PBS television stations began working with local school districts to select programming to align with the school curriculum and to engage student learning (Diallo 2020). Some schools were developing creative ways to have students drop off handwritten assignments (Diallo 2020).

Eight months into the pandemic, 4.4 million households with students still lacked consistent access to an adequate device, and 3.7 million still lack internet access (USAFacts.org 2020). This is most prevalent in rural areas and in poor/low-income households nationwide. A photo that went viral in August of 2020 showed two young girls sitting on a sidewalk outside of a Taco Bell to connect to free Wi-Fi and do their school work (Ebrahimji 2020).

For students and teachers that do have access to the internet, online synchronized classroom time was organized. Zoom, a nine-year-old online conferencing software service used by businesses, schools, and groups, suddenly jumped in popularity. Many teachers started setting up Zoom classrooms. Video conferencing by Zoom instantly became the "go to" software; the number of users skyrocketed from 10 million users in December 2019 to 200 million participants in March (Patnaik 2020). While K-12 schools, colleges and universities, and office workers began working remotely and connecting online with Zoom, a phenomenon referred to as zoombombings occurred. Zoombombings are cyber-attacks where a hacker enters, uninvited, a private Zoom conference session, spewing hate, racist or threatening comments, displaying racist or sexually explicit content, or threatening/taunting participants (Read 2020). Families, educational institutions, and workplaces became aware of the increased need for cybersecurity. However, in spite of security issues and zoombombings, Zoom participants increased to 300 million by late April (Warren 2020). Google Meets and M.S. Teams were able to capture some of the educational market emphasizing cybersecurity.

## Online Social Interaction

Online platforms were used, not just for remote work but also for social interactions. Online technology use increased during the early months of the COVID-19 pandemic. In a survey conducted by the Pew Research Center, over 85 percent of people in a survey reported that the internet was either essential (53 percent) or important (34 percent) to them during the pandemic (Vogels, Perrin, Rainie, and Anderson 2020). In that same study, 80 percent of the respondents reported that schools should either provide all students computers (37 percent) or provide computers to students whose families could not afford computers (43 percent). The digital divide was real, and the gaps in access to technology via the internet and cell phones became very pronounced during the pandemic. Anderson and Vogels (2020) found that 76 percent of people in their study used email or online messaging services to communicate with others; 70 percent used the internet to learn more about the coronavirus, and 25 percent used some kind of online video conferencing for work meetings.

Social interaction online has changed dramatically since the coronavirus was identified in January of 2020. Over a third of US adults reported participating in live online social gatherings such as parties, happy hours, or social events (Vogels 2020). Zoom happy hours, birthdays, and other special events were restructured virtually to connect people during "social distancing" and "stay-at-home" orders. In April 2020, Kent State University East Liverpool was one of the first to convert their Annual Earth Day Environmental Justice Conference to an online event where students were able to present their research. Actor John Krasinski, known for his roles in "The Office" and "A Quiet Place," started a YouTube series called SNG, "Some Good News," to bring positivity during the COVID 19 pandemic (Adams 2020). He used his channel to host a live, Virtual Prom to replace proms that were canceled. On April 28, Krasinski (2020) tweeted, "Alright, that's it, enough is enough. All you graduates of 2020? After all those long hours you've put in. All the hard work you've put in . . . you're gettin a graduation! And that's all there is to it! This week! I'm there with tassels on! #SGNgraduation!!!" He put out a call for all valedictorians to dust off their speeches, put on their cap and gowns, and send in a video of their speech (Adams 2020).

Since the COVID 19 outbreak, people have begun using the internet for many different kinds of social interactions, such as online exercise classes, art classes, music lessons, and socializing (Vogel 2020). However, there are still some major social determinants that are correlated with these kinds of online usage: age gaps, education gaps, and the rural/urban gap (Vogel 2020). Not surprisingly, younger people are more likely to use the internet. As the "stay-at-home" orders merged into "stay safe" and "shelter-in place" during this pandemic, online usage expanded and became a more significant part of the norm. New norms on how to do virtual meetings were emerging as people figured out what worked and what did not work. With 2020 being a presidential election year, there were some discussions on how to redesign democracy to allow full participation without the risk of spreading COVID-19. Such discussions were met with polarizing rhetoric and extreme responses.

## MISINFORMATION, LIES, AND THE ATTACK ON AMERICAN DEMOCRACY

The pernicious political tactics of the Trump administration in response to the outbreak emerged as the most significant environmental justice issue of 2020, with deadly outcomes resulting from a profound amount of misinformation. As of November 14, 2020, there have been 251,132 COVID deaths throughout all 50 US states and territories; over 33,975 of these deaths were in New York (WOM 2020); a disproportionate number of American Natives and Black Americans suffer exposure and death from COVID-19. Trump's rhetoric and behavior at press conferences caused confusion and enhanced divides within the United States. Trump's purposeful downplaying of the seriousness of COVID-19 made it nearly impossible to mitigate the strain to the healthcare systems and create a united front to battle COVID-19. Trump politicized and polarized the nation. People that supported him were encouraged not to wear masks or practice social distancing. Trump claimed that some Americans are not wearing masks to protect themselves but rather to show their disapproval of him (Sheth 2020). This messaging went counter to the recommendations of the CDC, public health officials, and mandates within states that were experiencing high levels of COVID-19 cases.

## POLITICAL CONFRONTATION WITH GOVERNORS

The state governors, who were dealing with major outbreaks at the onset of the pandemic, found themselves in direct confrontation with Trump. Those that were critical of Trump, and his response to the pandemic, were ignored or a target for ridicule. Trump told Vice President Mike Pence not to contact the governors of Washington and Michigan, calling Washington governor Jay Inslee a "failed presidential candidate" and a "nasty person" and referring to Michigan governor Gretchen Whitmer as "the woman in Michigan." Trump, frustrated with the shutdown of the economy, held a press conference on April 13, where he misidentified his authority over governors:

> When somebody's president of the United States, the authority is total. And that's the way it's got to to [*sic*] be. It's total. It's total. And the governors know that. They will agree to it. But the authority of the president of the United States, having to do with the subject we're talking about, is total. (Behrmann 2020)

The US Constitution does not give the president of the United States total authority over state governors. Trump's conception of authority was completely inaccurate. Ultimately, the Trump administration, and some Republican governors, decided that economic concerns took precedence over health concerns. Trump's overly ambitious timeline to end "stay-at-home" measures resulted in his harmful medical suggestion that an injection of disinfectants or ultraviolet light could potentially treat the disease. Trump fanned political divides by telling people to liberate their states from the stay-at-home orders (Wingrove 2020). Washington's governor, Jay Inslee, stated, "The president's statements this morning encourage illegal and dangerous acts. He [Trump] is putting millions of people in danger of contracting COVID-19. His unhinged rantings and calls for people to 'liberate' states could also lead to violence" (Wingrove 2020).

Protests against stay-at-home orders resulted in the public gathering of groups (Andone 2020). In Colorado, health care workers opposed the stay-at-home protests by blocking vehicles at crosswalks (Williams 2020). The people protesting the stay-at-home orders in the various states were not just typical citizens but rather included paid partisan political groups (Wilson 2020).

> It [the protests] was organized by the Michigan Conservative Coalition, which Michigan state corporate filings show has also operated under the name of Michigan Trump Republicans. It was also heavily promoted by the Michigan Freedom Fund, a group linked to the Trump cabinet member Betsy DeVos. (Willson 2020)

What is disturbing about this political conflict is that Trump is clearly playing a mixed-up partisan game that even goes against his own administration's guidelines to mitigate the spread of COVID-19.

Georgia's governor, Republican Brian Kemp, was the first to lift the stay-at-home orders for gyms, hairdressers, barbers, bowling alleys, and tattoo parlors beginning April 25, just a couple of weeks into the outbreak in his state. As of November 28, 2020, Georgia, as a state, was ranked sixth in the number of COVID-19 cases and ranked ninth in deaths attributed to the virus. Although Trump originally stated that states should start reopening, he quickly backpedaled after Georgia began lifting the orders and stated that Georgia should take it more slowly. While many city mayors in Georgia criticized the governor and instructed their citizens to stay-at-home, residents were forming lines at hair salons, barbershops, nail salons, and tattoo parlors. As more non-essential shops were given the go-ahead to open, people began to tire of pandemic social distancing. The spread of COVID-19 continued, and a new surge of the virus began in November, causing major concern as hospitals began to be overwhelmed. As the number of COVID cases rose, governors began taking action. In North Dakota, the governor announced that healthcare workers who test positive but do not have symptoms could continue to work in COVID wards (Silva 2020). As hospitals across Massachusetts reached capacity, a garage at UMass Memorial hospital was converted into a field hospital to care for the overflow of patients (Baker-Polito 2020).

## COVID-19 and Immigration

On April 20, 2020, Trump declared via Twitter: "In light of the attack from the Invisible Enemy, as well as the need to protect the jobs of our GREAT

American Citizens, I will be signing an Executive Order to temporarily suspend immigration into the United States!"

This tweet implied that the executive order to suspend immigration was made in an effort to save American jobs (Rogers et al. 2020). However, this was just hyperbole, as a means to pander to xenophobic supporters. In reality, the executive order he signed merely "limited the order to a 60-day freeze on most green cards while still allowing visa-processing for hundreds of thousands of temporary employees like farm workers and crop pickers, who make up the majority of immigrants" (Luthi 2020). When it comes to developing policy and discussing issues related to immigration, Trump relies on misinformation, anti-immigration stereotyping, and false information. Mackenzie and Bhatt (2020), in their research on lies, bullshit (B.S.), and fake news, examine the role of B.S. as "the strategy to achieve credulity and support for the desired outcome through cynical and manipulative means." Trump's reckless manner propagated ignorance, fear, and hatred toward immigrants among his fans and political support base.

"People who strongly identify with Trump say they are more willing to commit violence against immigrants" (Whyte 2020). Political divides and protests increased substantially between those who believed in the lies, half-truths, and rhetoric of Trump and those who rely on scientific findings and trusted health professionals. Since 1984, both Democratic and Republican presidents have been advised by Anthony Fauci, the director of the National Institute of Allergy and Infectious Diseases (NIAID). While Trump initially worked with Fauci at the beginning of the pandemic, he eventually rejected his advice and explanations.

Kunst, Fischer, Sidanius, and Thomsen (2017) have found support that there is a link between the role of government and social cues that support inequality. They attribute this link to a psychological mindset or subconscious support of group-based hegemony. Trump's statement that the latest executive order would secure jobs for Americans, at a time when 30 million Americans had lost their jobs, was a calculated stance meant to enhance his favorability among his supporters and win a second term in office. President Trump continually misled the nature of his orders and incited fear and hatred of immigrants through his tweets.

In January, before COVID 19 disrupted immigration,

> the State Department granted 5,536 green cards to Mexicans (Chalfant and Bernal, 2020). Out of those, nearly 3,000 were spouses and children of U.S. citizens. The largest groups of Mexican nationals who would have fallen under the suspension are children and spouses of legal permanent residents and the foreign national parents of U.S. citizen adults. (Chalfant and Bernal, 2020)

These immigrants are not taking jobs away from US citizens. Many immigrants that reside in the United States, and work, typically work in low-paying and precarious jobs, such as migrant farm jobs. These are the kinds of jobs that are considered "essential" during the pandemic but typically undesirable. Furthermore, these jobs have been a low priority in procuring personal protective equipment (PPE), leaving workers vulnerable to the virus. Although these jobs put immigrants at a higher risk for contracting the virus, many have no choice but to go to work because they do not qualify for unemployment benefits (McFarling 2020). In late February, the federal governments' "public charge" immigration rule (put into place prior to COVID-19) went into effect. This limited noncitizens' use of government programs (Fessler and Rose 2020) and caused many immigrants to become afraid of seeking public services such as housing and food supplements, and medical care. Many feared that seeking these services could lead to deportation or prevent them from receiving permanent residency in the future.

Margot Kushel, a physician who directs the Center for Vulnerable Populations at the University of California, San Francisco, said, "We are seeing this virus disproportionately impact racial minority populations. We are seeing it hit people who are in poorly paid, yet risky jobs . . . jobs that cannot be done via Zoom meeting" (McFarling 2020). Immigrants know they are in a precarious situation and are fearful of testing for the virus due to fears of deportation (McFarling 2020).

In late April and early May 2020, the Trump administration moved swiftly to bar asylum seekers and undocumented immigrants from entering the country. Immigration advocates have said Trump and his advisers are using a global pandemic to further hard-line immigration policies.

## COVID-19, VOTER SUPPRESSION, AND CHALLENGES TO DEMOCRACY

A national concern regarding citizen voting rights emerged as the pandemic impacted voting norms. As the projections of Trump losing the presidential re-election grew, Trump and his supporters reinvigorated false claims of voter fraud. With the election of former president Barack Obama in 2010, a number of politicians, claiming that there was widespread voter fraud, worked to put restrictions on who could vote. In reality, it was the Republican Party that engaged in a number of tactics to disenfranchise Black, Latinx, Native Americans, and other minoritized groups from participating in our democracy. Carol Anderson (2018), in *One Person, No Vote: How Voter Suppression Is Destroying Our Democracy*, documents how the American people were "harassed, obstructed, frustrated, and excluded from voting in 2016." The purpose is racist sentiment, "white rage," traced to the civil war and Reconstruction to ensure that Black Americans would not gain political power (Anderson 2016; Anderson 2018).

Since the Obama administration, Trump had been making false claims of voter fraud. During his 2016 presidential campaign, Trump cited unsubstantiated urban myths about rampant voter fraud in the United States and the likelihood of a "rigged" election (Farley 2016). Since his election into the White House, the most common voter legislation enacted was voter identification laws. These laws are identified as "voter suppression laws," and include restricting the terms and requirements of registration (Rafei 2020). Some of the restrictions included requiring documents to prove citizenship or identification and limiting the window of time in which voters can register (Rafei 2020). Many states also engaged in voter purges.

> The most common excuses for purging voter rolls are to filter out voters who have changed their address, died, or have failed to vote in recent elections. States often conduct such purges using inaccurate data, booting voters who don't even fall under the targeted category. In 2016, Arkansas purged thousands of voters for so-called felony convictions, even though some of the voters had never been convicted of a felony at all. And in 2013, Virginia purged 39,000 voters based on data that was later found to have an error rate of up to 17 percent. (Rafei 2020)

With "stay at home," "shelter in place," and "stay safe" orders limiting people from going out in large numbers, 15 states postponed or delayed 2020 primary elections, and one state canceled it altogether (Corasaniti and Saul 2020). Many states extended deadlines to register and submit absentee ballots by mail. There were major political organizers that called for expanding the use of voting by mail, no-excuse absentee voting, curbside ballot drop-offs, and early voting.

On April 7, 2020, at a press briefing, Trump was asked a question about the primary election in Wisconsin. Despite the "safer at home" order in place since March 24, 2020, the Supreme Court decided that Wisconsin could not extend the voter absentee deadline. This caused thousands of people to be forced to wait in hours-long lines and risk their health in order to vote (Hains 2020). When asked if the Supreme Court's decision was right, Trump stated that he supported the decision, and then went on to make false claims regarding mail ballots. Trump stated: "Mail ballots—they cheat. OK? People cheat." "There's a lot of dishonesty going along with mail-in voting" (Hains 2020). Fact-checkers found these claims to be false and provided reports and studies showing that there was no evidence of voter fraud (Farley 2020; Timm 2020).

Using these kinds of statements, Trump began laying the groundwork to contest the outcome of the presidential election should he lose. Since the beginning of this pandemic, civil rights leaders have been worried about voter participation. The NAACP articulates this issue the best:

> The fundamental right of every eligible voter to cast their ballot and every resident to be counted as a member of society are the cornerstones of our democracy. How we deploy resources, make real the social norms and standards across every community, shape our daily lives through policy, and move forward the shared values of this country are all based on this foundation. The Covid-19 pandemic has called into question how we as a nation can ensure elections are free of barriers for all eligible voters and that the 2020 Census counts all persons living in the country. This crisis requires the federal government, in partnership with states, to provide dedicated resources guaranteeing all communities—especially those systematically left behind—are included. (NAACP 2020)

Since Trump's election, the divide between those who believed wholeheartedly in Trump, and those who no longer trusted him, increased in far greater numbers, as did their respective political activism. The 2020 presidential election recorded the highest voter turnout for a presidential election ever. Over 100 million people participated in early voting, and an estimated 158 million citizens voted in total (McDonald 2020). On the night of the election (Tuesday, November 3, 2020), no winner was announced. The divide between American voters was reflected in a race that was too close to call and required additional time to count all votes. This did not stop Trump from falsely claiming he won the election. On Saturday, November 7, 2020, most outlets called the election in favor of President-elect Joe Biden and Vice-President-elect Kamala Harris. However, Trump continued to refuse to concede the election and inhibited the transition of power. He claimed, without evidence, that widespread fraud in counting votes had taken place. Not only did Trump try to stop the counting of votes, but his campaign filed multiple lawsuits in an attempt to ultimately invalidate the election results. In an unprecedented move, Trump fired top officials at the pentagon, and he hired strong loyalists. On Friday, November 13, Trump stated that time would tell if he would remain president despite the fact that the election had ended, and Joe Biden had been declared president-elect by news outlets.

## ENVIRONMENTAL AND ECOLOGICAL DISRUPTIONS IN POLLUTING PRACTICES

COVID-19, and the ensuing shutdown of society, non-essential businesses, and stay-in-place orders, provided a view into the healing that can take place on our planet if fossil fuel use is reduced and $CO_2$ emissions stopped. Cities around the world reported having extended periods of cleanest air. Such outcomes bring to the forefront the necessity to seek clean air alternatives.

The detrimental effects of long-term exposure to air pollution have been found to increase the likelihood of death from COVID-19 (Wu et al. 2020). The ecological mapping of racial minorities and low/poor income communities exposes environmental justice issues. Toxic and polluting industries that cause air, water, and soil contamination are more likely to be located in communities of color and income-disadvantaged communities. People who live in health-compromising environments, and contract COVID-19, tend to fare less well than those that live in or have access to healthy environments. For example, the Navajo Nation, which has been dealing with the deadly legacy of uranium mining, is currently experiencing a higher per/capita rate of COVID-19 than New York. Uranium contamination is linked to health conditions such as a weakened auto-immune system, kidney failure, and cancer. This contamination is continually found in members of the Navajo Nation, including newborn babies. On November 13, with a resurgence of COVID-19 cases and deaths, the Navajo Nation issued a new three-week "Stay-at-home" (Shelter-in-place) order.

### Animals

As people retreat into dwellings and attempt to mitigate the spread of COVID-19, the impact on companion animals, service animals, and livestock has been understudied. Early in the pandemic, a public official in China warned people to be careful with pets because mammals can spread the illness. This unsubstantiated comment resulted in a severe public response; many pets (mostly cats and dogs) were killed or abandoned (McNamara et al. 2020). While there is little evidence that companion animals are carriers, some pets are known to have had COVID along with their owners.

An ecofeminist lens brings attention to the oppression and domination that animals are subjected to by humans. Denmark recently announced that a mutated COVID-19 virus was found in mink farms and that this could interfere with a human vaccine. Initially, this outbreak resulted in over 5,000 mink deaths. After the announcements that this outbreak could interfere with a vaccine, more than ten million minks were slaughtered as a precaution.

Fur-farming, in general, will be phased out in Denmark over a three-year buy-out period. No action as of November 15, 2020, has been taken for mink farms in the United States other than quarantining the farm and their animals. The mass slaughter of minks, and the humane treatment of animals, has been under scrutiny by animal activists. Globally, the mink fur industry may be coming to an end due to COVID-19 concerns.

As human activity reduced with the "shelter-in-place" orders, wild animals ventured into abandoned cities and parks. In Hong Kong, there was a significant rise in sightings of the endangered pink dolphins. With less traffic on the road, fewer animals were killed by vehicles. Around the world, stray animals (like cats, dogs, birds, rodents, and many others), who typically relied on human food waste for survival, faced starvation. The overall impact and fallout of the pandemic on animals, both wild and domesticated, have been understudied. In time, this impact will need to be researched to understand both the positive and negative outcomes of human interaction on the larger natural ecosystem.

## Green Spaces

The relationship between access to green spaces and overall health and well-being has been well documented (Coombes et al. 2010). Gatekeeping practices have limited access to green walking paths, accessible parks, and bike trails resulting in an environmental justice issue. Minoritized groups tend to face many barriers to green spaces due to structural inequality. Such social determinants negatively impact health. Environmental activists have worked to increase green open spaces, access to green spaces, community gardening, and nature walking trails. During COVID-19, these social inequalities became more apparent. Although the "stay-in-place" orders specifically stated that people could leave their homes to walk and exercise, not all people have access to green spaces or even safe streets where they can walk.

## Trash Production during COVID-19

The basic values of ecofeminism create opportunities to address many injustices and can serve to enhance problem-solving by emphasizing ecosystems within society, the built environment, and the planet. During COVID-19, overpackaging became more intense, leading to more trash than ever before. Being mindful of the need to limit trash projection can start with individual commitments. In 2016, a viral Buzzfeed video titled "I Tried to Make Zero Trash for 30 Days" and showcased a young woman attempting to live for 30 days without making any trash. The struggle she documents is real and difficult. In this video, she needed to figure out how to procure food that is not overly packaged. Concern over the spread of COVID-19 has put environmental issues, such as overpackaging, reusable grocery bags, and limiting trash production, on the sidelines.

Environmental justice issues are embedded in an array of social justice issues/policies and emerged on the political forefront in the last five decades. Some of these issues were addressed in this chapter rather than chapter 4 because the issues have become more evident during the COVID-19 pandemic.

## CONCLUSION

The COVID-19 global pandemic will be known as a time of strong political division and participation. Trump's inability, and unwillingness, to mitigate the spread of the virus resulted in mass deaths. This critical time in history was also riddled with many other hardships and divides. While one side worked to institute voter suppression, others worked to counter those tactics. Many changes took place to balance "stay-in-place" measures and figure out an effective way to conduct national elections, reinvent work, redesign home spaces, and reimagine education.

While Trump rejected a medical response, refused to develop a national plan, and politicized the use of masks and social distancing, hospitals were once again faced with trying to serve an overwhelming number of sick patients in need of critical care. As governors instituted measures to flatten the curve, Trump thwarted them. Although political action increased, the virus continued to spread.

As "stay-in-place" orders were enacted, work, family, and educational spaces all conflated within the home. Social issues such as family abuse and the mental health of individuals emerged during the pandemic. The food system was challenged, and the economy left many essential workers and their families vulnerable. Grocery store food supplies were tested during the pandemic when panic buying occurred. The resulting new norms on shopping for household supplies and food, and the increased use of food banks for those that were economically challenged, exposed the many vulnerabilities in our food system. Essential workers who stocked shelves in stores, while constructed as heroes, worked precarious hours with low pay and found themselves overly exposed to COVID-19.

Structural changes in daily living emphasized the many ways that technology also had structural holes—particularly highlighting the digital divide. New ways of interacting using video conferencing software served to connect people. Celebrations, such as the virtual proms, graduations, and birthdays, went virtual, showing that people could still connect with others during "stay-at-home" measures.

Trump's mishandling of COVID-19 and his partisan politics when working with governors created a chaotic and politicized environment in the United States. Despite the major health issues in the United States, Trump continued his political attacks on immigration. This caused many immigrants to fear that using social services would get them deported. The false claims of voter fraud and Trump's questioning of mail-in ballots resulted in the most divisive election in US history. This challenge to democracy diverted attention away from other important issues such as environmental issues.

The pandemic gave the world an opportunity to see the impact that lowering $CO_2$ emissions and reducing the burning of fossil fuels could have on our environment. Environmental justice issues were not a concern for the Trump administration. Issues such as animal oppression and domination were only addressed when they impacted humans. The infection of COVID-19 in mink farms, and the resulting slaughter of thousands of minks, brought animal abuse to the forefront. Additionally, it is important to consider the ecological impact of animals that rely on humans for survival. This pandemic may end up being an opportunity to establish a new vision for how to redesign lifestyles, take care of animals, and ensure that green spaces are fairly accessible to all. Redesigning life can take into consideration environmental justice.

# *Chapter 7*

# Police Brutality and the Black Lives Matter Movement

Amid 2020's global COVID-19 pandemic and ensuing national medical crisis, a graphic cell phone video of Minneapolis police officers killing George Floyd went viral. The video sparked massive outrage and nationwide protests that would continue throughout 2020. The Black Lives Matter movement (BLM) had already been emotionally and politically charged with the killings of Ahmaud Arbery (pursued and shot by vigilantes while jogging on February 23, 2020) and Breonna Taylor (killed by police who entered her apartment by mistake on March 13, 2020).

The surge of activism that began with the killing of George Floyd was a serious call to address the long history of systemic racism in the United States, rooted in enslavement and policing. To understand the current rise in Black activism, it is important to first understand the US socio-cultural history of systemic racism and policing, the Black Power movement of the 1960s, and the development of the #BlackLivesMatter movement.

The current surge in the BLM movement is comparable to the civil rights movement of the 1960s, where nationwide protests included whites and other racial groups. As the protests in the 1960s, the current BLM movement is a protest of systemic racism, police brutality, and vigilante killings. The activist work of Black women is covered in this chapter; specifically, this chapter will describe the role of Black women in eliminating slavery, women in the Black Power movement, and women in the BLM movement. The chapter will conclude with a description and analysis of the political activism and strife fueled by the continued killing of Black people and a discussion of the 2020 BLM movement within the ecofeminist goals of documenting and addressing oppression and domination.

## SOCIO-CULTURAL FOUNDING OF SYSTEMIC RACISM AND POLICING IN THE UNITED STATES

Systemic racism in the United States is attributed to the acceptance of enslaved Africans that were captured, kidnapped, and brought to shore in 1619 (i.e., human trafficking) (Hannah-Jones et al. 2019). By 1662, the enslavement of Black people became codified into law by the declaration that children born of enslaved mothers would be the property of the mother's owner (History 2020). Initially, approximately 400,000 Africans were brought to the shores of North America. However, due to this law, nearly four million descendants of enslaved Africans were placed into the American racial caste system (Wilkinson 2020).

Although the slave trade was outlawed in 1807, chattel slavery continued. Chattel slavery refers to a slave with no rights, who exists only as of the property of his or her master (Miers 2003). Chattel slavery fueled the exploitation of the land through cash crops like tobacco, cotton, and sugar (History 2020). By 1860, enslaved peoples in the United States made up about 13 percent of the total population (U.S. Census 1860). The many contributions of Black women in the resistance and abolishment of slavery are often overlooked. Although western history typically only focuses on a few Black women, such as Harriet Tubman and Sojourner Truth, in reality, they were a part of a larger network of Black female activists. Black women (both enslaved and free) have always played a strong role in both activism and politics.

### Black Women and Underground Railroad Quilts

The term "Underground Railroad" was used to describe a collection of people, a network, that used a variety of strategies and routes to help Black people escape slavery; this term was part of the common language by the 1840s. Harriette Tubman, Mary Ann Shadd, and many other unnamed Black women abolitionists openly opposed and thwarted the laws by assisting enslaved Black people in escaping to the North and Canada (Sutton 2019; Presley 2016). Many enslaved Black women who worked in slave owner's houses, known as "house slaves," created and displayed quilts that were used to teach, communicate, and assist escaping slaves (Abernathy 2013; Tobin and Dobard 1999).

Quilting is known as feminine handiwork. The work and design in quilts are purposeful. The designs and shapes are developed, named, and given meaning. Embedded in the quilts of the Underground Railroad were hidden instructions and tips for escape. The names of the designs had specific meanings (Abernathy 2013; Tobin and Dobard 1999). For example, "monkey wrench," design meant preparation are in place to escape; A "wagon wheel," meant you would probably be leaving by wagon; A "log cabin," meant you would be looking for a safe house; and the "north star," design meant as a reminder to follow the north star (Abernathy 2013; Tobin and Dobard 1999). There were many more of these signs, and as the meaning of these shapes were articulated, documented, and shared knowledge spread. The handiwork of designing and sewing a meaningful quilt is a political, social action to overcome oppression. Warren (2000) uses the metaphor of the quilt as a way to describe how theory-building and the many different ways ecofeminism is a "theory-in-process." Utilizing an oral history, writing it down (documentation), sharing it (dissemination), and giving it new life is "theory-in-process."

The oral tradition of sharing information about the Underground Railroad developed because keeping written records was dangerous. Participation in the Underground Railroad involved transforming homes, schools, and churches into "arenas for politicization" (Sutton 2019)—places that women prevailed in making space for resistance to oppression and domination. Sutton (2019) describes the many unnamed Black women of the Underground Railroad who were able to offer shelter, prepare food, take care of the sick/injured, sew quilts, provide clothing, and raise money to assist those escaping enslavement.

## Black Women Abolitionists

While the Underground Railroad was activism that directly thwarted laws to assist enslaved people in escaping slavery, the Abolitionist movement worked to change laws. This social and political movement denounced slavery and worked for systemic change. The socio-historical writings of the era typically only mention a few prominent Black Women abolitionists, such as Sojourner Truth, Harriet Tubman, Maria W. Stewart, and Mary Ann Shadd. However, there were many more women than the few written about in history books who spoke out in gatherings to condemn slavery. Political action took many forms, such as informational fairs, petition drives, published leaflets, newspaper articles, books, lectures, and talks (Presley 2016). Many of these actions were led and supported by unnamed Black women. The political work to eliminate the enslavement of Black people coincided with the establishment of formal policing.

## The Racial Politics of Policing in America

The creation of publicly funded police forces in the United States was influenced by politics, economics, and the "changing notions of public order" (Waxman 2017). Perceptions about the need for policing have changed throughout history in the United States but clearly have been influenced by policing's history. In the South, the first police forces were created in 1704 for one primary purpose: to preserve the system of slavery. The beginning police forces in the South were known as "slave patrols," and they existed to capture individuals who were escaping enslavement (Waxman 2017). These slave patrols eventually evolved into the police departments of today (Malka 2018). After the Civil War, defending public order meant enforcing the disenfranchisement of freed slaves. The racial caste system was embedded within the criminal justice system and has continued to be the driving force in police brutality (Wilkerson 2020).

## Police Brutality

Police brutality is defined as the unwarranted or excessive force by police officers against civilians. The types of force used are illegal and include assault, beatings, mayhem, torture, and murder. Included in this definition of police brutality are harassment based on intimidation, verbal abuse, false arrest, and other forms of mistreatment (Moore 2010). W. E. B. DuBois (1940) referred to police brutality when he wrote, "No one who does not know can realize what a tyranny a low-grade white policeman can exercise in a colored neighborhood" (181). Although police brutality has been experienced by all races, classes, and genders, Black Americans have been victimized the most (Malka 2018; Niedermeier 2019).

Since the inception of police in the United States, there has been ongoing resistance. Women have been a strong force in this resistance. Williams (2008), in her article "Black Women and Black Power," notes that photos and film clearly show women's participation in the Black Power movement. However, mention of women in the written text was not articulated or "fade" in much of written history. The social imagination of the Black Power movement of the 1960s and 1970s brings to mind images of Black men. The era supported hypermasculinized Black Power politics, which obscured the critical contributions of women to Black Power projects. While the powerful contributions of women such as Angela Davis (scholar, political activist), Fannie Lou Hamer (activist, community organizer, and civil rights leader), and Patricia Robinson (advocate for mental health, reproductive rights, and socialism) are known, many of the women who were very much a part of the Black Power movement and civil rights campaigns, especially so at the local level, are unknown or unnamed (Williams 2008). These women formed and participated in a variety of "urban-neighborhood based" organizations such as housing tenant councils, welfare rights groups, and religious organizations. During the civil rights era, black women engaged in many political battles not just on the national level but on micro and macro levels of home and community. Women used multiple strategies to fight for housing rights and welfare rights and to counter police brutality.

One of the main issues addressed in the Black Power movement was police brutality and killings. This issue is still being addressed today. Among the many problems inherent within police departments is the lack of accountability. Fatal shootings of civilians by police officers are often never reported to the FBI because police departments are not required to do so; the reporting of fatal shootings by police officers is voluntary. In 2015, the *Washington Post* began logging every fatal shooting by an on-duty police officer in the United States (Tate, Jenkins, and Rich 2020; McCarthy 2020). The data collected revealed that the FBI had undercounted fatal police shootings by more than half; since the collection of this data, officers have killed approximately 1,000 people each year. Black Americans are killed at a much higher rate than any other group (Tate, Jenkins and Rich 2020; McCarthy 2020). A view of the raw numbers shows that half of the people killed by police are white; however, when you take into consideration that Black Americans only account for less than 13 percent of the US population, Black Americans are shot and killed more than twice the rate of white Americans.

The lack of mandatory reporting of police shootings and killings by police departments have motivated researchers around the country to gather their own data. Nearly 45 percent of Black Americans responded that they had been unfairly stopped by police because of their race or ethnicity (Pierson et al. 2020). In an examination of nearly 100 million traffic stops across the United States, Black drivers were approximately 20 percent more likely to be stopped by police officers than white drivers (Pierson et al. 2020). In that same study, Black drivers were found to be subjected to car searches 1.5 to 2 times more often than white drivers, even though Black drivers are less likely "to be carrying drugs, guns, or other illegal contraband compared to their white peers" (Pierson et al. 2020).

Police departments do not typically analyze data detailing interactions between police and civilians. The Stanford Open Policing Project (2020) was created with an interdisciplinary team of researchers and journalists at Stanford University with a mission to "combine the academic rigor of statistical analysis with the explanatory power of data journalism." Data on police stops throughout the United States is being collected and standardized. Side-by-side maps of the racial make-up of residents and the people stopped by police clearly show the racial disparity in policing citizens (Stanford Open Policing Project 2020). Under the "veil of darkness," Grogger and Ridgeway (2006) found that when the sun went down (making it difficult to determine a driver's race), Black drivers comprised a smaller proportion of drivers stopped by police. Police stops of Black drivers were linked to sunlight and the ability to see the race of the driver (Grogger and Ridgeway 2006).

## Black Men and White Rage

Increased interactions with police officers are many times instigated by "white rage." Individuals (motivated by a racial caste system) call and activate police interactions. In the past few years, there has been an increase in cell phone videos that recorded white individuals calling or threatening to call the police to report Black Americans who were engaged in ordinary activities such as jogging, walking from a store, or bird watching in a park. Several of the videos made public show white women behaving as if they were distressed while calling 911, claiming danger from Black men when video evidence showed there was no danger. Such calls escalate the situation with the police, despite the lack of any danger. On Memorial Day of 2020, Christian Cooper, an avid birdwatcher, was in Central Park enjoying the day when Amy Cooper's dog approached him. Christian asked her to leash her dog. She refused and proceeded to call 911, telling the dispatcher about the man's race in dramatic fashion, claiming that an "African-American man" was threatening her.

These incidents are identified as an attempt to maintain Jim Crow, the laws that enforced segregation, to exclude people of color from public spaces and activities. Black men already know that interactions with the police can lead to a deadly situation; as such, "white rage" behavior is an act of intimidation and terrorism. This behavior is linked to enslavement. Wilkerson (2020) describes the American caste system in *Caste: The Origins of Our Discontents*. She writes,

> The vast majority of African-Americans who lived in this land in the first 246 years of what is now the United States lived the terror of people who had absolute power over their bodies and their very breath, subject to people who faced no sanction for any atrocity they could conjure. (Wilkerson 2020: 47)

The terror exists not only because of formal policing but the informal policing as well. Citizens and vigilantes have always participated in reinforcing the racial caste system. The killing of Treyvon Martin, a teenager, by a "neighborhood watch captain" inspired the "Million Hoodie March."

## TREYVON MARTIN: MILLION HOODIE MARCH AND #BLACKLIVESMATTER

In 2012, Treyvon Martin, a 17-year-old boy wearing a hoodie, was murdered after leaving a convenience store where he had purchased an iced tea and skittles. Martin was stalked, attacked, and murdered by a neighborhood watch captain, George Zimmerman, for "looking suspicious." Treyvon Martin's murder hurt the heart of African Americans, and Treyvon quickly became a representation of "every black man" (Rowley 2012). President Barak Obama made a statement that if he had a son, he would have looked like Treyvon (Thompson and Wilson 2012; Rowley 2012).

A mass protest was organized; The "Million Hoodie March," held in New York City, March 21, 2012, was a call for justice (Flock 2012) and an end to racial profiling (Peralta 2012). The global significance of March 21 was purposeful and profound in that it is the International Day for the Elimination of Racial Discrimination, a day that is to kick off "a week of solidarity with people struggling against racism and racial discrimination" (U.N. 2020).

On July 13, 2013, Zimmerman was acquitted (Luscombe 2013). Following the acquittal, Alicia Garza posted on Facebook using the phrase "Black lives matter," and her friend Patrisse Cullors added the hashtag. Another friend, Opal Tometti, created the online site, BlackLivesMater.com. This website would become the organizational foundation for the global network of Black Lives Matter chapters (Roberts 2018; Chase 2018; Anderson 2016), connecting online conversations with social movements for political action. The hashtag, #BlackLivesMatter, was used over the following year to call attention to the violent racial killings of black men and women by police (Anderson 2016). The use of the hashtag increased with the killing of two unarmed black males (Chase 2018; Anderson 2016). The first was Eric Garner, whose death from a police chokehold on July 17, 2014 (Anderson 2016) was videotaped and shared via social media, going viral. Then less than a month later, on August 9, unarmed 18-year-old Michael Brown of Ferguson, Missouri, was killed by a police officer (Anderson 2016; *NYT* 2014). The many incidents of Black men being killed by police are represented in the killings of James Garner and Michael Brown.

## "I Can't Breathe" and "No Justice, No Peace"

On July 17, 2014, New York City police officers decided to arrest 43-year-old Eric Garner, an unarmed father of six, for allegedly selling loose cigarettes on a street corner in Staten Island. The videotaped encounter was recorded on a cellphone by Mr. Garner's friend, Ramsey Orta, who witnessed the incident. The videotape showed a white police officer grabbing the unarmed Mr. Garner by the neck and pulling him down to the sidewalk, where the officer wrapped his arm around Mr. Garner's neck in a chokehold. Mr. Garner "gasped, wailing "I can't breathe" eleven times before he died" (Prokupecz 2019). "I Can't Breathe" came to symbolize police brutality and the oppression and domination of Black people.

The New York Police Department had banned the use of "bar-arm chokeholds" in 1993—except when an officer's life is in danger" (Evstatieva and

Mak 2020). The Reverend Al Sharpton of the National Action Network called for a federal civil rights investigation into the case. At Garner's funeral, Sharpton began planning a demonstration to protest the police killing of Garner. However, before a protest could be planned, Michael Brown, unarmed, was killed by police in Ferguson, Missouri.

Within hours and days of Brown's killing, the streets of Ferguson, Missouri, were the site of political protest and unrest (*NYT* 2014). "After a candlelight vigil on Sunday evening, protesters flood into the streets near the scene of the shooting, chanting, "No justice, no peace." They were met by police officers in riot gear, carrying rifles and shields" (*NYT* 2014). This kicked off a confrontation that led to rioting, looting, and a call for social action (*NYT* 2014). Major political unrest continued, and a series of national protests against state violence toward black Americans in the United States emerged. There were two weeks of protest and unrest in Ferguson. The governor of Missouri declared a state of emergency, instituted a curfew, and called in the National Guard. At Michael Brown's funeral, civil rights leaders from around the country attended and made the call to "work for justice, not just for Michael Brown, but for others" (*NYT* 2014).

The first major protest of Garner's murder was held on August 23, 2014; thousands of people traveled to Staten Island to protest the killing of Graner and to insist that police who break the law be held accountable. The use of the hashtag, #BlackLivesMatter, once again exploded in use, just four months later (November 22, 2014), when Tamir Rice, a 12-year old Black boy, was shot and killed by police while playing with a toy gun (Anderson 2016). Protests were organized and planned as police killings continued, and the officers involved in the killings were not held accountable. The Black Lives Matter movement became a global human rights movement (Roberts 2018), with the focus on racial profiling, police brutality, and police killings of Black Americans. Protests and gatherings around the United States gained momentum against police brutality. These events included the 19th Annual National Day of Protest to Stop Police Brutality, Repression, and the Criminalization of a Generation (October 22, 2020). Over 70 "Die In" protests nationwide were held by young professionals (medical and law students). Multiple student activists held grassroots civil rights campaigns to keep the attention on police brutality (Laughland 2014).

Viral videos of blatant racial-based police brutality and murder around the US moved people to protest and riot. The lack of consequences for the police officers involved in the high-profile, unjust killings of Trevon Martin, Eric Garner, and Michael Brown was indicative of the systemic, institutionalized. These deaths highlighted what Attorney Garret Chase (2018) names the "Disease of Racial Police Violence."

## Black Women Subjected to Police Brutality, #SayHer Name

Black women are particularly vulnerable to police brutality and are more likely than white or Latinx women to be unfairly stopped by the police (Parker et al. 2020). Black women have also been preyed upon and raped by police (McLaughlin and Sidner 2016). An intersectional perspective can provide insight into the increased level of danger in society for Black women. In 2014, the African American Policy Forum (AAPF) and the Center for Intersectionality and Social Policy Studies (CISPS) launched the #SayHerName campaign to bring awareness to Black women and girls who have been victimized by police brutality. Girls as young as seven years old and women as old as 93 have been killed by the police (AAPF and CISP).

The names and stories of Black women and girls killed by police are many times ignored, much like the protest work of Black women throughout history. On May 20, 2015, in New York City, the AAPF hosted #SayHerName: A Vigil in Memory of Black Women and Girls Killed by the Police. This group brought together the families who lost a daughter, sister, or partner to police violence.

The vulnerability of Black women is exemplified in the case of an Oklahoma police officer, who was a serial rapist. This officer specifically preyed on Black women, selecting victims from one of the poorest neighborhoods in Oklahoma City. He would then use the police database to narrow his selection of victims to those who had a criminal history in drugs or prostitution so that any claims made against him would be undermined (McLaughlin and Sidner 2016). The police officer used gender, race, and criminal history to select victims, knowing that the combination of these identities already produced a high level of discrimination in society, and he would have a low risk of being held accountable for his actions. Since 2015, 48 Black women have been killed by the police.

## Breonna Taylor and the Longest Ongoing Protest Against Police Brutality

Breonna Taylor, a 26-year-old Black woman, was killed in her own home in Louisville, Kentucky. She had been working on the front lines during the COVID pandemic as an emergency room technician. The night that Breonna Taylor was killed by police, she had just finished four overnight shifts at the hospital (Callimachi 2020). Just after midnight on March 13, 2020, three plain-clothed police officers used a battering ram, broke down the door, and entered Taylor's home. Breonna Taylor and her boyfriend called out, asking who was there. When her boyfriend heard the intruders inside the home, he fired a single shot, striking one of the officers in the thigh. In retaliation, the officers fired a total of 32 shots into the home. Breonna Taylor was shot six times.

Breonna Taylor struggled to breathe, and, according to dispatch logs, she was not given any medical attention for more than 20 minutes after being shot. Although an ambulance was on standby outside the home, against standard practice, the ambulance was told to leave before the raid. Breonna Taylor's boyfriend did not know that the intruders were plain-clothed police officers and called 911. Prior to the raid, the police officers had received court approval for a "no-knock" warrant based on an investigation of two men who were selling drugs from a house that was far from Breonna Taylor's home. Before the raid, the orders were changed from a "no-knock" entry to a "knock and announce" entry that required the police to identify themselves. The police never identified themselves, nor were there any drugs in Breonna Taylor's home. No charges were filed for two of the police officers responsible for killing Taylor. The third officer was only charged with reckless endangerment for firing his gun into the home without a line of sight.

Activists Linda Sarsour and Tamika Mallory, two of the co-founders of the 2017 Women's March, moved from New York to Louisville to organize protests. Their goal was to bring attention to Breonna Taylor's killing and demand justice. As the United States was three months into the coronavirus pandemic, the protests were delayed. On May 28, 2020, the frantic 911 call made by Breonna's boyfriend was released. Taylor's boyfriend can be heard saying, "I don't know what is happening. Somebody kicked in the door and shot my girlfriend." The protests began when this tape was released.

Protesters took to the streets chanting "No Justice, No Peace," and as the protests escalated, the National Guard was called. Over 871 protest-related arrests were made between May 29 and September 28. The protests have been ongoing (as of December 4, 2020, at the time of writing this monograph) and are considered the longest ongoing demonstrations against aggressive policing.

The Breonna Taylor protests in Kentucky brought attention to an Atlanta-based Black militia group called Not F**king Around Coalition (NFAC). The NFAC came out (heavily armed) in support of the protests. The group was formed in 2017, and they made their first public during the protest of Ahmaud Arbery's murder. NFAC intends to protect, self-police, and educate Black communities on firearms and their constitutional rights. The group marched twice in Louisville for transparency in the killing of Taylor. (On December 3, 2020, the leader was arrested by the FBI for allegedly pointing a rifle at police during the Taylor protest on September 5.)

## The Killing of George Floyd

On May 25, George Floyd bought a pack of cigarettes from a neighborhood grocery store in Minneapolis. After he left, the teenaged clerk suspected that the $20 bill used by Floyd might have been counterfeit. The employee followed protocol and called the police. Within 30 minutes, George Floyd was dead. The brutal murder of Floyd was captured on cellphone video by horrified witnesses who called for help and begged police officers to stop the killing. The videos were posted on social media and went viral around the United States and the world, turning social media participants into virtual witnesses of one of the most graphic and disturbing examples of police brutality in the United States.

The videos of George Floyd's killing show the unarmed man, lying face down on the street, handcuffed with his arms behind his back, while three white police officers hold him down and one police officer uses his entire body weight to kneel on Floyd's neck.

Police body camera videos reveal that the encounter began with police officers immediately pulling their weapons on George Floyd, who was quietly sitting in a parked car. The video lays bare the fear in Floyd's facial expression as he turns to see a gun pointed at his face just outside his car door window. A terrified Mr. Floyd begins pleading several times, "Please don't shoot me, Mr. Officer, please." The pleas for George Floyd's life would continue from Floyd and from multiple bystanders. Floyd begged for his life, telling police officers, "I can't breathe." Transcripts from police bodycam footage show that Floyd said that he could not breathe more than 20 times, as he was being asphyxiated by a white police officer's knee grinding into his neck.

Just before George Floyd lost consciousness, he called out for his mother, "Mama," he shouted. "Mama . . . I'm through!" (Longman 2020). When blood flowed from Floyd's nose, a female bystander pleaded again for police to stop what they were doing. When Floyd became non-responsive, bystanders pleaded and urged officers to check his pulse. One officer checked for a pulse and determined that Floyd did not have a pulse. And yet, the officer who was kneeling on George Floyd's neck did not move.

The cellphone videos of white police officers killing George Floyd went viral. For Black Americans who have disproportionately suffered the negative outcomes of the coronavirus pandemic, the viral video of another Black man being brutalized by police was too much to take. Around the world, "eight minutes and 46 seconds" and "I Can't Breathe" came to symbolize police brutality. Mom's around the world felt the pain when George Floyd called out to his mom. Black mothers and mothers of color are intimately familiar with the fear that comes from knowing that one's own child, because of race, is not safe in a racist society. The message, "All mothers were summoned when he called out for his mama," was on posters, online, and on graffiti. Many white suburban moms heard the call and joined the BLM movement.

## SYSTEMIC RACISM AND THE CALL FOR SOCIAL ACTION: UNDERSTANDING THE IMPACT OF DIVIDED IDEOLOGY

Within hours of George Floyd's killing, thousands of people descended upon the streets of Minneapolis to protest police brutality and the killing of George Floyd. The powerful momentum of the Black Lives Matter movement resulted in a nationwide uprising against racial oppression and police brutality. The language of systemic racism became mainstream in these protests. The protests extended beyond the United States, as the Black Lives Matter became a global movement. Although the world was experiencing a global pandemic, protesters donned a mask, risked police violence, arrest, and their own health to march in the streets in solidarity against racism and police brutality.

In recent years, there have been multiple cell phone videos shared on social media that have documented unwarranted police brutality against unarmed Black Americans, and there have been many protest marches initiated by those incidents. However, something was different in the case of George Floyd. The number of protesters began growing into massive gatherings throughout the United States. Protests have erupted in more than 1,700 places and across all 50 states (Haseman et al. 2020). Also different from previous BLM protests is the demographic of the protesters. People from all walks of life, every age, gender, and race have participated in the 2020 Black Lives Matter protests in mass numbers (Parker et al. 2020). Most notable is the rise of white protesters who began participating. The Black Lives Matter protests in 2020 have attracted an unprecedented number of both white protesters and white supporters. The video of George Floyd's killing has garnered overwhelming and widespread support for the Black Lives Matter movement beyond the Black community.

The strong support from a majority of Americans makes the 2020 Black Lives Matter protests similar to the protests of the 1960s and has led to an opportunity to put forth a call to political leaders to address systemic racism in the United States. Researchers found that two-thirds of all US adults support the Black Lives Matter movement, including 60 percent of white Americans, 77 percent of Hispanic Americans, and 75 percent of Asian Americans (Parker et al. 2020). Aside from protesting, the movement has led to more Americans talking to family and friends about race and racial equity (69 percent). Many people have also begun sharing content related to race and racial issues on social media sites (37 percent) (Parker et al. 2020). With an increase in non-Blacks participating in the Black Lives Matter protests, even white suburban moms had to endure police brutality. On July 20, 2020, a group of moms in Portland, Oregon, came out to form a protective wall between BLM protesters and federal police. They chanted, "Feds stay clear, moms are here!" and "Feds go home!" Although the moms were peaceful, police, in full riot gear, still used tear gas and rubber bullets on both the moms and protesters (Givetash 2020). Several state governors activated the National Guard to assist police with protests (Haseman et al. 2020). Much of the reaction of police can be attributed to Trump's rhetoric about the protests. Nearly half of all Americans say that Trump has made race relations worse (Parker et al. 2020).

According to national polls, the percentage of "high attention" that Americans devoted to news about George Floyd was almost the same as the percentage of high attention devoted to news about the COVID-19 pandemic (Mitchell et al. 2020). In addition, the vast number of people affected by the pandemic through unexpected unemployment, financial loss, illness, or death has created new levels of vulnerability among individuals in society and may have changed the lens by which people viewed George Floyd's killing.

While social media allowed for the viral documentation of the unjust killings of Black Americans, the balkanized media ecosystem became the vehicle for racist fabrications and conspiracy theories. As most of the country was engaged in conversations about race, racism, and how to make systemic change, Trump continued endeavors to energize his base with overt racism. Trump redefined the protests as riots, and he attacked emancipatory pedagogy. On September 22, 2020, Trump signed Executive Order 13950 banning "malign ideology" such as the use of "critical race theory," other emancipatory theories, and the removal of the 1619 Project from the school curriculum. The order eliminated racial sensitivity training for federal agencies or those with federal funding. The language of the executive order is confusing and claims to combat race and sex stereotyping. The effect was the elimination of gains made in diversity, equity, and inclusion, which squelch the conversation on systemic racism that has been a significant part of the Black Lives Matter movements across the United States.

After the killing of George Floyd, 6 out of 10 adults in the United States viewed Trump's messages as "wrong" (Mitchell et al. 2020). According to a national poll, 50 percent of respondents identified Trump as a racist, and 76 percent believed that "the country is currently out of control" (Lemon 2020). The racism of our nation and the brutality of police cannot be denied when faced with graphic videos that expose the realities of police killings.

The Black Lives Matter movement has brought an awareness to mainstream systemic racism in America. Critical Race Theory (CRT) intersects with ecofeminism in examining institutional power and privilege as well as seeking out praxis for social change to eliminate oppression and domination. CRT can provide a greater understanding of the ways social systems and social institutions create and maintain the power and privilege of the dominant group while perpetuating the unjustified domination of minoritized groups.

## CONCLUSION

In August of 2019, the *New York Times Magazine* began an ongoing initiative to share Black American history with what is called the "1619 Project." Not surprisingly, the Trump administration has attacked the project and has attempted to reinstate a project that ignores the roles of slavery in creating systemic racism, with a cleaned-up version of US history that begins in 1776 and omits the hardship enslavement of Black people. There will be much work for a new administration to overcome the many executive orders, memos, and proclamations made during the Trump administration that has propagated systemic racism.

Slavery and systemic racism have always been a major divide in the United States. This divide resulted in a four-year Civil War (1861 to 1865). The Emancipation Proclamation, signed by Abraham Lincoln in 1862, redefined the Civil War from a war to save the Union to a war against slavery. It was the 13th Amendment to the US Constitution, ratified in 1865 after the Civil War, that abolished slavery in the United States.

The 13th Amendment states: "Neither slavery nor involuntary servitude, except as a punishment for crime whereof the party shall have been duly convicted, shall exist within the United States, or any place subject to their jurisdiction" (U.S. Const.; Balkin and Levinson 2012). This Amendment is a key to transforming society into one without oppression and domination. Balkin and Levinson (2012) recognize that the Amendment has been very literally interpreted more so than any other amendment because of the implications to change public and private power relations. Political governance, market and work practices, family structure, and even the way animals are treated can be transformed to eliminate oppression and domination with the 13th Amendment. There were many political and social struggles for Black Americans over the next hundred years. The Civil Rights era of the 1960s did not happen in a vacuum; the upheaval was part of a larger structure situated within enslavement and an ongoing struggle to eliminate and overcome racism.

# Conclusion

## *Ecofeminist Healing Strategies—Equity, Diversity, and Inclusion*

Women's political activism during the age of Trump, the coronavirus, and the Black Lives Matter movement was studied with a dedication to ecofeminist values that opposed domination and oppression. Ecofeminism relates to politics in its examination of the extraordinary surge in women's political activism. The research in this monograph emphasizes the correlation between the increase in women's political activism and the hyper-dramatic shift in the dominant social and political ideology toward misogyny and racism, initiated by Trump's 2016 presidential campaign. By using the political system to address issues related to humans, non-humans, and the environment, while upholding the protection of democratic principles and ideals, women become a powerful force in transforming society.

As research linking ecofeminism with politics, this analysis was guided by the intention to expose harmful domination in American society from 2016 to 2020. The principles addressed in the preamble of the US Constitution provide significant idealistic goals, and basic principles, for the democracy of the United States. The opening phrase, "We, the people," attributes control and power of the government, not to a monarchy or dictator but to the people of the nation. The statement implies inclusion and diversity. The constitution clearly establishes grounds for equity in phrases mentioned in the preamble: "establish justice," "promote the general welfare," and "secure the blessings of liberty to ourselves and our posterity." The Constitution of the United States is the foundational document that unites the American people. As responsible citizens, there must be agreement that the ideals and goals established by the constitution should be the criteria by which all federal policies are measured. As ecofeminists, there is a broad understanding that action and research should serve to eliminate oppression and domination while respecting all life (human, non-human, nature, and environment).

The evidence-based examples presented in this ecofeminist analysis of women's political activism conclude that the Trump administration's rhetoric and policies were a rejection of equity, diversity, and inclusion. The Trump administration's oppressive conceptual frameworks, based on sexism, racism, and other -isms of domination, resulted in significant harm and death to women, people of color, and the environment. The practices and federal policies of the Trump administration valorized white male supremacy and further polarized the nation. Trump's influence in emboldening alt-right white supremacist groups resulted in the escalation of hate group membership and activity, including a drastic increase of hate crimes in the United States; Trump's xenophobic rhetoric altered public discourse by mainstreaming hate and establishing federal policies directly founded on isms of domination.

The shift in social and political ideology represented a threat to democracy, the reassertion of patriarchy, the capitalistic exploitation of the environment, and the promotion of a political agenda grounded in white supremacy. This shift is responsible for the surge of women's political activism, resulting in increased participation in both protest marches and running for political offices.

The historic 2017 Women's March included a call to be more politically involved. Following the march, a historic number of women were elected for public office in both 2018 and 2020. Many of them had never served in a government position. Most of the women elected in 2018 opposed the politics of the Trump administration. However, in 2020, there was a strong split between the party affiliations of Democrats and Republicans. This is likely a result of the increased polarization of Trump's rhetoric and the shifting ideology, as well as the realization that women, regardless of party affiliation, can play a significant role in government. The increased number of women of color elected to office in both elections (2018 and 2020) is also historic. However, although this election marked the highest percentage of women elected to Congress (26 percent), it is still well below the percentage of women in society overall (52 percent). There is still much work to be done to overcome the inequality of women and other marginalized groups.

Trump did inspire political activism, but perhaps not always in a good way. Those that opposed Trump celebrated his loss in the 2020 Presidential election. However, Trump refused to accept those results. Instead of conceding, Trump spent the days and weeks after the election attempting to stop the count of votes, invalidate votes, rally his supporters to overturn the election, and filing multiple lawsuits to overturn the election results. Trump attacked the fundamental shared norm of American democracy—accepting the results. Trump, with his lies that he won, and with false and unsubstantiated claims that there is widespread voter fraud, created language and norms to contest and not accept future elections. As of November 23, 2020, Republican (GOP) members of Congress are slowly starting to side with democracy and are making soft statements acknowledging that Trump lost.

Undoubtedly, the divide is ever pronounced both for our political leaders that were selected to work together across party lines and those outside of government working to influence elected leaders. The schism among Americans, profoundly enhanced by the Trump administration, will leave deep scars. Ecofeminism, as a multidimensional, layered praxis, can accelerate that healing by creating a shared value system of respecting all life (human and non-human) and understanding our connection to nature and the impact of climate change. The new administration, President-elect Joe Biden, and Vice-President-elect Kamala Harris bring with them hope for healing this schism and a renewed sense of developing consensus for the values of equity, diversity, and inclusion.

## EQUITY, DIVERSITY, AND INCLUSION

Looking back at the 2017 Women's March (remembering the millions of diverse women standing together, marching together around the world, seeing the sea of pink hats), it is clear that an ecofeminist, purposeful response is not going to be a singular, unified, response. The response will have to be grounded in equity, informed by multiple perspectives and worldviews, and respectful to all. The needs of all Americans will have to be balanced so that the changes that take place are equitable for both the plethora of different human groups in society and non-human life. The social structural needs that led to the emergence of Trump will also have to be addressed.

The ecofeminist movements of the past 100 years are still viable. There are multiple distinctions among ecofeminists. To ground the multiplicity of issues in equity and justice—providing for the many varied needs of society's members with concern for the environment at the forefront—is to reset norms. One way to do this is to embrace and teach the value of eliminating oppression. All the different ways that one can see themselves (ethnicity, race, class, gender, sexuality, ability, education, etc.) can fit under the umbrella of "ecofeminism." Ecofeminism is a strategy to spotlight different ecosystems (many times represented as social movements) that require immediate attention, such as #BlackLivesMatter, #MeToo, climate change, or global health and hunger.

Classifying the socio-historical history of feminism into waves is merely a tool to help visualize, share this history, see where women have been, the effective strategies that have been used, and the mistakes that were made. With that understanding, action plans and strategies to work toward equitable change in society can be realized. Using both a scientific tradition and a communicative tradition, the imagery of the waves is significant in keeping the history alive and sharing it cognitively with the next generation of feminists/ecofeminists. As the next generation studies, describes and explains inequality in society as a means to identify oppression and create solutions to ending oppressions, it will be important to be mindful of the historical settings and documentation of the denigration of women, minoritized groups, and the environment.

There is much to learn from the feminist and ecofeminist activists that have come before. The simplicity of discussing ecofeminism as historically situated in metaphorical waves (be it four waves, five waves, overlapping waves, or more) contributes to sharing this history with the next generation of people willing to work for environmental justice and the betterment of all people (including the Trump supporters), non-human life, and the natural world. The wave metaphor is to keep one's thoughts organized to ease the articulation of ecofeminist history. But be mindful, in practice, ecofeminism praxis and thought have many elusive and tenuous elements. The malleability of ecofeminism is what makes this theory, this praxis, viable and relevant. Ecofeminists can work to guide this messiness in accepting the possibility of developing a holistic, systematic knowledge base to inform action and praxis—knowing it is an ongoing process or task and that wrong moves will be made—so be ready to adjust and pivot.

Environmental justice and working to mitigate the exploitation of the earth (air, water, soil, all life, non-renewable resources) must be consistently and diligently sought to achieve equity. (Idiom: We do not want to make the sheep cry, but we cannot starve the wolf.) The world is dynamic, and as such, people have the capacity to use their imagination and creativity in living life beyond merely the basics of survival (food, water, shelter). New and unimagined harm is likely to emerge from the elements of social and environmental ecosystems that are interconnected and layered. Stepping back and listening, reflecting, strategizing, and knowing to allow a person to understand that there are other ecosystems, both social and environmental, that may have to be prioritized.

*Pink Hats and Ballots* contributes to the knowledge and theory of ecofeminism as an upgraded, multidimensional, multilayered theory that accommodates all social and environmental ecosystems with the hope of a participatory model that works to eliminate oppressions. Striving for balance is linear thinking—all merely exist until they do not. Harsh barriers and divides can be harmful and inhibit equity; ecofeminism is a space to limit harm. This analysis took the liberty to "call out," "to name," the agendas of the 2018 new freshman class of politicians as ecofeminism if their agenda included identifying and rooting out oppression. There is always room for others to reject the label of "ecofeminism," despite their discernible ecofeminist focus.

The Midterm Election was just a start. In the last year and a half since, many women have taken office, not just in Congress, but in every level of government. While this monograph focused on women who won elections, it is also important to honor those who took the initiative to run for office but did not win. Ultimately, the varied voices of women who ran for public office contributed to the bringing about of a consensus. If anything, it is hoped that the significant issues to be addressed by political leaders will include more than just environmental justice issues and the stewardship of non-human life; ecofeminism includes healthcare, equality for women, protections for immigrants and refugees, and protections for the LGBTQ+ community.

The health of our planet is based on the health of all communities. To treat human and non-human life on this planet equitably will require information, data, knowledge, awareness, and perseverance. It is difficult to know the plight of others unless it is brought to the forefront. Self-education, individual intellectual growth, and a desire to empathize are important strategies. A start might be to develop a level of respect and care in our everyday interactions by listening to others. Be committed to seeking different kinds of information in the balkanized media landscape to broaden the scope of needs in the world; embrace the perseverance needed to monitor the natural environment, alongside built environments, to ensure a healthy planet is prioritized. Addressing complex issues such as climate change, the depletion of natural resources, and the destruction of biodiversity takes commitment to working cohesively with other groups. Experts from many different nations, and people who take the time to gather information and knowledge on specific topics outside of capitalism, need to unite. Much more research is needed.

Back in the first few months of his presidency, nothing communicated Trump's position on diversity and inclusion as accurately as the photographs of him signing executive orders that affected women. One of Trump's first executive orders reinstated a "global gag order" that prevented international health organizations from providing important advice on contraception, family planning options, or abortion. Non-compliance would result in the elimination of vital American funding. The infamous photo depicts Trump holding the signed order that would negatively affect the health of women around the world while being surrounded by white men. Images such as these would continue throughout the Trump presidency. Some examples include the following: the large male-only White House meeting to discuss a health care bill and whether maternity services should be considered an "essential benefit" (Wolf 2017); or the White House Health Care Event, where the majority of the participants were white men, to make decisions about health care that would disproportionately affect women (Groppe 2017).

The dramatic shift in government toward white patriarchy was especially poignant considering the diversity and inclusion of women established by previous presidential administrations. The Obama administration included eight women in cabinet positions. Trump's regression to white male patriarchy, and the exclusion of women and diversity, was not based on Republican convictions. Many recent Republican administrations appointed women to prominent government positions. For example, Elizabeth Dole served in two different Republican cabinets, and Condoleezza Rice served as secretary of state in George W. Bush's cabinet. The lack of diversity, and the exclusion of women, while not an inherent principle of Republican ideology, was embraced by Republican President Donald Trump and therefore represented a growing shift within the political party. The Trump administration's adherence to patriarchy granted men power and position over women, minoritized groups, and nature. Warren (2000) explains "male power and privilege" in patriarchies is not based on merit, effort, or ability, but is due to benefits and power that men receive "at birth by virtue of their being male" (64). The power given to men in Trump's administration intensified patriarchal notions grounded in oppressive conceptual frameworks that allowed them to establish and maintain power. Sexism, racism, classism, and other "isms" of domination were used as guiding principles to create and maintain domination through government institutions and federal policies.

Patriarchy's power to dominate women minoritized others, and nature is established by the lack of diversity and inclusion. What characterizes the position of women in a patriarchy is that they "are excluded from political and economic institutions of power and privilege" (Warren 2000: 64). The lack of inclusion, as well as the lack of diversity within institutional structures of power, prevent both the power and perspective of women/minoritized groups from transforming oppressive policies and practices within government institutions.

It is incumbent upon women to transform society with diversity and inclusion. Rather than waiting for an invitation, the current women's movement is not about getting out to vote; the movement is about having a higher level of political engagement, which includes running for political office.

## CURRENT AREAS OF ECOFEMINIST RESEARCH

There are several areas of current ecofeminist research where issues of equity in policy development and commitment to resources are sorely needed: feminization of poverty, femicide, and health inequity. Poverty is an environmental issue. Within the United States, women experience higher rates of poverty than men, and among women who live in poverty, 54 percent are women of color (Bleiweis et al. 2020). While this issue is addressed to some extent in chapter 3, it is a growing issue that should be front and center in ecofeminist research.

Femicide, the murder of a woman due to being a woman, is on the rise both within the United States and globally. A key example is the murder of 20-year-old Vanessa Guillén, a Mexican-American Army specialist who disappeared from Fort Hood, Texas, on April 22, 2020. Her remains were found two months later. She had been a victim of sexual harassment in the Army and was killed while on duty; her body was chopped up into pieces and scattered near the fort. Her killing, as femicide, was just one of many, not just in the United States, but globally.

The United States collects data on intimate partner violence, but not on femicide. A Facebook site ran by Donna Wilcox, Woman Count USA: Femicide Accountability Project, aims to bring awareness to this issue in the United States (Anguiano 2019). Additionally, in the United States, there are over 2,300 missing and 1,800 murdered Native American women and girls (Ortiz 2020; Abinanti, Cavaliere, Nulph, and George 2020). These two issues, the feminization of poverty and femicide, are understudied, undercounted, and inadequately addressed in US legislation.

## RACIALIZED INEQUITIES IN HEALTHCARE AND ECONOMICS

Although some research based on the theory of intersectionality has demonstrated health disparities between a person's identities (race, gender, class, etc.) and the level and quality of care they receive in the US healthcare systems, much more health equity research is needed. The intersectionality between being a woman and being a person of color has produced deadly outcomes for Black women and their babies. Studies have confirmed that women of color face healthcare inequities, which create an increased risk to their health that others do not face.

According to the American Medical Association in 1999, Black American women are two to six times more likely to die from pregnancy complications than white women, depending on where they live. However, more recent data collected from the CDC shows that Black women in New York City are 12 times more likely to die from complications of pregnancy (Chuck 2018). The infant mortality rate for Black babies is double what it is for white babies. The most disappointing discovery from both of these studies is that class had no impact on these findings; higher education and higher incomes do not protect Black women or their babies from these high mortality rates. In fact, the babies of well-educated, middle-class Black mothers "are more likely to die before their first birthday than babies born to poor white mothers with less than a high school education" (Reeves and Matthew 2016). The fact that economics had no effect on health care disparities indicates that racism and bias, inherent within the healthcare system, impact the care one receives. Health risks for women of color stem from the discrimination of health care professionals, lack of access to healthcare, disproportionate exposure to environmental hazards, and chronic stress.

These same types of disparities exist when examining household income and wealth in America; the economic divide between Black households and White households has not changed since 1968. Kuhn and Steins (2018) examined household-level data regarding income and wealth since 1949. The conclusion of their study revealed that "no progress has been made in reducing income and wealth inequities between Black and white households over the past 70 years." In 1968, the typical middle-class white household had $70,786 in wealth compared to the typical middle-class Black household that had $6,674 in wealth. In 2016, the numbers reflected an even larger gap, with middle-class white households having $149,703 in wealth and middle-class Black households having $13,024 in wealth (Long and Van Dam 2020). Much more ecofeminist research, and social involvement, is necessary to address these social and ecological inequities.

## THE POWER OF PINK

Women heard the call to get politically active; they heard the call to vote in their interests, and they heard the call to run for political office. The current surge of women becoming candidates and getting elected to local, state, and federal political offices indicates that social change toward enhancing social equity is at the forefront. Of course, the major divide between those that supported Donald Trump for president, and those that did not, means that much work is necessary. The leadership of our nation must adhere to democratic ideals and the principles that protect democracy. Decisions at the highest levels of government must be made with integrity, adherence to facts, and in the best interest of the people, not based on the possibility of retaliation by extremists who engage in propagating fabricated social media slander in an effort to expel politicians from office. The links between ecofeminism and democracy have been addressed by numerous ecofeminist scholars, bringing attention to shortcomings in democratic governance, but acknowledging the capacity for democracy to self-correct through social and political change. There are very significant issues at stake for both our nation as a whole and for the individuals living within the United States. Ultimately, it was the environment that was harmed by the Trump administration—the physical environment (nature) as well as the social environment (individuals, communities, and institutions).

Democracy requires that the voting rights of all citizens be protected; methods of voter suppression must be exposed and eliminated. Elections are vital to the quality of democratic governance, as is the adherence to political processes. Propaganda and efforts aimed at suppressing the votes of citizens and circumvent established political processes are an undeniable threat to democracy. Activism to protect voter rights must continue. The lesson learned from Stacey Abrams and her success in Georgia is that ongoing dedicated activism produces results. Abrams's 10-year voter registration project resulted in the largest increase in voter turnout of any other state in the country at the 2018 Midterm Election and in the 2020 election. Stacey Abrams is credited with Georgia's new status as a Democratic state. The record-breaking turnout among Black voters in the swing state was a contributing factor in President Joe Biden's election, and the Democrats' control of the Senate, with Georgia's election of the first two Democratic senators in 20 years.

Coming to consensus and voting is an important duty for all US citizens. However, there must be a focus on selecting candidates that are willing to learn about the multiplicity of issues and the ways that different groups are negatively affected. Furthermore, the future leaders of the country must study ethics and the Constitution of the United States of America before engaging in public service as our political leaders. It is important to elect more individuals from under-represented groups. Becoming knowledgeable on the contributions of ecofeminism, and the major ways that voices can be heard, allow for equity, diversity, and inclusion. This will ultimately make the world a better place.

# References

Abernathy, Regina. 2013. "Quilts of the Underground Railway Hidden Codes, Secret Messages." The Knowledge Exchange, Lakeland Community College, September 18, 2020. https://www.youtube.com/watch?v=LU6y0YUHSZc. Accessed December 1, 2020.

Abernethy, Laura. 2019. "Photographer Laura Dodsworth Shows What Vulvas Look Like in 100 Photographs of Different Women." *MetroNews*, February 13, 1019. https://metro.co.uk/2019/02/13/photographer-laura-dodsworth-shows-vulvas-look-like-100-photographs-different-women-8578196/. Accessed April 15, 2020.

Abinanti, Abby, Angi Cavaliere, Alanna Nulph, and Blythe K. George. 2020. "To 'Kee Skuy' Soo Ney-Wo-Chek' I Will See You Again in a Good Way: A Year 1 Project Report on Missing and Murdered Indigenous Women, Girls, and Two Spirit People of Northern California." Progress Report. July 2020. Accessed November 23, 2020. https://2a840442-f49a-45b0-b1a1-7531a7cd3d30.filesusr.com/ugd/6b33f7_a83c3e5d9fed4906b70413a985321ac4.pdf?index=true

Abramson, Alana. 2016. "How Donald Trump Perpetuated the 'Birther' Movement for Years." *ABC News*. September 16, 2016. https://abcnews.go.com/Politics/donald-trump-perpetuated-birther-movement-years/story?id=42138176. Accessed April 29, 2020.

Acevedo, Nicole, and Minyvonne Burke. 2020. "Washington State Man becomes First U.S. Death from Coronavirus." *NBCNews*, Feb. 29th, 2020. https://www.nbcnews.com/news/us-news/1st-coronavirus-death-u-s-officials-say-n1145931.

Adams, Carol. 1995. *The Sexual Politics of Meat: A Feminist-Vegetarian Critical Theory*. New York: Continuum.

Adams, Heather. 2020. "John Krasinski To Host Virtual Graduation Amid Coronavirus Pandemic on 'Some Good News' Show for 2020 Class Whose Graduations Might Have Been Canceled." *MassLive*, April 30, 2020. https://www.masslive.com/coronavirus/2020/04/john-krasinski-to-host-virtual-graduation-amid-coronavirus-pandemic-on-some-good-news-show-for-2020-class-whose-graduations-might-have-been-canceled.html. Accessed May 2, 2020.

Adams, John. 2011. "O.C. Tea Party Member Sends Picture of Obama as Ape." *NBC News*. April 19, 2011. https://www.nbclosangeles.com/news/local/oc-tea-party-member-sends-picture-of-obama-as-ape/1921463/. Accessed November 14, 2020.

Age of Revolution. 2017. "The Pussyhat: Political Revolution," *Revolutionary Ideas, French Revolution*. https://ageofrevolution.org/200-object/the-pussyhat/. Accessed April 16, 2020.

Ahmed, Tufayel. 2019. "Trump Teen Rape Allegation Resurfaces, Ronan Farrrow Claims National Enquirer Tried To Protect Him in New Book." *Newsweek*. October 16, 2019. https://www.newsweek.com/trump-teen-rape-allegation-national-enquirer-ronan-farrow-jane-doe-1465652. Accessed March 11, 2020.

Alcoff, Linda Martín. 2012. "Feminism: Then and Now." *The Journal of Speculative Philosophy*, 26(2): 268–290. https://www.jstor.org/stable/10.5325/jspecphil.26.2.0268.

Allard, Sam. 2020. "DeWine Orders State Water Utilities to Halt Shutoffs, Restore Service During COVID-19 Crisis." *Cleveland Scene*, March 31, 2020. https://www.clevescene.com/scene-and-heard/archives/2020/03/31/dewine-orders-state-water-utilities-to-halt-shutoffs-restore-service-during-covid-19-crisis. Accessed May 1, 2020.

Allman, Dan. 2013. "The Sociology of Social Inclusion." *Sage-Open Journal*. January 8, 2013. https://journals.sagepub.com/doi/full/10.1177/2158244012471957. Accessed May 1, 2020.

Almukhtar, Sarah, Jugal K. Patel, Derek Watkins and Karen Yourish. 2018. "Where Migrant Children Are Being Held Across the U.S." *New York Times*. June 21, 2018. Accessed March 11, 2020. https://www.nytimes.com/interactive/2018/06/21/us/where-are-the-border-children.html.

Alter, Charlotte. 2018. "A Year Ago They Marched. Now a Record Number of Women are Running for Office." *Time*, January 18, 2018. https://time.com/5107499/record-number-of-women-are-running-for-office/. Accessed April 21, 2020.

American Bar Association. 2018. "What Is an Executive Order?" November 27, 2018 https://www.americanbar.org/groups/public_education/publications/teaching-legal-docswhat-is-an-executive-order-/. Accessed April 29, 2020.

American Medical Association. 1999. "State-Specific Mortality among Black and White Women: United States." *Journal of the American Medical Association*, 282(13): 1220–1222.

American Medical Association. 2019. "Ethics of Privacy, Confidentiality & Medical Records." *AMA*. November 14, 20119. Accessed March 10, 2020. https://www.ama-assn.org/topics/ethics-privacy-confidentiality-medical-records.

Ancelovici, Marcos. 2016. "Occupy Montreal and the Politics of Horizontalism," in *Street Politics in the Age of Austerity: From the Indignados to Occupy*, edited by Marcos Ancelovici, Pascale Dufour, and Héloïse Nez. Amsterdam University Press. https://www.jstor.org/stable/j.ctt1d8hb8t.10.

Anderson, Carol. 2016. *White Rage: The Unspoken Truth of Our Racial Divide*. Bloomsbury Publishing: New York.

Anderson, Carol. 2018. *One Person, No Vote: How Voter Suppression Is Destroying Our Democracy*. Bloomsbury Publishing: New York.

Anderson, Monica. 2016. "Social Media Conversations about Race. How social media users see, Share and Discuss Race and The Rise of Hashtags Like #BlackLivesMatter." *Pew Research Center: Internet & Technology*, August 15, 2016. https://www.pewresearch.org/internet/2016/08/15/social-edia-conversations-about-race/. Accessed April 14, 2020.

Anderson, Monica and Emily A. Vogels. 2020. Americans Turn to Technology during COVID-19 Outbreak, Say an Outage Would Be a Problem." *Pew Research, Internet and Technology*, March 31, 2020. https://www.pewresearch.org/fact-tank/2020/03/31/americans-turn-to-technology-during-covid-19-outbreak-say-an-outage-would-be-a-problem/. Accessed May 2, 2020.

Andone, Dakin, 20220. "Protests Are Popping Up Across the US Over Stay-At-Home Restrictions." *CNN*, April 17, 2020. https://www.cnn.com/2020/04/16/us/protests-coronavirus-stay-home-orders/index.html. Accessed April 26, 2020.

Anguiano, Dani. 2019. "The Nurse Tracking America's 'Epidemic' of Murdered Women." *Guardian*, April 11, 2019. Accessed November 23, 2020. https://www.theguardian.com/us-news/2019/apr/11/the-nurse-tracking-americas-epidemic-of-murdered-women.

Anti-Defamation League. 2016. *How Hate Groups Form.* https://www.adl.org/resources/backgrounders/how-hate-groups-form Accessed April 29, 2020.

Anti-Defamation League. 2016. *Murder and Extremism in the United States in 2016: An ADL Center on Extremism Report.* https://www.adl.org/sites/default/files/documents/MurderAndExtremismInUS2016.pdf.

AP Archive. 2015. "USA: Thousands of African Americans March on Capitol Hill – 1995. Video Footage of the Million Man March." https://www.youtube.com/watch?time_continue=61&v=JQPbv_OalQ8&feature=emb_title. Accessed April 30, 2020.

Agarwal, Bina. 1992. "The Gender and Environment Debate: Lessons from India." *Feminist Studies,* 18(1): 119–158. http://www.jstor.org/stable/3178217. Accessed September 1, 2020.

Aubrey, Allison. 2020. "Who's Hit Hardest By COVID-19? Why Obesity, Stress And Race All Matter." *NPR, Health News*, April 18, 2020. https://www.npr.org/sections/health-shots/2020/04/18/835563340/whos-hit-hardest-by-covid-19-why-obesity-stress-and-race-all-matter. Accessed May 1, 2020.

Austin Kelly F. and Laura A. McKinney. 2016. "Disaster Devastation in Poor Nations: The Direct and Indirect Effects of Gender Equality, Ecological Losses, and Development." *Social Forces*, 95(1): 355–380. https://doi.org/10.1093/sf/sow056.

Azar II, Alex M. 2020. "Determination that a Public Health Emergency Exists." https://www.phe.gov/emergency/news/healthactions/phe/Pages/2019-nCoV.aspx.

Bagenstose, Kyle, Sky Chadde, and Matt Wynn. 2020. "Coronavirus at Meatpacking Plants Worse than First Thought, USA TODAY Investigation Finds." *USA Today*, April 22, 2020. https://www.usatoday.com/in-depth/news/investigations/2020/04/22/meat-packing-plants-covid-may-force-choice-worker-health-food/2995232001/. Accessed May 2, 2020.

Bahr, Lindsey. 2017. "Harvey Weinstein to Take Leave of Absence After Bombshell New York Times Sex Harassment Report." *Chicago Tribune, Los Angeles.* October 5, 2017. https://www.chicagotribune.com/entertainment/movies/ct-harvey

-weinstein-new-york-times-sexual-harassment-report-20171005-story.html. Accessed April 20, 2020.

Bailey, Martha, Brad Hershbein, and Amalia Miller. 2012. "The Opt-In Revolution? Contraception and the Gender Gap in Wages." *American Economic Journal: Applied Economics,* 4(3): 225–254. https://www.ncbi.nlm.nih.gov/pmc/articles/PMC3684076/. Accessed June 3, 2021.

Baker, Mike, Hartocollis, Anemona, and Weise, Karen. 2020. "First U.S. Colleges Close Classrooms as Virus Spreads. More Could Follow." *New York Times*, March 6, 2020 (Updated March 11, 2020). https://www.nytimes.com/2020/03/06/us/coronavirus-college-campus-closings.html. Accessed April 26, 2020.

Baker-Polito. 2020 Baker-Polito Administration Announces Re-establishment of a Field Hospital at the DCU Center in Worcester. Mass.gov *Press Release*, November 13, 2020. Accessed November 15, 2020. https://www.mass.gov/news/baker-polito-administration-announces-re-establishment-of-a-field-hospital-at-the-dcu-center.

Balkin, Jack M. and Sanford Levinson. 2012. The Dangerous Thirteenth Amendment. *Columbia Law Review*, 112(7): 1459–1499. Symposium: The Thirteenth Amendment: Meaning, Enforcement, and Contemporary Implications. https://www.jstor.org/stable/41708156. Accessed December 2, 2020.

Bankoff, Caroline. 2014. "Thousands Show Up to Protest Death of Eric Garner." *Intelligencer*, Aug. 23, 2014. Accessed December 5, 2020. https://nymag.com/intelligencer/2014/08/thousands-show-up-to-protest-eric-garners-death.html.

Barbaro, Michael and Twohey Megan. 2016. "Crossing the Line: How Donald Trump Bahaved With Women In Private." *New York Times*. May 16. 2014. Accessed March 10, 2020. https://www.nytimes.com/2016/05/15/us/politics/donald-trump-women.html.

Barbaro, Michael. 2016. "Donald Trump Clung to 'Birther' Lie for Years, and Still Isn't Apologetic." *New York Times*. September 16, 2016. Accessed March 10, 2020. https://www.nytimes.com/2016/09/17/us/politics/donald-trump-obama-birther.html.

Barrow, Bill. 2016. "Trump again Disavows Alt-Right, White Supremacists." *APNews*, November 22, 2016. https://apnews.com/decb7c1cae4e4c19ba5cf117a2eaf04e. Accessed April 29, 2020.

Bartoli, Teresa and Lydia Rose. 2019. "Ecofeminist Analysis of the 2018 Midterm Election of Women in the United States Congress." Paper presented at the American Sociological Association Meetings in New York.

Bates, Karen Grigsby. 2017. "Race and Feminism: Women's March Recalls The Touchy History." *NPR*, January 21, 2017. Accessed November 23, 2020. https://www.npr.org/sections/codeswitch/2017/01/21/510859909/race-and-feminism-womens-march-recalls-the-touchy-history.

Bayly, Lucy. 2020. "New Weekly Figures Show Almost 40 Million People Lost Their Job Since the Pandemic." *NBC News*. May 21, 2020. https://www.nbcnews.com/business/economy/new-weekly-figures-show-almost-40-million-people-lost-their-n1211886. Accessed November 15, 2020.

BBC News. 2018. "Over 1,600 Scientists Condemn Trump Transgender Proposal." November 2, 2018 https://www.bbc.com/news/world-us-canada-46067559. Accessed April 30, 2020.

Beckwith, Ryan Teague. 2016. "Read Donald Trump's Acceptance Speech at the Republican Convention." *Time*. July 21, 2016. https://time.com/4418493/republican-convention-donald-trump-transcript/. Accessed April 29, 2020.

Bedera, Nicole. 2020. "Trump's New Rule Governing College Sex Assault is Nearly Impossible for Survivors to Use. That's the Point." *Time*. May 14, 2020. https://time.com/5836774/trump-new-title-ix-rules/. Accessed November 25, 2020.

Begley, Sarah. 2018. "White Supremacist and Black Nationalist Groups Both Grew During Trump's First Year as President." *Time*, February 21, 2018. https://time.com/5168677/donald-trump-hate-groups-splc/. Accessed April 29, 2020.

Behrmann, Savannah. 2020. "'We Don't Have a king:' Trump's Claim of 'Total' Authority Over States Gets Pushback Across Spectrum." *Politics, USA Today*, April 13, 2020. https://www.usatoday.com/story/news/politics/2020/04/13/trumps-claim-presidential-powers-gets-pushback-across-spectrum/2987065001/. Accessed April 24, 2020.

Bekkar, Bruce, Susan Pacheco, Rupa Basu, and Nathaniel DeNicola. 2020. "Association of Air Pollution and Heat Exposure with Preterm Birth, Low Birth Weight, and Stillborn in the U.S." *Journal of the American Medical Association*. June 18, 2020. https://jamanetwork.com/journals/jamanetworkopen/fullarticle/10.1001/jamanetworkopen.2020.8243?utm_source=For_The_Media&utm_medium=referral&utm_campaign=ftm_links&utm_term=061820. Accessed November 19, 2020.

Bekkar, Bruce, Susan Pacheco, Rupa Basu, and Nathaniel DeNicola. 2020. Association of Air Pollution and Heat Exposure with Preterm Birth, Low Birth Weight, and Stillbirth in the US: A Systematic Review. *JAMA Network Open*. 1; 3(6): e208243.DOI: 10.1001/jamanetworkopen.2020.8243.

Benen, Steve. 2016. "Trump's 'Birther' Crusade Was a Scam Wrapped in a Con." *MSNBC*, July 5, 2016. http://www.msnbc.com/rachel-maddow-show/trumps-birther-crusade-was-scam-wrapped-con. Accessed April 29, 20.

Benen, Steve. 2018. "Team Trump's War on Science Reaches a New Level." *MSNBC* March 5, 2018. http://www.msnbc.com/rachel-maddow-show/team-trumps-war-science-reaches-new-level. Accessed April 29, 20.

Benería, Lourdes and Gita Sen. 1981. "Accumulation, Reproduction, and 'Women's Role in Economic Development': Boserup Revisited." *Development and the Sexual Division of Labor* (Winter, 1981), pp. 279–298. https://www-jstor-org.proxy.library.kent.edu/stable/pdf/3173878.pdf?ab_segments=0%2Fbasic_SYC-5187_SYC-5188%2F5187&refreqid=fastly-default%3A76959d3e3da3fa78e9112f191e8a4159. Accessed November 20, 2020.

Berbrier, Mitch. 2000. "The Victim Ideology of White Supremacists and White Separatists in the United States." *Sociological Focus*, 33(2): 175–191. https://www.jstor.org/stable/20832074. Accessed April 28, 2020.

Berenson, Tessa. 2015. Here Are Some of the Tough Questions Megyn Kelly Asked at the Debate. *Time*. August 6, 2016. Accessed March 10, 2020. https://time.com/3988288/republican-debate-megyn-kelly/.

Berenson, Tessa. 2016. "Donald Trump Defends Tweet About Military Sexual Assault." *Time*. September 7, 2016. Accessed March 10, 2020. https://time.com/4483354/donald-trump-military-sexual-assault-forum/.

Berman, Mark. 2017. "U.N. Experts Say Trump Immigration Order Violates U.S. Human Rights Obligations." *Washington Post*. February 1, 2017, 11:45 AM. EST. Accessed March 10, 2020. https://www.washingtonpost.com/news/post-nation/wp/2017/02/01/u-n-experts-say-trump-immigration-order-violates-u-s-human-rights-obligations/.

Bernstein, Jennifer. 2017. "On Mother Earth and Earth Mothers: Why Environmentalism Has a Gender Problem." *Breakthrough Journal*, 7. Accessed November 17, 2020. https://thebreakthrough.org/journal/issue-7/on-mother-earth-and-earth-mothers.

Biesecker, Michael. 2017. "DOE Staffer Claims Retaliation Over Photos of Secret Meeting." *Associated Press*. January 17, 2018. https://apnews.com/30c6de5c24e14e0f832cccc6fae993eb. Accessed August 12, 2020.

Biesecker, Michael. 2018. "Ex-chemical Industry Lawyer to Lead Superfund Task Force." *Associated Press*. June 2, 2018. Accessed August 11, 2020. https://apnews.com/c2ef5e4050fd4fe69f3469a5f4d731dc/Ex-chemical-industry-lawyer-to-lead-Superfund-task-force.

Biesecker, Michael and Flesher, John. 2017. "EPA Contact [sic] Freeze in Place." *U.S. News*. January 24, 2017. Accessed March 10, 2010. https://www.usnews.com/news/politics/articles/2017-01-24/trump-admin-orders-epa-contract-freeze-and-media-blackout.

Blake, Aaron. 2017. "What Is An Executive Order? And How Do President Trump's Stack Up?" *Washington Post*. January 27, 2017. https://www.washingtonpost.com/news/the-fix/wp/2017/01/27/what-is-an-executive-order-and-how-do-president-trumps-stack-up/. Accessed April 29, 2020.

Bleiweis,Robin, Diana Boesch, and Alexandra Cawthorne Gaines. 2020. "The Basic Facts About Women in Poverty." *Center for American Progress*, August 3, 2020. Accessed November 23, 2020. https://www.americanprogress.org/issues/women/reports/2020/08/03/488536/basic-facts-women-poverty/.

Bleseker, Michael. 2018. "EPA head Scott Pruitt Lived in D.C. Condo Connected to Energy Lobbyist." *PBS*. March 30, 2018, 10:56 AM EDT. Accessed March 10, 2020. https://www.pbs.org/newshour/politics/epa-head-scott-pruitt-lived-in-d-c-condo-connected-to-energy-lobbyist.

Blow, Charles M. 2017. "Trump's Obama Obsession." *New York Times*. June 29, 2017. https://www.nytimes.com/2017/06/29/opinion/trumps-obama-obsession.html. Accessed March 10, 2020.

Bona, Marc. 2020. "Giant Eagle Looks to the Future, Adding 2nd Store for Curbside-Pickup-Delivery Only." *Cleveland.com*, April 9, 2020. https://www.cleveland.com/entertainment/2020/04/giant-eagle-looks-to-the-future-adding-2nd-store-for-curbside-pickup-delivery-only.html.

Booker, Brakkton. 2020. "Georgia Businesses Start To Reopen As Trump Distances Himself From State's Governor." *NPR*, April 24, 2020.

Boserup, Ester. (1970; 2007). *Women's Role in Economic Development*. Earthscan: New York.

Boxer, Marilyn J. 2002. "Women's Studies as Women's History." *Women's Studies Quarterly*, 30(3/4): 42–51. https://www.jstor.org/stable/40003241.

Bracho-Sanchez, Edith. 2019. "Transgender Teens in Schools with Bathroom Restrictions Are At Higher Risk of Sexual Assault, Study Says." *CNN*. May 6, 2019. https://www.cnn.com/2019/05/06/health/trans-teens-bathroom-policies-sexual-assault-study/index.html. Accessed April 29, 2020.

Branswell, Hellen and Joseph, Andrew. 2020. "WHO Declares the Coronavirus Outbreak A Pandemic." *STATNews*, March 11, 2020. https://www.statnews.com/2020/03/11/who-declares-the-coronavirus-outbreak-a-pandemic/. Accessed April 26, 2020.

Breiding, Matthew J., Sharon G. Smith, Kathleen C. Basile, Mikel L. Walters, Jieru Chen, and Melissa T. Merrick. 2014. "Prevalence and Characteristics of Sexual Violence, Stalking, and Intimate Partner Violence Victimization—National Intimate Partner and Sexual Violence Survey, United States, 2011." *Morbidity and Mortality Weekly Report*, 63:8. http://www.cdc.gov/mmwr/pdf/ss/ss6308.pdf. Accessed April 29, 2020.

Brigham, Tess. 2019. "A 'Millennial Therapist' Explains Why Young People Hate Their Jobs—And What To Do About It." *CNBC, Make it*, July 29, 2019. https://www.cnbc.com/2019/07/29/millennial-therapist-why-young-people-hate-their-jobs-so-much.html. Accessed May 2, 2020.

Brooks, Katherine. 2016. "Where The Hell Does the Word 'P***y' Come From, Anyway? How A Word Potentially Derived from "Pocket" Became One of the Nastiest Terms in the Dictionary." *HuffPost*, October 12, 2016; updated October 25, 2016. https://www.huffpost.com/entry/where-does-pussy-come-from_n_57fc0968e4b0b6a43034e7ac. Accessed April 16, 2020.

Browne, Stephanie and Sara LaLumia. 2014. "The Effects of Contraception on Female Poverty." *Journal of Policy Analysis and Management,* 33(3): 602–622.

Brownstein, Ronald. 2020. "The Most Important 2020 States Already Have Vote by Mail: But the battle over expanding access is only getting started." *Atlantic*, April 11, 2020. https://www.theatlantic.com/politics/archive/2020/04/voting-mail-2020-race-between-biden-and-trump/609799/. Accessed May 2, 2020.

Budowsky, Brent. 2016. "Colin Powell Is Right: Birtherism Is Racism." *Observer*, September 16, 2016. https://observer.com/2016/09/colin-powell-is-right-birtherism-is-racism/. Accessed April 29, 2020.

Bullard, Robert D. 2000. *Dumping in Dixie: Race, Class, and Environmental Quality*, Third Edition. New York: Routledge.

Bullock, Penn. 2016. "Transcript of 2005 Audio of Trump Making Vulgar Remarks about Women and Video." *New York Times*, October 8, 2016. https://www.nytimes.com/2016/10/08/us/donald-trump-tape-transcript.html. Accessed April 4, 2020.

Bump, Philip. 2017. "What Trump Has Undone." *Washington Post*. April 9, 2019, at 12:42 p.m. EDT. Accessed March 10, 2010. https://www.washingtonpost.com/news/politics/wp/2017/08/24/what-trump-has-undone/.

Bump, Philip. 2019. "The Surge in Migrants Seeking Asylum, Explained." *Washington Post*. April 9, 2019, at 12:42 p.m. EDT. Accessed March 10, 2010. https://www.washingtonpost.com/politics/2019/04/09/surge-migrants-seeking-asylum-explained/.

Buncombe, Andrew. 2018. "Donald Trump One Year On: How the Twitter President Changed Social Media and the Country's Top Office." *Independent*, January 17, 2018 https://www.independent.co.uk/news/world/americas/us-politics/the-twitter-president-how-potus-changed-social-media-and-the-presidency-a8164161.html. Accessed March 15, 2020.

Butler, Judith. 1990. *Gender Trouble*. Routledge: New York.

Butler, Judith. 1993. *Bodies That Matter: On the Discursive Limits of "Sex."* Routledge: New York.

BuzzFeedVideo. "I Tried to Make Zero Trash for 30 Days" https://www.youtube.com/watch?v=KtTTnEEPeAQ.

Callimachi, Rukmini. 2020. "Breonna Taylor's Life Was Changing. Then Police Came to Her Door." *New York Times*. August 30, 2020. https://www.nytimes.com/2020/08/30/us/breonna-taylor-police-killing.html. Accessed November 15, 2020.

Campbell, Horace. 1997. "The Million Woman March." *Agenda: Empowering Women for Gender Equity*, 35: 86–89. https://www.jstor.org/stable/4066098. Accessed April 4, 2020.

Campbell, Monica and Julienne Gage. 2018. "The Government Faces Deadlines to Reunite Migrant Families. It's Unclear If It Will Meet Them." *The World*, June 28, 2018. Accessed November 17, 2020. https://www.pri.org/stories/2018-06-28/government-faces-deadlines-reunite-migrant-families-it-s-unclear-if-it-will-meet.

Canovan, Margaret. 1999. "Trust the People! Populism and the Two Faces of Democracy." *Political Studies*, 47(1): 2–16. https://doi.org/10.1111/1467-9248.00184. Accessed April 29, 2020.

Cantor, David. Fisher, Bonnie. Chibnall, Sussan and Townsend, Reane. 2015. "Report on the AAU Campus Climate Survey on Sexual Assault and Sexual Misconduct." *Association of American Universities*. October 20, 2017. Accessed March 10, 2020. https://www.aau.edu/sites/default/files/AAU-Files/Key-Issues/Campus-Safety/AAU-Campus-Climate-Survey-FINAL-10-20-17.pdf.

Capatides, Christina. 2017. "Moments after Donald Trump Became President, The White House's LGBT Rights Page Disappeared." *CBS News*. January 20, 2017. https://www.cbsnews.com/news/moments-after-donald-trump-became-president-the-white-houses-lgbt-rights-page-disappeared/. Accessed April 29, 2020.

Cardyn, Lisa. 2002. "Sexualized Racism/Gendered Violence: Outraging the Body Politic in the Reconstruction South." *Michigan Law Review*, 100(4): 675–867. https://repository.law.umich.edu/cgi/viewcontent.cgi?article=1904&context=mlr.

Carlassare, Elizabeth. 1994. "Essentialism in Ecofeminist Discourse." In *Ecology: Key Concepts in Critical Theory* edited by Carolyn Merchant. Humanity Books: Amherst, New York.

Carranza, Rafael and Daniel Gonzales. 2018. "Attorney General Jeff Sessions Vows To Separate Kids from Parents, Prosecute All Illegal Border-Crossers." *AZCentral*. May 8, 2018. Accessed April 28, 2020. https://www.azcentral.com/story/news/politics/immigration/2018/05/08/ag-jeff-sessions-vows-separate-kids-parents-border/591924002/.

Carroll, E. Jean. 2019. "Hideous Men: Donald Trump Assaulted Me in a Bergdorf Goodman Dressing Room 23 Years Ago. But He's Not Alone on the List of Awful

Men in My Life." *New York, The Cut*. June 21, 2019. https://www.thecut.com/2019/06/donald-trump-assault-e-jean-carroll-other-hideous-men.html#_ga=2.175472930.1808467948.1561391109-1177717110.1558358450. Accessed April 29, 2020.

Carson, Rachel. 1962. *Silent Spring*. Houghton Mifflin Company, The Riverside Press: Boston, MA.

Carter, Niambi M. 2012. "Intimacy without Consent: Lynching as Sexual Violence." *Politics & Gender*, 8(3): 414–421.

Caty, Laura. 2019. "The Social Effects of Detention on Undocumented Children." *Immigration and Human Rights Law Review*. February 25, 2019. https://lawblogs.uc.edu/ihrlr/2019/02/25/the-social-effects-of-detention-on-undocumented-children/. Accessed April 29, 2020.

Cauterucci, Christina. 2016. "Getting the Women's March on Washington on the Road." *Slate*, November 23, 2016. https://slate.com/human-interest/2016/11/the-womens-march-on-washington-faces-uncertain-logistics-on-inauguration-weekend.html. Accessed March 19, 2020.

CDC—Centers for Disease Control and Prevention, National Center for Emerging and Zoonotic Infectious Diseases (NCEZID), Division of Global Migration and Quarantine (DGMQ). 2020. "Legal Authorities for Isolation and Quarantine." February 24, 2020. https://www.cdc.gov/quarantine/aboutlawsregulations quarantineisolation.html. Accessed April 30, 2020.

Center for American Women and Politics at Rutgers University. 2018. "Summary of Women Candidates." (updated 11/14/18) https://cawp.rutgers.edu/potential-candidate-summary-2018. Accessed April 21, 2020.

Chalfant, Morgan and Rafael Bernal. 2020. "Trump Signs Executive Order Limiting Immigration." *The Hill*, April 22, 2020. https://thehill.com/homenews/administration/494230-trump-signs-executive-order-limiting-immigration. Accessed May 2, 2020.

Chandler, D.L. 2019. "Little Known Black History Fact: Million Man March" https://blackamericaweb.com/2019/10/16/little-known-black-history-fact-million-man-march/. Accessed April 30, 2020.

Chappell, Neena L. and Havens, Betty. 1980. "Old and Female: Testing the Double Jeopardy Hypothesis." *Sociological Quarterly*, 21(2): 157–171. https://www.jstor.org/stable/4106148.

Chase, Garrett. 2018. "The Early History of the Black Lives Matter Movement and the Implications Thereof." *Nevada Law Journal*, 18: 1091–1112. https://scholars.law.unlv.edu/cgi/viewcontent.cgi?article=1757&context=nlj. Accessed April 15, 2020.

Chen, Michelle. 2017. "Donald Trump's War on Science." *The Nation*. March 2, 2017. https://www.thenation.com/article/archive/donald-trumps-war-on-science/. Accessed April 29, 2020.

Chenoweth, Erica and Jeremy Pressman. 2017. "This is what we learned by counting the women's marches." *Washington Post*, February 7, 2017. https://www.washingtonpost.com/news/monkey-cage/wp/2017/02/07/this-is-what-we-learned-by-counting-the-womens-marches/. Accessed April 4, 2020.

Chuck, Elizabeth. 2018. "How Training Doctors in Implicit Bias Could Save the Lives of Black Mothers." *NBC News*. May 11, 2018. https://www.nbcnews.com/news/us-news/how-training-doctors-implicit-bias-could-save-lives-black-mothers-n873036. Accessed November 14, 2020.

Cillizza, Chris. 2020. "Donald Trump Would Like Everyone To Say 'Thank You' for His Coronavirus Actions." *The Point with Chris Cillizza*, CNN, March 17, 2020. https://www.cnn.com/2020/03/17/politics/donald-trump-coronavirus-response/index.html. Accessed April 27, 2020.

Cillizza, Chris and Sam Petulla. 2017. "Trump is On Pace to Sign More Executive Orders Than Any President in the Last 50 Years." *CNN*. October 13, 2017. https://www.cnn.com/2017/10/13/politics/donald-trump-executive-orders/index.html. Accessed April 29, 2020.

Clay, Karen and Nicholas Z. Muller. 2019. "Recent Increases in Air Pollution: Evidence and Implications for Mortality." *National Bureau of Economic Research*. October 2019. https://www.nber.org/papers/w26381. Accessed November 17, 2020.

Clarke, Kristen. 2020. "What Trump Has Done to the Justice Department's Civil Rights Division Is a Disgrace." *CNN*. September 11, 2020. https://edition.cnn.com/2020/09/11/opinions/trump-barr-undercutting-doj-civil-rights-division-clarke/index.html. Accessed November 2, 2020.

Cogburn, Courtney. 2018. "Every Woman You Know Has Been Assaulted, Narrowly Avoided Assault, Had to Calculate the Possibility of Being Assaulted or Has Held the Hand of Another Woman Who Was Assaulted." *Twitter*, September 27, 2018, 10:39pm. https://twitter.com/CourtneyCogburn/status/1045503173446664192.

Cohen, Elena L., Melissa M. Forbis, and Deepti Misri. 2018. "Introduction: Protest." *Women's Studies Quarterly*, 46(3 & 4): 14–28. https://www.jstor.org/stable/10.2307/26511329. Accessed March 19, 2020.

Collins, Patricia Hill. 1990. *Black Feminist Thought: Knowledge, Consciousness, and the Politics of Empowerment,* First Edition. Routledge: New York.

Collins, Patricia Hill and Sirma Bilge. 2020. *Intersectionality,* Second Edition. Polity Press: Cambridge, England.

Coombes, Emma, Andrew P. Jones, and Melvyn Hillsdon. 2010. "The Relationship of Physical Activity and Overweight to Objectively Measured Green Space Accessibility and Use." *Social Science & Medicine,* 70: 816–822. Accessed November 15, 2020. doi:10.1016/j.socscimed.2009.11.020.

Condon, Stephanie. 2011. "Poll: One in Four Americans Think Obama Was Not Born in U.S." *CBS News*. April 21, 2011. Accessed August 10, 2020. https://www.cbsnews.com/news/poll-one-in-four-americans-think-obama-was-not-born-in-us/.

Connell, R.W. 1995. *Masculinities*. University of California Press, Berkeley and Los Angeles, California.

Connell, R.W. and James W. Messerschmidt. 2005. "Hegemonic Masculinity: Rethinking the Concept." *Gender and Society,* 19(6): 829–859. http://www.jstor.org/stable/27640853.

Cook, James. 2016. "U.S. Election: Trump and the Rise of the Alt-Right." *BBC News*. November 7, 2016. Accessed April 28, 2020. https://www.bbc.com/news/election-us-2016-37899026.

Cook, J., Oreskes, N., Doran, P. T., Anderegg, W. R. L., Verheggen, B., Maibach, E. W., Carlton, J. S., Lewandowsky, S., Skuce, A. G., Green, S. A., Nuccitelli, D., Jacobs, P., Richardson, M., Winkler, B., Painting, R., and Rice, K. 2016. "Consensus on consensus: a synthesis of consensus estimates on human-caused global warming." *Environmental Research Letters*, 11(4): 1–7. https://doi.org/10.1088/1748-9326/11/4/048002. Accessed April 29, 2020.

Coppedge, Michael, Angel Alvarez, and Claudia Maldonado. 2008. "Two Persistent Dimensions of Democracy: Contestation and Inclusiveness." *Journal of Politics*, 70(3): 632–547. Accessed May 1, 2020. doi:10.1017/s0022381608080663.

Corasaniti, Nick and Stephanie Saul. 2020. "15 States Have Postponed Primaries During the Pandemic. One Has Canceled." *New York Times*, April 27, 2020. https://www.nytimes.com/article/2020-campaign-primary-calendar-coronavirus.html. Accessed May 2, 2020.

Crenshaw, Kimberlé. 1989. "Demarginalizing the Intersection of Race and Sex: A Black Feminist Critique of Antidiscrimination Doctrine, Feminist Theory, and Antiracist Politics." University of Chicago Legal Forum 1(8). http://chicagounbound.uchicago.edu/uclf/vol1989/iss1/8. Accessed on June 3, 2021

Crenshaw, Kimberlé. 1991. Mapping the Margins: Intersectionality, Identity Politics, and Violence against Women of Color. *Stanford Law Review*, 43(6): 1241–1299. https://www.jstor.org/stable/1229039.

Crutzen Paul .J. 2006. The "Anthropocene". In *Earth System Science in the Anthropocene*, edited by E. Ehlers and T. Krafft. Springer: Berlin, Heidelberg.

Crutzen, Paul J. and Schwägerl, Christian. 2011. "Living in the Anthropocene: Toward a New Global Ethos." *Yale Environment* 360, January 24, 2011. Accessed April 26, 2020 from https://e360.yale.edu/features/living_in_the_anthropocene_toward_a_new_global_ethos.

CT—Chicago Tribune. 2020. "#MeToo: A Timeline of Events." *Chicago Tribune*, March 11, 2020. https://www.chicagotribune.com/lifestyles/ct-me-too-timeline-20171208-htmlstory.html.

Cumming-Brice, Nick. 2018. "Taking Migrant Children from Parents is Illegal, U.N. Tells U.S." *New York Times*. June 5, 2018. https://www.nytimes.com/2018/06/05/world/americas/us-un-migrant-children-families.html. Accessed April 28, 2020.

Cumming-Brice, Nick. 2018. "U.N. Rights Chief Tells U.S. to Stop Taking Migrant Children From Parents." *New York Times*. June 18, 2018. https://www.nytimes.com/2018/06/18/world/europe/trump-migrant-children-un.html.

Cummings, William. 2018. "Alternative Facts to Witch Hunt: A Glossary of Trump Terms." *USA Today*. January 16, 2018. https://www.usatoday.com/story/news/politics/onpolitics/2018/01/16/alternative-facts-witch-hunt-glossary-trump-terms/1029963001/. Accessed April 29, 2020.

Cutler, David and Francesca Dominici. 2018. "A Breath of Bad Air: Cost of the Trump Environmental Agenda May Lead to 80,000 Extra Deaths per Decade."

*JAMA*. October 22, 2020. https://jamanetwork.com/article.aspx?doi=10.1001/jama.2018.7351. Accessed November 18, 2020.

Dahl, Robert A. 1971. *Polyarchy: Participation and Opposition.* Yale University Press: New Haven.

Dahl, Robert A. 1977. "On Removing Certain Impediments to Democracy in the United States." *Political Science Quarterly*. 92: 1–20 https://www.jstor.org/stable/2148546. Accessed May 1, 2020.

Daly, Kathleen. 1993. "Class-Race-Gender: Sloganeering in Search of Meaning." *Social Justice*, 20(1/2): 56–71. https://www.jstor.org/stable/29766732.

Daniels, Kimberly and William D. Mosher. 2013. "Contraceptive Methods Women Have Ever Used: United States, 1982–2010." *National Health Statistics Report*, 62: 1–15.

DaSilva, Chantal. 2019. "More than 5,400 Children were Separated From their Parents by the Trump Administration, 'Shocking' New Tally Shows." *Newsweek*. October 25, 2019. https://www.newsweek.com/trump-administration-family-separation-policy-aclu-1467715. Accessed March 29, 2020.

Davenport, Coral. 2017. "With Trump in Charge, Climate Change References Purged From Website." *New York Times*. January 20, 2017. https://www.nytimes.com/2017/01/20/us/politics/trump-white-house-website.html. Accessed May 1, 2020.

Davenport, Coral. 2017. "With Trump in Charge, Climate Change References Purged From Website." *New York Times*. January 20, 2017. https://www.nytimes.com/2017/01/20/us/politics/trump-white-house-website.html. Accessed May 1, 2020.

Davis, Angela. 1981. *Women, Race & Class*. New York: Random House.

Davis, Angela. 2017. "Angela Davis' Women's March Speech: 'This Country's History Cannot Be Deleted.'" *Guardian*, January 22, 2017. https://www.theguardian.com/commentisfree/2017/jan/22/angela-davis-womens-march-speech-countrys-history-cannot-be-deleted. Accessed April 30, 2020.

Dawsey, Josh. 2018. "Trump Derides Protections for Immigrants from 'Shithole' Countries." *Washington Post*. January 12, 2018. https://www.washingtonpost.com/politics/trump-attacks-protections-for-immigrants-from-shithole-countries-in-oval-office-meeting/2018/01/11/bfc0725c-f711-11e7-91af-31ac729add94_story.html. Accessed April 28, 2020.

Deckha, Maneesha. 2013. "Animal Advocacy, Feminism, and Intersectionality." DEP: Deporta, esuli, profughe: Rivista telematica di studi sulla memoria femminile, 23: 48–65. https://www.unive.it/pag/fileadmin/user_upload/dipartimenti/DSLCC/documenti/DEP/numeri/n23/Dep_04.pdf. Accessed on June 3, 2021

Delaney, Arthur and Alissa Scheller. 2015. "Who Gets Food Stamps? White People, Mostly." *Huffpost Politics*, February 28, 2015 (updated December 6, 2017). Accessed November 20, 2020. https://www.huffpost.com/entry/food-stamp-demographics_n_6771938.

Dennis, Brady. 2016. "Scientists Are Frantically Copying U.S. Climate Data, Fearing It Might Vanish under Trump." *Washington Post*. December 13, 2016. https://www.washingtonpost.com/news/energy-environment/wp/2016/12/13/scientists-are-frantically-copying-u-s-climate-data-fearing-it-might-vanish-under-trump/. Accessed April 29, 2020.

Dennis, Brady and Juliet Eilperin. 2020. "EPA Overhauls Mercury Pollution Rule, Despite Opposition From Industry and Activists Alike." *Washington Post*. April 16, 2020. https://www.washingtonpost.com/climate-environment/2020/04/16/epa-overhauls-mercury-pollution-rule-despite-opposition-industry-activists-alike/. Accessed November 18, 2020.

Dennis, Brady and Steven Mufson. 2017. "Thousands of Emails Detail EPA Head's Close Ties to Fossil Fuel Industry." *Washington Post*. February 22, 2017. https://www.washingtonpost.com/news/energy-environment/wp/2017/02/22/oklahoma-attorney-generals-office-releases-7500-pages-of-emails-between-scott-pruitt-and-fossil-fuel-industry/. Accessed April 29, 2020.

Desilver, Drew. 2018. "A Record Number of Women Will Be Serving in the New Congress." *Pew Research Center*. December 18, 2018. https://www.pewresearch.org/fact-tank/2018/12/18/record-number-women-in-congress/. Accessed April 21, 2020.

Diallo, Amadou. 2020. "How To Reach Students Without Internet Access During Coronavirus? Schools Get Creative." *NBC News*, The Hechinger Report, April 19, 2020. https://www.nbcnews.com/news/education/how-reach-students-without-internet-access-during-coronavirus-schools-get-n1186251. Accessed May 2, 2020.

Diamond, Jeremy. 2015. "Lawyer: Donald Trump Called Me 'Disgusting' for Request to Pump Breast Milk." *CNN*. July 29, 2015. https://www.cnn.com/2015/07/29/politics/trump-breast-pump-statement/index.html. Accessed March 10, 2020.

Diaz, Daniella. 2016. "Trump Calls Clinton 'A Nasty Woman." *CNN* October 20, 2016. https://edition.cnn.com/2016/10/19/politics/donald-trump-hillary-clinton-nasty-woman/index.html. Accessed November 24, 2020.

Diaz, Daniella. 2017. "Kelly: DHS is Considering Separating Undocumented Children from their Parents at the Border." *CNN*. March 7, 2017. Accessed April 28, 2020. https://www.cnn.com/2017/03/06/politics/john-kelly-separating-children-from-parents-immigration.

DiChristopher, Tom. 2017. "Trump Revives a Misleading Claim that Global Warming Isn't Happening Because It's Cold Outside." *CNBC*. December 29, 2017. https://www.cnbc.com/2017/12/29/trump-revives-misleading-claim-its-cold-so-global-warming-isnt-real.html. Accessed March 11, 2020.

Dickerson, Caitlin. 2018. "Trump Administration in Chaotic Scramble to Reunify Migrant Families" *New York Times*, July 5, 2018. Accessed November 17, 2020. https://www.nytimes.com/2018/07/05/us/migrant-children-chaos-family-separation.html.

Dickerson, Caitlin. 2020. "Parents of 545 Children Separated at the Border Cannot Be Found." *New York Times*, October 21, 2020. Accessed November 17, 2020. https://www.nytimes.com/2020/10/21/us/migrant-children-separated.html.

Dickerson, John. 2011. "The Birther Controversy: Who's to Blame?" *CBS News*. April 28, 2011. Accessed March 11, 2020 https://www.cbsnews.com/news/the-birther-controversy-whos-to-blame/.

Dinkelspiel, Frances. 2016. "Thousands of Women Knit Pink Pussy Hats to Wear at Trump Protest Marches." *BerkeleySide*, Dec. 29, 2016. https://www.berkeleyside.com/2016/12/29/thousands-of-women-knit-pink-pussy-hats-to-wear-at-trump-protest-marches. Accessed April 16, 2020.

Dobratz, Betty and Shanks-Meile, Stephanie. 1997. *White Power, White Pride!: The White Separatist Movement in the United States.* Twayne Publishers, Social Movements Series.Simon and Schuster: New York.

Dodsworth, Laura. 2019. *Womanhood: The Bare Reality*. Pinter & Martin: London, UK.

Donaghue, Erin. 2020. "2,120 Hate Incidents against Asian Americans Reported during the Coronavirus Pandemic." *CBSNews*, July 2, 2020.

Drabold, Will. "Donald Trump Heads for Coal Industry Fundraiser in West Virginia." *Time*. June 27, 2017. https://time.com/4384957/donald-trump-coal-global-warming-murray/. Accessed August 12, 2020.

Du Bois, W. E. B. 1940. *Dusk of Dawn: An Essay toward an Autobiography of a Race Concept*. Harcourt, Brace and Company: New York.

Eadens, Savannah. 2020. "Viral Photo Shows Line of White People between Police, Black Protesters at Thursday Rally." *Courier Journal*. May 29, 2020. https://www.courier-journal.com/story/news/local/2020/05/29/breonna-taylor-photo-white-women-between-police-black-protesters/5286416002/. Accessed November 14, 2020.

Ebrahimji, Alisha. 2020. School Sends California Family a Hotspot after Students Went to Taco Bell to Use their free WiFi. *CNN*. Accessed November 14, 2020 https://www.cnn.com/2020/08/31/us/taco-bell-california-students-wifi-trnd/.

Einbinder, Nicole. 2018. "Coal Executive's "Action Plan" for Trump Made Public." *PBS* January 10, 2018. https://www.pbs.org/wgbh/frontline/article/a-coal-executives-action-plan-for-trump-is-made-public/. Accessed November 17, 2020.

Eldeib, Duaa. 2016. "Women Plan March on Washington Day after Trump's Inauguration." *Chicago Tribune*, November 29, 2016. https://www.chicagotribune.com/news/ct-womens-march-on-washington-met-20161128-story.html. Accessed April 4, 2020.

Engle, Gigi. 2017. "Where Does the Word Pussy Come From and Should Feminists Really Use It?" *Glamour: Sex-Love-Life*, April 24, 2017. https://www.glamour.com/story/origin-of-the-word-pussy. Accessed April 15, 2020.

Environmental Protection Agency. "History." https://www.epa.gov/history

Environmental Protection Agency. 2017. Superfund Task Force. Accessed August 11, 2020. https://www.epa.gov/superfund/superfund-task-force.

Erturk, Yakin. 2009. "Towards a Post-Patriarchal Gender Order: Confronting the Universality and the Particularity of Violence against Women." *Sociologisk Forskning*, 46(4): 61–70 Published by: Sveriges Sociologförbund (Swedish Sociological Association) Stable URL: https://www.jstor.org/stable/20853687.

Estes, Carroll L. 2018. Women's Rights, Women's Status, Women's Resistance in the Age of Trump. Generations: *Journal of the American Society on Aging*, 41(4): 36–44. https://www.jstor.org/stable/10.2307/26556315. Accessed March 30, 2020.

Fahrenthold, David A. 2016. "Trump Recorded Having Extremely Lewd Conversation About Women in 2005." *Washington Post*. October 8, 2016. https://www.washingtonpost.com/politics/trump-recorded-having-extremely-lewd-conversation-about-women-in-2005/2016/10/07/3b9ce776-8cb4-11e6-bf8a-3d26847eeed4_story.html?postshare=2491475870527101. Accessed March 10, 2020.

Fahrenthold, David A. and Johnathan O'Connell. 2018. "'I Like Them Very Much:' Trump has Long-Standing Business ties with Saudis, Who Have Boosted His Hotels Since he Took Office." *Washington Post*. October 11, 2018. https://www.washingtonpost.com/politics/i-like-them-very-much-trump-has-long-standing-business-ties-with-saudis-who-have-boosted-his-hotels-since-he-took-office/2018/10/11/0870df24-cd67-11e8-a360-85875bac0b1f_story.html. Accessed April 29, 2020.

Faludi, Susan. 1991. *Backlash: The Undeclared War against American Women*. New York: Three Rivers Press.

Fantz, Ashley. 2009. "Obama as Witch Doctor: Racist or Satirical?" CNN. https://edition.cnn.com/2009/POLITICS/09/17/obama.witchdoctor.teaparty/. Accessed November 4, 2020.

Farley, Robert. 2016. "Trump's Bogus Voter Fraud Claims." *FactCheck*, October 19, 2016. https://www.factcheck.org/2016/10/trumps-bogus-voter-fraud-claims/. Accessed May 2, 2020.

Farley, Robert. 2020. "Trump's Latest Voter Fraud Misinformation." *FactCheck*, April 10, 2020. https://www.factcheck.org/2020/04/trumps-latest-voter-fraud-misinformation/. Accessed May 2, 2020.

Feimster, Crystal N. 2009. *Southern Horrors: Women and the Politics of Rape and Lynching*. Cambridge, MA: Harvard University Press.

Fessler, Pam and Joel Rose. 2020. "Trump Administration Rule Would Penalize Immigrants for Needing Benefits." *NPR*, August 12, 2019. https://www.npr.org/2019/08/12/748328652/trump-administration-rule-would-penalize-immigrants-for-using-benefits. Accessed May 2, 2020.

Feuer, Alan. 2020. "Justice Dept. Intervenes to Help Trump in E. Jean Carroll Defamation Lawsuit." *New York Times*. October 27, 2020. https://www.nytimes.com/2020/09/08/nyregion/donald-trump-jean-carroll-lawsuit-rape.html. Accessed November 24, 2020.

Filipovic, Jill. 2017. "Our President Has Always Degraded Women—And We've Always Let Him." *Time*. December 5, 2017. https://time.com/5047771/donald-trump-comments-billy-bush/. Accessed March 10, 2020.

Fisher, Max and Bubola, Emma. 2020. "As Coronavirus Deepens Inequality, Inequality Worsens Its Spread." *New York Times*, March 15, 2020. https://www.nytimes.com/2020/03/15/world/europe/coronavirus-inequality.html. Accessed April 20, 2020.

Fitzsimons, Tim. 2019. "Trans Teens Face Higher Sexual Assault Risk When Schools Restrict Bathrooms, Study Finds." *NBC News*. May 6, 2019. https://www.nbcnews.com/feature/nbc-out/trans-teens-face-higher-sexual-assault-risk-when-schools-restrict-n1002601. Accessed April 29, 2020.

Flock, Elizabeth. 2012. "Trayvon Martin 'Million Hoodie March': A Short History of the Hoodie." *Washington Post*, March 22, 2012. https://www.washingtonpost.com/blogs/blogpost/post/trayvon-martin-million-hoodie-march-a-short-history-of-the-hoodie/2012/03/22/gIQAeGCnTS_blog.html. Accessed April 10, 2020.

Fortin, Jacey. 2018. "Trump's History of Defending Men Accused of Hurting Women." *New York Times*. February 11, 2018. https://www.nytimes.com/2018/02/11/us/trump-sexual-misconduct.html. Accessed March 10, 2020.

France-Presse, Agence. 2020. "A Man Lies Dead in the Street: The Image that Captures the Wuhan Coronavirus Crisis." *Guardian*, January 30, 2020. https://www.theguardian.com/world/2020/jan/31/a-man-lies-dead-in-the-street-the-image-that-captures-the-wuhan-coronavirus-crisis. Accessed April 27, 2020.

Fredrickson, Barbara L. and Tomi-Ann Roberts. 1997. "Objectification Theory: Toward Understanding Women's Lived Experiences and Mental Health Risks." *Psychology of Women Quarterly,* 21: 173–206.

Freking, Kevin. 2019. "Trump Outstripping Obama on Pace of Executive Orders." *AP News*, October 19, 2019. https://apnews.com/25ca8d3b39024f9e828df7ebeb718274. Accessed April 30, 2020.

Fried, Susana T. (2003). Violence against Women. *Health and Human Rights*, 6(2): 88–111. https://www.researchgate.net/publication/261903514_Violence_against_Women. Accessed April 28, 2020.

Friedman, Lisa. 2018. "How a Coal Baron's Wish List Became President Trump's To-Do List." *New York Times*. January 9, 2018. https://www.nytimes.com/2018/01/09/climate/coal-murray-trump-memo.html. Accessed November 17, 2020.

Friedman, Lisa. 2019. "A Coal Baron Funded Climate Change Denial as His Company Spiraled Into Bankruptcy." *New York Times*, December 17, 2019. https://www.nytimes.com/2019/12/17/climate/murray-energy-climate-denial-coal.html. Accessed August 12, 2020.

Friedman, Lisa. 2019. "E.P.A. to Limit Science Used to Write Public Health Rules." *New York Times*. November 11, 2019. https://www.nytimes.com/2019/11/11/climate/epa-science-trump.html. Accessed April 29, 2020.

Friedman, Lisa. 2020. "Trump Serves Notice to Quit Paris Climate Agreement." *New York Times*. November 4, 2020.

Friedman, Lisa and Coral Davenport. 2020. "EPA Weakens Controls on Mercury." *New York Times.* April 16, 2020. https://www.nytimes.com/2020/04/16/climate/epa-mercury-coal.html. Accessed November 19, 2020.

Fuller, Thomas and Baker, Mike. 2020. "Coronavirus Death in California Came Weeks Before First Known U.S. Death." *New York Times*, April 22, 2020. https://www.nytimes.com/2020/04/22/us/coronavirus-first-united-states-death.html. Accessed April 26, 2020.

Gaard, Greta. 1993. "Living Interconnections with Animals and Nature." In *Ecofeminism: Women, Animals, Nature*, edited by Greta Gaard. Temple University Press: Philadelphia, PA.

Gaard, G. and Gruen L. 1993. "Ecofeminism: Toward Global Justice and Planetary Health." *Society and Nature* 2, : 1–35.

Gangel, Jamie, Jeremy Herb, and Elizabeth Stuart. 2020. "'Play it down': Trump admits to concealing the true threat of coronavirus in new Woodward book." *CNN Politics*, September, 9, 2020. https://www.cnn.com/2020/09/09/politics/bob-woodward-rage-book-trump-coronavirus/index.html. Accessed October 23, 2020.

Gangitano, Alex. 2020. "Trump uses Defense Production Act to Order Meat Processing Plants to Stay Open." *Hill*, April 28, 2020. https://thehill.com/homenews/administration/495175-trump-uses-defense-production-act-to-order-meat-processing-plants-to. Accessed May 2, 2020.

Gaouette, Nicole. 2019. "Pentagon Transgender Ban Goes into Effect." *CNN*. April 13, 2019. https://www.cnnphilippines.com/world/2019/4/13/pentagon-transgender-ban.html. Accessed April 29, 2020.

Garcia, Sandra E. 2017. "The Woman Who Created #MeToo Long Before Hashtags." *New York Times*, Oct. 20, 2017. Accessed April 19, 2020 from https://www.nytimes.com/2017/10/20/us/me-too-movement-tarana-burke.html. Accessed April 30, 2020.

Gay-Stolberg, Sheryl and Brian M. Rosenthal. 2017. "Man Charged After White Nationalist Rally in Charlottesville Ends in Deadly Violence." *New York Times*. August 12, 2017. https://www.nytimes.com/2017/08/12/us/charlottesville-protest-white-nationalist.html?action=click&contentCollection=U.S.&module=RelatedCoverage&region=Marginalia&pgtype=article. Accessed November 21, 2020.

Geewax, Marilyn and Michel Martin. 2017. "Countries Listed on Trump's Refugee Ban Don't Include Those He Has Business With." *NPR*. January 28, 2017. https://www.npr.org/2017/01/28/512199324/countries-listed-on-trumps-refugee-ban-dont-include-those-he-has-business-with. Accessed April 29, 2020.

Geller, Eric. 2020. "Coronavirus Boosts Push for Online Voting Despite Security Risks." *Atlantic*, May, 1, 2020. https://www.theatlantic.com/politics/archive/2020/04/voting-mail-2020-race-between-biden-and-trump/609799/. Accessed May 2, 2020.

Genz, Stéphanie, and Benjamin A. Brabon. 2018. "Do-Me Feminism and Raunch Culture." In *Postfeminism: Cultural Texts and Theories*, 139–54. Edinburgh University Press" Edinburgh. www.jstor.org/stable/10.3366/j.ctt1tqxv9w.9. Accessed April 16, 2020.

Goffman, Erving. 1959. *The Presentation of Self in Everyday Life*. New York: Anchor Books.

Goldman, Gretchen. 2019. "EPA Administrator Wheeler Worsens Particulate Pollution Review Process." *Union of Concerned Scientists*. August 22, 2019. https://blog.ucsusa.org/gretchen-goldman/wheeler-worsens-particulate-pollution-review-process?_ga=2.101617160.86448406.1571689449-1606488785.1571689449. Accessed November 17, 2020.

Gomez, Antoinette M., Fatemeh Shafiei, and Glenn S. Johnson. 2011. "Black Women's Involvement in the Environmental Justice Movement: An Analysis of Three Communities in Atlanta, Georgia. *Race, Gender & Class*, 18(1/2): 189–214. https://www.jstor.org/stable/23884875. Accessed December 7, 2020.

Gordon, Paul and Francesca Klug. 1986. *New Right, New Racism*. Searchlight Publications: London.

Grabell, Michael, Bernice Yeung and Maryam Jameel. 2020. "Millions of Essential Workers Are Being Left Out of COVID-19 Workplace Safety Protections, Thanks to OSHA." *ProPublica*, April 16, 2020. https://www.propublica.org/article/millions-of-essential-workers-are-being-left-out-of-covid-19-workplace-safety-protections-thanks-to-osha. Accessed May 2, 2020.

Gramlich, John. 2019. "Far More Immigration Cases Are Being Prosecuted Criminally under Trump Administration." *Pew Research Center*. September 27, 2019. https://www.pewresearch.org/fact-tank/2019/09/27/far-more-immigration-cases

-are-being-prosecuted-criminally-under-trump-administration/. Accessed April 29, 2020.

Grandoni, Dino 2018. "EPA Chief Scott Pruitt Relied on Obscure Law To Hire Ex-Lobbyists, Schedulers and Spokesmen." *Washington Post*. April 3, 2018. Accessed August 11, 2020.https://www.washingtonpost.com/news/powerpost/wp/2018/04/03/epa-chief-scott-pruitt-relied-on-obscure-law-to-hire-ex-lobbyists-schedulers-and-spokespeople/.

Grandoni, Dino and Brady Dennis. 2019. "Former EPA Leaders Question Agency's Direction Under Trump. *Washington Post*. June 11, 2019. https://www.washingtonpost.com/climate-environment/2019/06/11/former-epa-leaders-question-agencys-direction-under-trump/. Accessed April 29, 2020.

Green, Miranda. 2017. "More Questions about a Trump Administration War on Science." *CNN*. August 24, 2017. https://www.cnn.com/2017/08/24/politics/trump-environmental-changes/index.html. Accessed April 29, 2020.

Grenell, Richard. 2016. "Donald Trump Holds High The Flag For Gay Equality." *Washington Times*. November 2, 2016. https://www.washingtontimes.com/news/2016/nov/2/donald-trump-holds-high-flag-gay-equality/. Accessed April 28, 2020.

Griswold, Eliza. 2012. "How "Silent Spring" Ignited the Environmental Movement." *New York Times Magazine*. September 21, 2012. https://www.nytimes.com/2012/09/23/magazine/how-silent-spring-ignited-the-environmental-movement.html. Accessed November 18, 2020.

Grogger, Jeffrey and Greg Ridgeway. 2006. "Testing for Racial Profiling in Traffic Stops From Behind a Veil of Darkness." *Journal of the American Statistical Association*, 101(475). DOI 10.1198/016214506000000168. Available at https://www.rand.org/content/dam/rand/pubs/reprints/2007/RAND_RP1253.pdf. Accessed December 3, 2020.

Groppe, Maureen. 2017. "White House Defends Lack of Women at Heath Care Event." *USA Today*. May 7, 2017. https://www.usatoday.com/story/news/politics/onpolitics/2017/05/07/white-house-defends-lack-women-health-care-event/101405436/. Accessed November 24, 2020.

Guillaumin, Colette. 1995. "Sexism, A Right-Wing Constant of Any Discourse: A Theoretical Note." In *Racism, Sexism, Power and Ideology* edited by Colette Guillaumin, 171–175. Translated by Caroline Kunstenaar. Routledge: London.

Gutierrez-Morfin, Noel. 2016. "Trump, Clinton Make Push for LGBTQ Voters on Campaign Trail." *NBC News*. October 31, 2016. https://www.nbcnews.com/feature/nbc-out/trump-clinton-make-push-lgbtq-voters-during-campaign-rallies-n675716. Accessed April 29, 2020.

Haberman, Maggie. 2016. "Donald Trump's Apology That Wasn't." *New York Times*, Oct. 8, 2016. https://www.nytimes.com/2016/10/08/us/politics/donald-trump-apology.html. Accessed April 4, 2020.

Hains, Tim. 2020. "Watch: White House Coronavirus News Conference for Tuesday, April 7." *Real Clear Politics*, April 7, 2020. https://www.realclearpolitics.com/video/2020/04/07/watch_live_white_house_coronavirus_news_conference_for_tuesday_april_7.html. Accessed May 2, 2020.

Hannah-Jones, Nikole, Mary Elliott, Jazmine Hughes, Jake Silverstein, New York Times Company. 2019. "The 1619 Project," *New York Times magazine*, August 18, 2019. *New York Times*. https://pulitzercenter.org/sites/default/files/full_issue_of_the_1619_project.pdf. Accessed December 5, 2020.

Harley, Sharon. 2019. African American Women and the Nineteenth Amendment. National Park Services. Accessed November 15, 2020. https://www.nps.gov/articles/african-american-women-and-the-nineteenth-amendment.htm.

Harrington, Rebecca. 2016. "Here's How Much Oil Has Spilled from US Pipelines since 2010." Business Insider. December 15, 2016. https://www.businessinsider.com/how-much-oil-spills-from-pipelines-us-america-natural-gas-2016-12?r=MX&IR=T. Accessed September 14, 2020.

Harris, Reginald. 2016. "Suicide in the Workplace." *Monthly Labor Review*, Dec 016. https://www.bls.gov/opub/mlr/2016/article/pdf/suicide-in-the-workplace.pdf.

Haseman, Janie, Karina Zaiets, Mitchell Thorson, Carlie Procell, George Petras, and Shawn J. Sullivan. "Tracking Protests Across the USA in the Wake of George Floyd's Death." *USA Today*. June 18, 2020. https://www.usatoday.com/in-depth/graphics/2020/06/03/map-protests-wake-george-floyds-death/5310149002/. Accessed November 14, 2020.

Hazards Magazine. 2020. "Work Suicides." http://www.hazards.org/suicide/.

Heilmann, Ann. 2005. "First-Wave Feminist Engagements with History: Introduction." *Victorian Review*, 31(1): 1–4. https://www.jstor.org/stable/27793561.

Heller, Mouchka. 2020. "How COVID-19 Is Showing Us We Might Be Wasting Our Tech Revolution." *Forbes*, April 1, 2020. https://www.forbes.com/sites/worldeconomicforum/2020/04/01/how-covid-19-is-showing-us-we-might-be-wasting-our-tech-revolution/#6d2aeaee5892. Accessed April 20, 2020.

Henry, Liz. 2017. "Here Is The Full Text of Ashley Judd's Powerful Speech At The Women's March." *Scarymommy.com* January 22, 2017. https://www.scarymommy.com/ashley-judd-speech-womens-march/. Accessed April 19, 2020.

Herrera, Marina. 1992. "Environmentalism and Political Participation: Toward a New System of Social Beliefs and Values?" *Journal of Applied Social Psychology*, 22(8:) 657–676. https://doi.org/10.1111/j.1559-1816.1992.tb00996.x.

Hershenov, Eileen. 2019. "Eileen Hershenov's Testimony Before the House Judiciary Committee on Hate Crimes and the Rise of White Nationalism." April 9, 2019. https://www.adl.org/news/article/eileen-hershenovs-testimony-before-the-house-judiciary-committee-on-hate-crimes-and.

Hershenov, Eileen. 2019. Congressional Testimony, April 9, 2019. https://www.adl.org/media/12760/download. Accessed April 29, 2020.

Herships, Sally and Cardiff Garcia. 2019. "'Curbside Pickup' Gains Steam In Grocery Shopping." *NPR, Heard on Morning Edition*, December 5, 2019. https://www.npr.org/2019/12/05/784994904/curbside-pickup-gains-steam-in-grocery-shopping. Accessed May 3, 2020.

Hewitt, Nancy A. 2012. "Feminist Frequencies: Regenerating the Wave Metaphor." *Feminist Studies*, 38(3): 658–680. https://www.jstor.org/stable/23720198.

Hickey, Georgina. 2008. "Barred from the Barroom: Second Wave Feminists and Public Accommodations in U.S. Cities." *Feminist Studies*, 34(3): 382–408.

Hillman, Anne. 2017. "Women's March Draws Thousands in Downtown Anchorage. *Alaska Public Media*, January 21, 2017. Accessed November 18, 2020. https://www.alaskapublic.org/2017/01/21/womens-march-draws-thousands-in-downtown-anchorage/.

Hirschfeld Davis, Julie and Helene Cooper. 2017. "Trump Says Transgender People Will Not Be Allowed in the Military." *New York Times*. July 26, 2017. https://www.nytimes.com/2017/07/26/us/politics/trump-transgender-military.html. Accessed April 29, 2020.

History.com Editors. 2020. "First Enslaved Africans Arrive in Jamestown, Setting the Stage for Slavery in North America." *A&E Television Networks*. History. Published August 13, 2019/updated August 18, 2020. https://www.history.com/this-day-in-history/first-african-slave-ship-arrives-jamestown-colony. Accessed December 1, 2020.

Hohmann, James. 2018. "The Daily 202: Trump Still Hasn't Nominated a Director for the Violence against Women Office at the Justice Department." *Washington Post*. February 15, 2018. https://www.washingtonpost.com/news/powerpost/paloma/daily-202/2018/02/15/daily-202-trump-still-hasn-t-nominated-a-director-for-the-violence-against-women-office-at-the-justice-department/5a84ebe730fb041c3c7d78e1/. Accessed April 29, 2020.

Holshue, Michelle L., Chas DeBolt, Scott Lindquist, Kathy H. Lofy, John Wiesman, Hollianne Bruce, Christopher Spitters, Keith Ericson, Sara Wilkerson, Ahmet Tural, George Diaz, and Amanda Cohn. 2020. "First Case of 2019 Novel Coronavirus in the United States." *New England Journal Medicine*, 382: 929–936. Accessed October 20, 2020. DOI: 10.1056/NEJMoa2001191.

Hudetz, Marry. 2019. "US official: Research Finds Uranium in Navajo Women, Babies." Associated Press, October 7, 2019. Accessed November 15, 2020. https://abcnews.go.com/Technology/wireStory/us-official-research-finds-uranium-navajo-women-babies-66124231.

Ifill, Sherrilyn. 2018. "President Trump's First Year Was an Affront to Civil Rights." *Time*. January 17, 2018. https://time.com/5106648/donald-trump-civil-rights-race/. Accessed November 15, 2020.

Ingram, Mathew. 2017. "Trump Administration Puts Gag Order on Several Government Agencies." *Fortune*, January 24, 17. Accessed November 22, 2020. https://fortune.com/2017/01/24/trump-gag-order/.

Ingraham, Christopher. 2019. "Air Pollution is Getting Worse and the Data Show More People Are Dying." *Washington Post*. October 23, 2019. https://www.washingtonpost.com/business/2019/10/23/air-pollution-is-getting-worse-data-show-more-people-are-dying/. Accessed November 17, 2020.

Iron Eyes, Chase. 2020. "What Really Happened at Standing Rock: I Was There." Testimonial Video. *Vice*. September 25, 2020. https://www.youtube.com/watch?v=J1yD2J8vHAk. Accessed December 16, 2020.

Itkowitz, Colby. 2017. "LGBT Rights Page Disappears From White House Web Site." *Washington Post*. January 20, 2017. Accessed April 29, 2020. https://www.washingtonpost.com/local/2017/live-updates/politics/live-coverage-of-trumps-inauguration/lgbt-rights-page-disappears-from-white-house-web-site/.

Jagannathan, Meera. 2018. "The Case against Pussyhats, Ahead of this Year's Women's March." *MarketWatch: Moneyish*. Jan. 12, 2018. https://www.marketwatch.com/story/the-case-against-pussyhats-ahead-of-this-years-womens-march-2018-01-12-0883824. Accessed April 15, 2020.

Jaimes*Guerrero, M. A. "'Patriarchal Colonialism' and Indigenism: Implications for Native Feminist Spirituality and Native Womanism." *Hypatia*, 18(2), Indigenous Women in the Americas (Spring, 2003): 58–69. https://www.jstor.org/stable/3811011.

Janofsky, Michael. 1997. "At Million Woman March, Focus Is on Family." *New York Times*, October 26, 1997. https://www.nytimes.com/1997/10/26/us/at-million-woman-march-focus-is-on-family.html. Accessed April 9, 2020.

Jewett, Chas. 2017. "The Standing Rock Water Protectors." Testimonial by Chas Jewett, from the Cheyenne River Sioux Tribe, and Standing Rock Water protector. *Afriireland*. https://www.youtube.com/watch?v=Wz8kDZ_a-8I.

Johnson, Chris. 2016. "Trump Makes History With LGBT Inclusion in Speech." *Washington Blade*. July 22, 2016. https://www.washingtonblade.com/2016/07/22/trump-makes-history-lgbt-inclusion-acceptance-speech/. Accessed April 29, 2020.

Johnson, Jenna. 2015. "Trump Calls For 'Total and Complete Shutdown of Muslims Entering the United States." *Washington Post*. December 7, 2015. https://www.washingtonpost.com/news/post-politics/wp/2015/12/07/donald-trump-calls-for-total-and-complete-shutdown-of-muslims-entering-the-united-states/. Accessed April 29, 2020.

Jones, Ashley. 2008. "Million Woman March, 1997." *Black Past*, February 26, 2008. https://www.blackpast.org/african-american-history/million-woman-march-1997/. Accessed April 30, 2020.

Jones, Charisse. 2020. "Jobless Claims Climb to 30 Million in Six Weeks as COVID-19 Layoffs Continue to rise." *USA Today*, April 30, 2020. https://www.usatoday.com/story/money/2020/04/30/unemployment-benefits-3-8-million-file-jobless-claims-amid-pandemic/3046759001/. Accessed November 25, 2020.

Jones, Jo, William Mosher, and Kimberly Daniels. 2012. "Current Contraceptive use in the United States, 2006–2010, and Changes in Patterns of Use Since 1995." *National Health Statistics Report*, 60: 1–25.

Jones, Martha S. 2020. *Vanguard: How Black Women Broke Barriers, Won the Vote, and Insisted on Equality for All*. Basic Books, Hatchette Book Group: New York, NY.

Just Saying, 2016. "Pink Pussy Power Hats!!" *Daily KOS*, December 27, 2016 https://www.dailykos.com/stories/2016/12/27/1614887/-Pink-Pussy-Power-Hats. Accessed April 30, 2020.

Kaczynski, Andrew, Chris Massie, and Nate McDermott. 2016. "Donald Trump to Howard Stern: It's Okay to Call My Daughter a 'Piece of Ass.'" *CNN*. October 9, 2016. https://www.cnn.com/2016/10/08/politics/trump-on-howard-stern/index.html. Accessed April 29, 2020.

Kano, Krista. 2020. "KSU Bringing Students Home from Florence Campus Due to Virus Crisis." *Record-Courier*, Feb 27, 2020 (updated Feb 29, 2020) https://www.

record-courier.com/news/20200227/ksu-bringing-students-home-from-florence-campus-due-to-virus-crisis. Accessed April 26, 2020.

Kassraie, Aaron. 2020. "Supermarkets Offer Special Hours for Older Shoppers: Move by Some Retailers Limits Coronavirus Exposure for At-Risk Customers." *AARP*, April 22, 2020. https://www.aarp.org/home-family/your-home/info-2020/coronavirus-supermarkets.html. Accessed May 2, 2020.

Kates, Graham. 2018. "Migrant Children at the Border—The Facts." *CBS News*. Juner 20, 2018. https://www.cbsnews.com/news/migrant-children-at-the-border-by-the-numbers/. Accessed April 29, 2020.

Kay, Susan Ann. 1985. "Feminist Ideology, Race, and Political Participation: A Second Look." *The Western Political Quarterly*, 38(3): 476–484. https://www.jstor.org/stable/448528.

Kearney, Laila. 2016. "Hawaii Grandma's Plea Launches Women's March in Washington." *Reuters*, December 5, 2016. https://www.reuters.com/article/us-usa-trump-women-idUSKBN13U0GW. Accessed April 4, 2020.

Keneally, Meghan. 2019. "List of Trump's Accusers and their Allegations of Sexual Misconduct." *ABC News*. June 25, 2019. https://abcnews.go.com/Politics/list-trumps-accusers-allegations-sexual-misconduct/story?id=51956410. Accessed April 29, 2020.

Kennedy, Merrit. 2016. "Lead-Laced Water in Flint: A Step-By-Step Look At the Makings of a Crisis." *NPR*, April 20, 2016. https://www.npr.org/sections/thetwo-way/2016/04/20/465545378/lead-laced-water-in-flint-a-step-by-step-look-at-the-makings-of-a-crisis. Accessed April 29, 2020.

Kessler, Glenn. 2020. "The 'Very Fine People' at Charlottesville: Who Were They?" *Washington Post.* May 8, 2020. https://www.washingtonpost.com/politics/2020/05/08/very-fine-people-charlottesville-who-were-they-2/. Accessed November 21, 2020.

Kilgannon, Corey. 2020. "As Morgues Fill, N.Y.C. to Bury Some Virus Victims in Potter's Field." *New York Times*, April 10, 2020. https://www.nytimes.com/2020/04/10/nyregion/coronavirus-deaths-hart-island-burial.html. Accessed May 1, 2020.

Kimble, Matthew, Andrada D. Neacsiu, William F. Flack, and Jessica Horner. 2010. "Risk of Unwanted Sex for College Women: Evidence for a Red Zone." *Journal of American College Health.* V.57, 3. https://www.tandfonline.com/doi/abs/10.3200/JACH.57.3.331-338. Accessed April 29, 2020.

King, Ynestra. 1995. "The Ecology of Feminism and the Feminism of Ecology." In *Readings in Ecology and Feminist Theology*, edited by MacKinnon and McIntyre. Sheed and Ward: Franklin.

Kings, A.E. 2017. "Intersectionality and the Changing Face of Ecofeminism." *Ethics and the Environment,* 22: 63–87. https://www.jstor.org/stable/10.2979/ethicsenviro.22.1.04?seq=1.

Kinser, Amber E. 2004. "Negotiating Spaces for/through Third-Wave Feminism." *NWSA Journal*, 16(3): 124–153. https://www.jstor.org/stable/4317084.

Klare, Michael T. 2020. "Covid-19's Third Shock Wave: The Global Food Crisis: Many people Are Already Going Hungry in the United States; Many More Will

Face Hunger or Starvation in Other Parts of the World." *The Nation*, May 1, 2020. https://www.thenation.com/article/society/coronavirus-global-food-crisis/.

Klare, Michael T. 2020. "Many People Are Already Going Hungry in the United States; Many More Will Face Hunger or Starvation in Other Parts of the World." *The Nation*, May 1, 2020. https://www.thenation.com/article/society/coronavirus-global-food-crisis/. Accessed May 2, 2020.

Klasfeld, Adam. 2020. "Trump Can't Pause Suit by Rape Accuser E. Jean Carroll." *Court House News*. August 7, 2020. https://www.courthousenews.com/trump-cant-pause-suit-by-rape-accuser-e-jean-carroll/. Accessed November 24, 2020.

Klinker, Philip. 2014. The Causes and Consequences of "Birtherism." Paper Presented at the 2014 Annual Meeting of the Western Political Science Association. http://www.wpsanet.org/papers/docs/Birthers.pdf. Accessed April 29, 2020.

Kocieniewski, David and Bloomberg. 2020. "4 U.S. Senators Sold Stock after Getting Coronavirus Threat Briefings in January." *Fortune*, March 20, 2020. https://fortune.com/2020/03/20/senators-burr-loeffler-sold-stock-coronavirus-threat-briefings-in-january/. Accessed April 29, 2020.

Kohut, Andrew, Doherty, Carroll Doherty, Michael Dimock, and Scott Keeter. 2012. "Partisan Polarization Surges in Bush, Obama Years." *Pew Research Center*. June 4, 2012. https://drive.google.com/drive/u/0/folders/1NcS1c2--JcNcokXDxKKL880GzGepqA6U?ths=true. Accessed August 22, 2020.

Krasinski, John. (2020) "Alright, That's It, Enough is Enough. All You Graduates of 2020? After All Those Long Hours You've Put In. All the Hard Work You've Put In . . . You're Gettin a Graduation! And That's All There Is To It! This Week! I'm There with Tassels On! #SGNgraduation !!!" *Twitter*, April 28, 2020. https://twitter.com/johnkrasinski/status/1255164795092901890. Accessed May 2, 2020.

Krauss, Lawrence M. 2016. "Donald Trump's War on Science." *New Yorker*. December 13, 2016. https://www.newyorker.com/tech/annals-of-technology/donald-trumps-war-on-science. Accessed April 29, 2020.

Krebs, Christopher, Christine Lindquist, Tara Warner, Bonnie Fisher, Sandra Martin. 2007. "The Campus Sexual Assault (CSA) Study." *NCJRS* 221153. https://www.ncjrs.gov/pdffiles1/nij/grants/221153.pdf. Accessed April 29, 2020.

Krieg, Gregory. 2016. "14 of Trump's Most Outrageous 'Birther' Claims—Half from After 2011." *CNN*. September 16, 2016. https://www.cnn.com/2016/09/09/politics/donald-trump-birther/index.html. Accessed February 20, 2020.

Kuhn, Moritz, Moritz Schularick and Ulrike I. Steins. 2018. "Income and Wealth Inequality in America, 1949–2016." *Opportunity and Inclusive Growth Institute*. June 2018. https://www.minneapolisfed.org/institute/working-papers-institute/iwp9.pdf. Accessed October 27, 2020.

Kulish, Nicholas. 2020. "'Never Seen Anything Like It': Cars Line Up for Miles at Food Banks: Millions are Flooding a Charitable System That Was Never Intended to Handle a Nationwide Crisis." *New York Times*, April 8, 2020. https://www.nytimes.com/2020/04/08/business/economy/coronavirus-food-banks.html. Accessed May 2, 2020.

Kunst, Jonas, Ronald Fischer, Jim Sidanius, and Lotte Thomsen. 2017. "Preferences for Group Dominance Track and Mediate the Effects of Macro-Level Social

Inequality and Violence Across Societies." *Proceedings of the National Academy of Sciences,* 114. 10.1073/pnas.1616572114. https://www.pnas.org/content/114/21/5407. Accessed May 2, 2020.

Lakhani, Nina. 2020. "'A Perfect Storm': US Facing Hunger Crisis as Demand for Food Banks Soars." *Guardian*, April 2, 2020. https://www.theguardian.com/environment/2020/apr/02/us-food-banks-coronavirus-demand-unemployment. Accessed May 2, 2020.

Latson, Jennifer. 2015. "The Burning River That Sparked a Revolution." *Time*. June 22, 2015. https://time.com/3921976/cuyahoga-fire/. Accessed April 29, 2020.

Laughland, Oliver. 2014. "US Medical Students Stage 'die-ins' Nationwide in Protest Against Police." *Guardian*, December 10, 2014. Accessed December 5, 2020. https://www.theguardian.com/us-news/2014/dec/10/us-medical-students-stage-die-insprotest-against-police.

Leach, Melissa. 2007. "Earth Mother Myths and Other Ecofeminist Fables: How a Strategic Notion Rose and Fell." *Development and Change*, 38(1), January 31, 2007.

Lee, Jasmine C. and Kevin Quealy. 2019. "The 598 People, Places, and Things Donald Trump Has Insulted on Twitter: A Complete List." *New York Times*. May 24, 2019. https://www.nytimes.com/interactive/2016/01/28/upshot/donald-trump-twitter-insults.html. Accessed March 15, 2020.

Lee, Tracy. 2018. "Trump Administration's Top Job Preventing Violence against Women Remains Unfilled." *Newsweek*. February 15, 2018. https://www.newsweek.com/trump-domestic-violence-against-women-808203. Accessed April 28, 2020.

Lemelle, Jr., Anthony J. 1995. "The Political Sociology of Black Masculinity and Tropes of Domination." *Journal of African American Men*, 1(2): 87–101. http://www.jstor.org/stable/41819284.

Lemelle, Jr., Anthony J. 2010. *Black Masculinity and Sexual Politics.* Routledge: New York.

Lemon, Jason. 2020. "Half of Americans think Trump is Racist and Additional 13 Percent are Unsure: Poll." *Newsweek*. July 16, 2020. https://www.newsweek.com/half-americans-think-trump-racist-additional-13-percent-are-unsure-poll-1518272. Accessed November 14, 2020.

Lenghi, Mola 2017. "Thousands mail pink p**sy hats ahead of Million Women March." *News Center Maine*. January 10, 2017. https://www.newscentermaine.com/article/news/local/thousands-mail-pink-psy-hats-ahead-of-million-women-march/97-384693526. Accessed April 20, 2020

Lenghi, Mola. 2017. "Pink Hat Project Gains Momentum Ahead of Women's March in DC: Healthcare and the Trump Administration's Agenda Will Be at the Center of a Protest on D.C. Streets the Day After the Inauguration." *12News*, January 9, 2017. https://www.12news.com/article/mobile/news/politics/national-politics/pink-hat-project-gains-momentum-ahead-of-womens-march-in-dc/384462659. Accessed April 27, 2020.

Lerner, Gerda. 1974. "Early Community Work of Black Club Women." *Journal of Negro History,* 59(2): (April 1974) 158–167. https://www-jstor-org.proxy.library.kent.edu/stable/pdf/2717327.pdf?ab_segments=0%2Fbasic_SYC-5187_SYC-51

88%2F5187&refreqid=fastly-default%3Af8b1588144a1e76484e267ea32c0fabc. Accessed November 19, 2020.

Levitan, Clarisse. 2019. "Why 85% of People Hate their Jobs." *Staff Squared*, December 3, 2019. https://www.staffsquared.com/blog/why-85-of-people-hate-their-jobs/.

Li, Shan. 2020. "New York City's Coronavirus Deaths Match Demographics in Other Hot Spots." *New York Times*, April 18, 2020. https://www.wsj.com/articles/new-york-citys-coronavirus-deaths-match-demographics-in-other-hot-spots-11587214800. Accessed April 20, 2020.

Lipton, Eric and Coral Davenport. 2017. "Scott Pruitt, Trump's E.P.A. Pick, Backed Industry Donors over Regulators." *New York Times*. January 14, 2017. https://www.nytimes.com/2017/01/14/us/scott-pruitt-trump-epa-pick.html. Accessed April 29, 2020.

Long, Heather and Andrew Van Dam. 2020. "The Black-White Economic Divide Is as Wide as it Was 1968." *Washington Post*. June 4, 2020. https://www.washingtonpost.com/business/2020/06/04/economic-divide-black-households/. Accessed November 1, 2020.

Lovelace, Jr., Berkeley. 2020. "Trump says some Americans wear coronavirus masks to signal disapproval of him." *CNBC*, June 19, 2020, updated July 14, 2020. https://www.cnbc.com/2020/06/18/trump-says-some-wear-coronavirus-masks-to-signal-disapproval-of-him.html. Accessed October 23, 2020.

Luscombe, Richard. 2013. "George Zimmerman Acquitted in Trayvon Martin Case. Neighbourhood Watch Leader Walks Free from Florida Court after Jury Finds Him Not Guilty over Death of 17-year-old." *Guardian*. July 14, 2013. https://www.theguardian.com/world/2013/jul/14/zimmerman-acquitted-killing-trayvon-martin. Accessed April 14, 2020.

Luthi, Susannah, 2020. "Court Upholds Trump's Coronavirus Immigration Ban." *Politico, Legal*. April 29, 2020. https://www.politico.com/news/2020/04/29/court-upholds-trumps-coronavirus-immigration-ban-224855. Accessed May 2, 2020.

MacKenzie, A., and I. Bhatt, 2020. "Lies, Bullshit and Fake News." 2020. *Postdigital Science and Education*, 2: 1–8. https://doi.org/10.1007/s42438-019-00085-4. Accessed May 2, 2020.

Malka, Adam. 2018. *The Men of Mobtown: Policing Baltimore in the Age of Slavery and Emancipation*. University of North Carolina Press: Chapel Hill, North Carolina.

Mangan, Dan. 2019. "Donald Trump Sexually Assulted E. Jean Carroll in the mid-1990s, Writer Says in New Book." *CNBC*. June 21, 2019. https://www.cnbc.com/2019/06/21/e-jean-carroll-says-donald-trump-sexually-assaulted-her.html. Accessed November 24, 2020.

Mandler, C. 2019. "Please Stop Wearing Those Pussy Hats To Women's Marches: A nonbinary Person's Thoughts on Trans Exclusion in Mainstream Social Movements . . ." *Seventeen*, Jan 18, 2019. https://www.seventeen.com/life/a15854506/stop-wearing-pussy-hats-womens-marches/. Accessed April 16, 2020.

Mann, Susan A. 2011. "Pioneers of U.S. Ecofeminism and Environmental Justice." *Feminist Formations*, 23(2): 1–25. https://www.jstor.org/stable/41301654.

Manning, Jennifer E and Brudnick, Ida A. 2018. "Women in Congress, 1917–2018: Service Dates and Committee Assignments by Member, and Lists by State and Congress." Congressional Research Service. https://crsreports.congress.gov/product/pdf/R/R43244. Accessed Dec. 10, 2018.

Markon, Jerry. 2016. "U.S. Illegal Immigrant Population Falls below 11 million, Continuing Nearly Decade-Long Decline, Report Says." *Washington Post*. January 20, 2016. https://www.washingtonpost.com/news/federal-eye/wp/2016/01/20/u-s-illegal-immigrant-population-falls-below-11-million-continuing-nearly-decade-long-decline-report-says/. Accessed April 29, 2020.

Marsh, Rene and Dan Merica. 2017. "Trump Administration Reviewing EPA Website, Curbs Agency Communication." *CNN*, January 26, 2017. Accessed April 28, 2020. https://www.cnn.com/2017/01/25/politics/trump-epa-lockdowns/index.html.

Martinez, Peter. 2019. "Hate Groups Hit New High, Up 30 Percent in Last 4 Years, Southern Poverty Law Center Says." *CBS News*. February 20, 2019. Accessed April 28, 2020. https://www.cbsnews.com/news/southern-poverty-law-center-new-hate-map-data-group-increase-splc-intelligence-report-today-2019-02-20/.

Martinovich, Milenko. 2017. "Stanford Scholars Analyze Trump's Revised Executive Order on Immigration." *Stanford News*. March 7, 2017. https://news.stanford.edu/2017/03/07/stanford-scholars-analyze-trumps-travel-ban/. Accessed April 29, 2020.

Mayer, Jane. 2016. "Documenting Trump's Abuse of Women." *New Yorker*. October 17, 2016. Accessed April 28, 2020. https://www.newyorker.com/magazine/2016/10/24/documenting-trumps-abuse-of-women.

Mayer, Jane. 2010. "Covert Operations." *New Yorker*. August 23, 2010. https://www.newyorker.com/magazine/2010/08/30/covert-operations. Accessed on June 6, 2021.

McCarthy, Niall. 2017. "America's Active Hate Groups." *Statista, Hate Groups*. https://www.statista.com/chart/10673/americas-active-hate-groups/.

McCarthy, Niall. 2020. Police Shootings: Black Americans Disproportionately Affected. Forbes. May 28, 2020. https://www.forbes.com/sites/niallmccarthy/2020/05/28/police-shootings-black-americans-disproportionately-affected-infographic/?sh=1e92608659f7. Accessed October 17, 2020.

McDonald, Michael. 2020. 2020 General Election Early Vote Statistics. U.S. Elections Project. Accessed November 14, 2020 https://electproject.github.io/Early-Vote-2020G/index.html.

McFarling, Usha Lee. "Fearing Deportation, Many Immigrants at Higher Risk of Covid-19 are Afraid to Seek Testing or Care." *StatNews, Health*, April 15, 2020. https://www.statnews.com/2020/04/15/fearing-deportation-many-immigrants-at-higher-risk-of-covid-19-are-afraid-to-seek-testing-or-care/. Accessed May 2, 2020.

McLaren, John. 2020. "Racial Disparity in COVID-19 Dealths: Seeking Economic Roots with Census Data. Working Paper 27407. http://www.nber.org/papers/w27407. National Bureau of Economic Research.

McLaughlin, Eliott C. and Sara Sidner. 2016. Oklahoma City Cop Convicted of Rape Sentenced to 263 Years in Prison. *CNN*. January 22, 2016. https://edition.cnn.com/2016/01/21/us/oklahoma-city-officer-daniel-holtzclaw-rape-sentencing/index.html. Accessed November 14, 2020.

McNamara,Tracey, Juergen A. Richt, and Larry Glickman. 2020. "A Critical Needs Assessment for Research in Companion Animals and Livestock Following the Pandemic of COVID-19 in Humans." *Vector-Borne and Zoonatic Diseases*, 20(6): 393–405. Accessed November 15, 2020. https://www.liebertpub.com/doi/pdf/10.1089/vbz.2020.2650.

Meckler, Laura. 2020. "Seven states, D.C. Order All Schools Closed in Effort to Prevent Spread of Covid-19." *Washington Post*, March 13, 2020. https://www.washingtonpost.com/local/education/ohio-maryland-order-all-schools-closed-in-effort-to-prevent-spread-of-covid-19/2020/03/12/e4078b3a-6499-11ea-845d-e35b0234b136_story.html. Accessed April 26, 2020.

Miers, Suzanne. 2003. "Slavery: A Question of Definition." *Slavery and Abolition*, 24(2): 1–16, https://doi.org/10.1080/01440390308559152. Accessed December 6, 2020.

Merchant, Carolyn. 1989. *The Death of Nature: Women, Ecology, and the Scientific Revolution*. Harper and Row: New York.

Merritt Johns, David and Karen Levy. 2019. "How Trump's War on Science is Borrowing From The Tobacco Industry Playbook." *Washington Post*. December 13, 2019. https://www.washingtonpost.com/outlook/2019/12/13/how-trumps-war-science-is-borrowing-tobacco-industry-playbook/. Accessed April 29, 2020.

Mervosh, Sarah, Lu, Denise, and Swales, Vanessa. 2020. "See Which States and Cities Have Told Residents to Stay at Home." *New York Times*, April 20, 2020. Accessed April 21, 2020 from https://www.nytimes.com/interactive/2020/us/coronavirus-stay-at-home-order.html.

Messner, Steven F., Richard Rosenfeld, and Susanne Karstedt. 2012. Social Institutions and Crime. The Oxford Handbook of Criminological Theory. December 2012. https://www.oxfordhandbooks.com/view/10.1093/oxfordhb/9780199747238.001.0001/oxfordhb-9780199747238-e-21. Accessed September 28, 2020.

Mies, Maria and Vandana Shiva. 1993/2014. *Ecofeminism*. Zed Books: London.

Milano, Alyssa. 2017. "If you've been sexually harassed or assaulted write 'me too' as a reply to this tweet." *Twitter*, October 15, 2017.

Mitchell, Amy, Mark Jurkowitz, J. Baxter Oliphant, and Elisa Shearer. 2020. "Majorities of Americans Say News Coverage of George Floyd Protests Has Been Good, Trump's Public Message Wrong." *Pew Research Center*. June 12, 2020. https://www.journalism.org/2020/06/12/majorities-of-americans-say-news-coverage-of-george-floyd-protests-has-been-good-trumps-public-message-wrong/. Accessed November 15, 2020.

Mohammed, Patricia. 2003. "Like Sugar in Coffee: Third Wave Feminism and the Caribbean." *Social and Economic Studies*, 52(3): 5–30. https://www.jstor.org/stable/27865339.

Montoya-Galvez, Camilo. 2020. "Chad Wolf Did Not Have the Authority to Restrict DACA program, Federal Judge Rules." *CBSNEWS*. Updated on November 16, 2020. https://www.cbsnews.com/news/chad-wolf-no-authority-daca-ruling/.

Moore, Leonard. 2010. *Black Rage in New Orleans: Police Brutality and African American Activism from World War II to Hurricane Katrina.* Louisiana State University Press: Baton Rouge, LA.

Mounk, Yascha. 2020. "Cancel Everything: Social Distancing Is the Only Way to Stop the Coronavirus. We Must Start Immediately." *The Atlantic*, March 10, 2020. https://www.theatlantic.com/ideas/archive/2020/03/coronavirus-cancel-everything/607675/. Accessed April 20, 2020.

MPI—Migration Policy Institute. 2019. "Deferred Action for Childhood Arrivals (DACA) Data Tools." September 30, 1019. https://www.migrationpolicy.org/programs/data-hub/deferred-action-childhood-arrivals-daca-profiles. Accessed April 30, 2020.

Mufson, Steven. 2017. "An American Energy Plan Straight From Coal Country." *Washington Post.* December 8, 2017. https://www.washingtonpost.com/business/economy/an-american-energy-plan-straight-from-coal-country/2017/12/08/1f207a26-d6ab-11e7-a986-d0a9770d9a3e_story.html?noredirect=on&utm_term=.6abdef747a28. Accessed August 12, 2020.

Mufson, Steven. 2018. "Scott Pruitt's Likely Successor Has Long Lobbying History on Issues Before the EPA." *Washington Post.* July 5, 2018. https://www.washingtonpost.com/business/economy/epas-acting-administrator-has-long-lobbying-record-on-issues-before-the-agency/2018/07/05/a591cd40-6a6b-11e8-bea7-c8eb28bc52b1_story.html. Accessed August 12, 2020.

Murchison, Gabriel R., Madina Agénor, Sari L. Reisner and Ryan J. Watson. 2019. "School Restroom and Locker Room Restrictions and Sexual Assault Risk Among Transgender Youth." *Pediatrics*, 143(6). https://doi.org/10.1542/peds.2018-2902. Accessed April 29, 2020.

Murphy Kelly, Samantha. 2020. "Zoom's Massive 'Overnight Success' Actually Took Nine Years." *CNN Business*, March 27, 2020. https://www.cnn.com/2020/03/27/tech/zoom-app-coronavirus/index.html. Accessed April 29, 2020.

Musumeci, Natalie. 2020. "Disturbing Video Shows Dead Bodies Loaded Onto Truck Outside NYC Hospitals." *New York Post*, March 30, 2020. https://nypost.com/2020/03/30/disturbing-footage-shows-dead-bodies-loaded-onto-truck-outside-brooklyn-hospital/. Accessed October 22, 2020.

NAACP—National Association for the Advancement of Colored People. 2020. "Voter Access and Participation during the Coronavirus Pandemic." *NAACP.* https://naacp.org/coronavirus/voter-access-and-participation-during-coronavirus-pandemic/. Accessed May 2, 2020.

Nagel, David. 2020. "Updated List of Statewide School Closures with Closure Dates. The Journal." Updated April 24, 2020/March 17, 2020. https://thejournal.com/Articles/2020/03/17/List-of-States-Shutting-Down-All-Their-Schools-Grows-to-36.aspx?p=1. Accessed April 26, 2020.

NCADV—*National Coalition against Domestic Violence.* 2018. https://www.ncadv.org/blog/posts/ncadv-denounces-president-trumps-fy19-budget-request.

NCSL—National Conference of State Legislatures. 2020. "2020 State Primary Election Dates." updated 4/20/2020. Accessed April 21, 2020 and November 11,

2020. https://www.ncsl.org/research/elections-and-campaigns/2020-state-primary-election-dates.aspx#Chronological.

Nebehay, Stephanie. 2018. "U.S. Should Stop Detaining Migrants, Separating Children: U.N." *Reuters*. June 5, 2018. https://www.reuters.com/article/us-usa-immigration-un-idUSKCN1J114A. Accessed April 29, 2020.

Neuhauser, Alan. 2019. "100,000 Americans Die From Air Pollution, Study Finds." *U.S. News and World Report*. April 8, 2019. https://www.usnews.com/news/national-news/articles/2019-04-08/100-000-americans-die-from-air-pollution-study-finds. Accessed November 17, 2020.

Niedermeier, Silvan. 2019. "Forced Confessions: Police Torture and the African American Struggle for Civil Rights in the 1930s and 1940s South." In *Crime and Punishment in the Jim Crow South,* edited by Amy Louise Wood and Natalie J. Ring. University of Illinois Press: Champaign, Illinois. https://www.jstor.org/stable/10.5406/j.ctvgs0c92.7. Accessed December 3, 2020.

NOI-Nation of Islam. 2020. "About the Million Man March: A Glimpse of Heaven." https://www.noi.org/about-million-man-march/. Accessed April 30, 2020.

NPR. 2018. "Transcript: White House Chief Of Staff John Kelly's Interview With NPR." *NPR*. May 11, 2018. https://www.npr.org/2018/05/11/610116389/transcript-white-house-chief-of-staff-john-kellys-interview-with-npr. Accessed April 29, 2020.

Nugent, Ciara. 2019. "Abuse is a Pattern. Why These Nations Took The Lead in Criminalizing Controlling Behavior in Relationships." *Time*. June 21, 2019. https://time.com/5610016/coercive-control-domestic-violence/. Accessed April 29, 2020.

*NYT* 2014. "Michael Brown's Shooting and Its Immediate Aftermath in Ferguson." *New York Times*, August 25, 2014. https://www.nytimes.com/interactive/2014/08/12/us/13police-shooting-of-black-teenager-michael-brown.html#/#time348_10376. Accessed April 15, 2020.

O'Hara, Mary Emily. 2017. "Trump Pulls Back Obama-Era Protections for Women Workers." *NBC News*. April 3, 2017. https://www.nbcnews.com/news/us-news/trump-pulls-back-obama-era-protections-women-workers-n741041. Accessed April 29, 2020.

Okolosie, Lola. 2014. "Beyond 'Talking' and 'Owning' Intersectionality." *Feminist Review*, 108: 90–96. https://www.jstor.org/stable/24571923.

Oppenheim, Maya. 2019. "Trump Administration 'Rolling Back Women's Rights by 50 Years' by Changing Definitions of Domestic Violence and Sexual Assault." *Independent*. January 24, 2019. Accessed April 29, 2020. https://www.independent.co.uk/news/world/americas/trump-dometic-abuse-sexual-assault-definition-womens-rights-justice-department-a8744546.html.

Orden, Erica. 2020. "Judge Rules E. Jean Carroll Can Continue to Seek Trump's DNA in Defamation Suit." *CNN*. August 7, 2020. https://edition.cnn.com/2020/08/07/politics/e-jean-carroll-trump-dna/index.html. Accessed November 24, 2020.

Ore, Ersula J. 2019. *Lynching: Violence, Rhetoric, and American Identity*. University Press of Mississippi.

Ortiz, Erik. 2020. Lack of Awareness, Data Hinders Cases of Missing and Murdered Native American Women, Study Finds. *NBCNews*, July 30, 2020. Accessed

November 23, 2020. https://www.nbcnews.com/news/us-news/lack-awareness-data-hinders-cases-missing-murdered-native-american-women-n1235233.

Ostler, Jeffrey. 2020. "Disease Has Never Been Just Disease for Native Americans: Native Communities' Vulnerability to Epidemics Is not a Historical Accident, but a Direct Result of Oppressive Policies and Ongoing Colonialism." *The Atlantic*, April 29, 2020. https://www.theatlantic.com/ideas/archive/2020/04/disease-has-never-been-just-disease-native-americans/610852/. Accessed May 1, 2020.

Overby, Peter. 2018. "There's a $500,000 Gender Gap When It Comes to Campaign Fundraising." *NPR*. September 26, 2018. https://www.npr.org/2018/09/26/651185105/theres-a-500-000-gender-gap-when-it-comes-to-campaign-fundraising. Accessed May 1, 2020.

Pain, Rachel. 2014. "Gendered Violence: Rotating Intimacy." *Area*, 46(4): 351–353. https://www.jstor.org/stable/24811739. Accessed April 29, 2020.

Pan, Deanna. 2020. "Black Americans, Suffering Disproportionately from COVID-19, Face a Mounting Mental Health Crisis." *Boston Globe*. September 7, 2020. https://www.bostonglobe.com/2020/09/07/metro/black-americans-suffering-disproportionately-covid-19-face-mounting-mental-health-crisis/. Accessed November 15, 2020.

Park, Haeyoun and Troy Griggs. 2017. "Could Trump Really Deport Millions of Unauthorized Immigrants?" *New York Times*. February 21, 2017. https://www.nytimes.com/interactive/2016/11/29/us/trump-unauthorized-immigrants.html. Accessed March 11, 2020.

Parker, Ashley. 2019. "How Trump Has Attempted to Recast his Response to Charlottesville." *Washington Post*. May 7, 2019. https://www.washingtonpost.com/politics/how-trump-has-attempted-to-recast-his-response-to-charlottesville/2019/05/06/8c4b7fc2-6b80-11e9-a66d-a82d3f3d96d5_story.html. Accessed November 21, 2020.

Parker, Ashley and Steve Eder, 2016. "Inside the Six Weeks Donald Trump Was a Nonstop Birther." *New York Times*. July 2, 2016. https://www.nytimes.com/2016/07/03/us/politics/donald-trump-birther-obama.html. Accessed April 29, 2020.

Parker, Kim, Juliana Menasce Horowitz, and Monica Anderson. 2020. "Amid Protests, Majorities Across Racial and Ethnic Groups Express Support for the Black Lives Matter Movement." *Pew Research Center*. June 12, 2020. https://www.pewsocialtrends.org/2020/06/12/amid-protests-majorities-across-racial-and-ethnic-groups-express-support-for-the-black-lives-matter-movement/. Accessed November 4, 2020.

Passel, Jeffrey S. and D'Vera Cohn. 2018. "U.S. Unauthorized Immigrant Total Dips to Lowest Level in a Decade." *Pew Research Center*. November 27, 2018. https://www.pewresearch.org/hispanic/2018/11/27/u-s-unauthorized-immigrant-total-dips-to-lowest-level-in-a-decade/. Accessed April 29, 2020.

Patnaik, Subrat. 2020. "Zoom's Daily Active Users Jumped from 10 Million to over 200 Million in 3 Months." *Reuters*, April 2, 2020. https://venturebeat.com/2020/04/02/zooms-daily-active-users-jumped-from-10-million-to-over-200-million-in-3-months/. Accessed April 30, 2020.

Peralta, Eyder. 2012. "'Million Hoodie March' Planned In New York To Protest Killing of Trayvon Martin." *The Two-Way, NPR*. https://www.npr.org/sections/thetwo-way/2012/03/21/149092286/million-hoodie-march-planned-in-new-york-to-protest-killing-of-trayvon-martin. Accessed April 14, 2020.

Peters, Jeremy W., Jo Becker and Julie Hirschfeld Davis. 2017. "Trump Rescinds Rules on Bathrooms for Transgender Students." *New York Times*. February 22, 2017. https://www.nytimes.com/2017/02/22/us/politics/devos-sessions-transgender-students-rights.html. Accessed April 29, 2020.

Phillip, Abby, Thomas Gibbons-Neff and Mike DeBonis. 2017. "Trump Announces That He Will Ban Transgender People From Serving In The Military." *Washington Post*. July 26, 2017. https://www.washingtonpost.com/world/national-security/trump-announces-that-he-will-ban-transgender-people-from-serving-in-the-military/2017/07/26/6415371e-723a-11e7-803f-a6c989606ac7_story.html. Accessed April 29, 2020.

Pierson, Emma, Camelia Simoiu, Jan Overgoor, Sam Corbett-Davies, Vignesh Ramachandran, Cheryl Phillips, and Sharad Goel. 2020. "A Large-Scale Analysis of Racial Disparities in Police Stops Across the United States." *Nature Human Behaviour*, 4: 736–745. https://5harad.com/papers/100M-stops.pdf. Accessed December 3, 2020.

Pilkington, Ed and Martin Pengelly. 2020. "Trump Was Warned in January of Covid-19's Devastating Impact, Memos Reveal." *Guardian*, April 7, 2020. https://www.theguardian.com/world/2020/apr/07/donald-trump-coronavirus-memos-warning-peter-navarro. Accessed October 23, 2020.

Plumwood, Val. 1996. "Nature, Self, and Gender: Feminism, Environmental Philosophy, and the Critique of Rationalism." In *Ecological Feminist Philosophies*, edited by Karen J. Warren, 155–180. Indiana University Press: Bloomington.

Pocock, David F. 1957. "Inclusion and Exclusion: A Process in the Caste System of Gujarat." *Southwestern Journal of Anthropology*, 13: 19–31.

Popovich, Nadja, Livia Albeck-Ripka, and Kendra Pierre-Louis. 2020. "The Trump Administration is Reversing Nearly 100 Environmental Rules. Here's the Full List." *New York Times*. October 15, 2020. https://www.nytimes.com/interactive/2020/climate/trump-environment-rollbacks.html. Accessed November 18, 2020.

Pramuk, Jacob. 2017. "Trump's Inaugural Committee Raised a Record $106.7 Million-Here's Who Donated." *CNBC*. April 19, 2017. https://www.cnbc.com/2017/04/19/trumps-inaugural-committee-raised-a-record-106-7-million-heres-who-donated.html. Accessed August 11, 2020.

Pramuk, Jacob. 2018. "The Number of Women Running for Office is Rising. 7 First-Time House Candidates Explain Why They're Running in the Age of Trump." *CNBC*. Wednesday, April 4, 2018. https://www.cnbc.com/2018/04/04/more-women-than-ever-are-running-for-office-this-year-7-first-time-house-candidates-explain-why-theyre-running.html.

Presley, Sharon. 2016. "Black Women Abolitionists and the Fight for Freedom in the 19th Century." *Libertarianism*. February 10, 2016. https://www.libertarianism.org/columns/black-women-abolitionists-fight-freedom-19th-century. Accessed December 1, 2020.

Prokhovnik, Raia. 1998. "Public and Private Citizenship: From Gender Invisibility to Feminist Inclusiveness." *Feminist Review*, 60: 84–104. Accessed May 1, 2020. www.jstor.org/stable/1395548.

Prokupecz, Shimon and Mark Morales. 2020. "Officials Removing Bodies from 'Overwhelmed' Brooklyn Funeral Home." *CNN*, April 30, 2020. https://www.cnn.com/2020/04/29/us/bodies-trucks-brooklyn-funeral-home/index.html. Accessed May 1, 2020.

Quarshie, Mabinty. 2018. "Is the Women's March More Inclusive This Year." *USA Today*. January 18, 208. https://www.usatoday.com/story/news/2018/01/18/womens-march-more-inclusive-year/1038859001/. Accessed May 1, 2020.

Rafei, Leila. 2020. "Block the Vote: Voter Suppression in 2020." *ACLU*, Feb. 3, 2020. 2020 https://www.aclu.org/news/civil-liberties/block-the-vote-voter-suppression-in-2020/. Accessed May 2, 2020.

Rakich, Nathaniel. 2020. "What Went Down in Ohio's Primary." May 7, 2020. 2020 Election. FiveThirtyEight. Accessed November 11, 2020 from https://fivethirtyeight.com/features/what-went-down-in-ohios-primary/.

Ramsey, Shawn D. 2012. "The Voices of Counsel: Women and Civic Rhetoric in the Middle Ages." *Rhetoric Society Quarterly*, 42(5): 472–489. https://doi.org/10.1080/02773945.2012.724513.

Ransom, Jan. 2020. "E. Jean Carroll, Who Accused Trump of Rape, Sues Him for Defamation." *New York Times*. October 19, 2020. https://www.nytimes.com/2019/11/04/nyregion/jean-carroll-sues-trump.html. Accessed November 24, 2020.

Ravesz, Rachael. 2017. "Donald Trump's New 'Muslim Ban' Still Does Not Include Countries That Have Produced Terrorists." *Independent*. March 6, 2017. https://www.independent.co.uk/news/world/americas/donald-trump-muslim-travel-ban-countries-terrorists-immigration-order-a7614701.html. Accessed April 29, 2020.

Read, Bridget. 2020. "Zoombombing' Is a Horrifying New Trend." *The Cut*, April 3, 2020. https://www.thecut.com/2020/04/what-is-zoombombing.html. Accessed May 1, 2020.

Reeves, Richard V. and Dayna Bowen Matthew. October 21, 2016. "6 Charts Showing Race Gaps within the American Middle Class." *Brookings*. https://www.brookings.edu/blog/social-mobility-memos/2016/10/21/6-charts-showing-race-gaps-within-the-american-middle-class/. Accessed November 14, 2020.

Reilly, Katie. 2016. "Here Are All the Times Donald Trump Insulted Mexico." *Time*, August 31, 2016. https://time.com/4473972/donald-trump-mexico-meeting-insult/. Accessed April 29, 2020.

Relman, Eliza. 2019. "Trump's War on Science is Being Led By A Climate Change Denier Who Compared Carbon Dioxide Pollution to 'Poor Jews Under Hitler.'" *Business Insider*. May 28, 2019. https://www.businessinsider.com/trump-war-on-science-is-led-by-climate-change-denier-2019-5. Accessed April 29, 2020.

Resurrección, Bernadette P. 2017. "Gender and Environment from 'Women, Environment and Development' to Feminist Political Ecology." In *Routledge Handbook of Gender and Environment*, edited by S. MacGregor, 71–85. Routledge: Oxon, Part I, Chapter 4.

Revesz, Rachael. 2016. "Survey Finds Hillary Clinton Has 'More Than 99% Chance' of Winning Election over Donald Trump." *Independent*, November 5, 2016. https://www.independent.co.uk/news/world/americas/sam-wang-princeton-election-consortium-poll-hillary-clinton-donald-trump-victory-a7399671.html. Accessed August 22, 2020.

Rice, Doyle. 2019. "Study Finds a Race Gap In Air Pollution-Whites Largely Cause It; Blacks and Hispanics Breathe It." *USA Today*. March 12, 2019. https://www.usatoday.com/story/news/nation/2019/03/11/air-pollution-inequality-minorities-breathe-air-polluted-whites/3130783002/. Accessed November 18, 2019

Richardson, Nikita. 2020. "More Than 40 Grocery Workers Have Died From COVID-19." *New Yorker*, April 13, 2020. https://www.grubstreet.com/2020/04/grocery-workers-covid19.html. Accessed May 3, 2020.

Riley, Kevin Jack and Hoffman, Bruce. 1995. *Domestic Terrorism: A National Assessment of State and Local Preparedness*. RAND: Santa Monica, CA. https://www.rand.org/pubs/monograph_reports/MR505.html. Accessed April 29, 2020.

Riotta, Chris. 2017. "When Has Trump Been Accused of Rape or Attempted Rape? Allegations Include A Child, His Wife and A Business Associate." *Newsweek*. November 16, 2017. https://www.newsweek.com/donald-trump-rape-sexual-assault-minor-wife-business-victims-roy-moore-713531. Accessed April 29, 2020.

Rizzo, Salvador. 2018. "The Facts about Trump's Policy of Separating Families at the Border." *Washington Post*. June 19, 2018. https://www.washingtonpost.com/news/fact-checker/wp/2018/06/19/the-facts-about-trumps-policy-of-separating-families-at-the-border/. Accessed April 29, 2020.

Robbins, Liz. 2018. "Hundreds of Separated Children Have Quietly Been Sent to New York." *New York Times*. June 20, 2018. https://www.nytimes.com/2018/06/20/nyregion/children-separated-border-new-york.html?login=smartlock&auth=login-smartlock. Accessed April 28, 2020.

Roberts, Frank Leon. 2018. "How Black Lives Matter Changed the Way Americans Fight for Freedom." July 13, 2018. https://www.aclu.org/blog/racial-justice/race-and-criminal-justice/how-black-lives-matter-changed-way-americans-fight. Accessed April 14, 2020.

Rogers, Katie, Shear, Michael D. and Kanno-Youngs, Zolan. 2020. "Trump Plans to Suspend Immigration to U.S." *New York Times*, April 20, 2020. https://www.nytimes.com/2020/04/20/us/politics/trump-immigration.html. Accessed April 21, 2020.

Rogers, Mary F. 2005. "Clarence Thomas, Patriarchal Discourse and Public/Private Spheres. *The Sociological Quarterly*, 39(2): 289–308. Accessed November 17, 2020. https://doi.org/10.1111/j.1533-8525.1998.tb00505.x.

Ropers-Huilman, Rebecca. 2011. "Editorial Introduction: Ecofeminism." *Feminist Formations*, 23(2): viii–xii. https://www.jstor.org/stable/41301653.

Rose, Lydia and Teresa Bartoli. 2019. "Agnotology and the Epistemology of Ignorance: a Framework for the Propagation of Ignorance as a Consequence of Technology in a Balkanized Media Ecosystem." *Postdigital Science and Education*, 2: 184–201 (2020). https://doi.org/10.1007/s42438-019-00084-5. Accessed April 29, 2020.

Rose, Lydia. 1993. "The Devil is A Fag: AIDS Origin Stories and Ideology." *Semiotic*, 178th Annual Meeting of the Semiotic Society of America, St. Louis.

Rose, Lydia. 1997. *The Social Construction of Acquired Immune Deficiency Syndrome: The Relationship Between AIDS Origin Stories and White Male Supremacist (Neo-Aryan) Ideology*. Dissertation, Purdue University. ProQuest Dissertations Publishing, 1997. 9808513. https://search.proquest.com/docview/304360357.

Rothe, Dawn L. and Victoria E. Collins. 2019. "Turning Back the Clock? Violence against Women and the Trump Administration." *Journal of Victims and Offenders,* 14: 965–978. https://www.tandfonline.com/doi/full/10.1080/15564886.2019.1671284?scroll=top&needAccess=true&. Accessed April 29, 2020.

Rowley, Michelle V. 2012. "'It Could Have Been Me' Really? Early Morning Meditations on Trayvon Martin's Death." *Feminist Studies*, 38(2): 519–529. https://www.jstor.org/stable/23269201. Accessed April 10, 2020.

Rucker, Philip. 2015. "Trump Says Fox's Megyn Kelly had 'Blood Coming Out of Her Wherever.'" *Washington Post*, August 8, 2015. Accessed November 17, 2020. https://www.washingtonpost.com/news/post-politics/wp/2015/08/07/trump-says-foxs-megyn-kelly-had-blood-coming-out-of-her-wherever/.

Ruether, Rosemary Radford. 1995. "Ecofeminism: Symbolic and Social Connections of the Oppression of Women and the Domination of Nature." *Feminist Theology,* 3(6): 35–50. http://journals.sagepub.com/doi/abs/10.1177/096673509500000903.

Ruwitch, John. 2020. "California Leans On National Guard To Help With Food Banks." *NPR*, National, March 29, 2020. https://www.npr.org/2020/03/29/823592895/california-leans-on-national-guard-to-help-with-food-banks. Accessed May 2, 2020.

Sacchetti, Maria. 2018a. "Still Separated: Nearly 500 Migrant Children Taken from their Parents Remain in U.S. Custody." *Washington Post*. August 31, 2018. https://www.washingtonpost.com/local/immigration/still-separated-nearly-500-separated-migrant-children-remain-in-us-custody/2018/08/30/6dbd8278-aa09-11e8-8a0c-70b618c98d3c_story.html. Accessed April 29, 2020.

Sacchetti, Maria. 2018b. "Top Homeland Security Officials Urge Criminal Prosecution of Parents Crossing Border with Children." *Washington Post*. April 26, 2018. https://www.washingtonpost.com/local/immigration/top-homeland-security-officials-urge-criminal-prosecution-of-parents-who-cross-border-with-children/2018/04/26/a0bdcee0-4964-11e8-8b5a-3b1697adcc2a_story.html. Accessed April 29, 2020.

Santucci, John. 2015. "Donald Trump's Ex-Wife Ivana Disavows Old Rape Allegation." *ABC News*. July 28, 2015. https://abcnews.go.com/Politics/donald-trumps-wife-ivana-disavows-rape-allegation/story?id=32732204. Accessed April 29, 2020.

Santucci, John, Matthew Mosk and Stephanie Ebbs. 2018. "EXCLUSIVE: More Cabinet Trouble for Trump? EPA Chief Lived in Condo Tied to Lobbyist 'power Couple.'" *ABC News*. March 29, 2018. https://abcnews.go.com/Politics/exclusive-cabinet-trouble-trump-epa-chief-lived-condo/story?id=54095310. Accessed April 29, 2020.

Schumaker, Erin. 2020. "Timeline: How Coronavirus Got Started: The Outbreak Spanning the Globe Began in December, in Wuhan, China." *ABC News*, April 23, 2020. https://abcnews.go.com/Health/timeline-coronavirus-started/story?id=69435165. Accessed April 26, 2020.

Schwartz, Brian. 2018. "Scott Pruitt's Replacement at the EPA Has a Long, Lucrative History of Working for Coal and Chemical Companies." *CNBC*. July 6, 2018. https://www.cnbc.com/2018/07/06/scott-pruitts-epa-successor-has-long-history-with-coal-companies.html. Accessed April 29, 2020.

Scott, Eugene. 2018. "Trump's History of Making Offensive Comments about Nonwhite Immigrants." *Washington Post*. January 11, 2018. https://www.washingtonpost.com/news/the-fix/wp/2018/01/11/trumps-history-of-controversial-remarks-about-nonwhite-immigrants/. Accessed April 29, 2020.

Sessions, George. 1987. "The Deep Ecology Movement: A Review." *Environmental Review*, 11(2): 105–125. https://www.jstor.org/stable/3984023.

Shah, Khushbu. 2019. "Women Still Face Hurdles in Running For Office." *US News and World Report*. November 11, 2019. https://www.usnews.com/news/elections/articles/2019-11-11/women-still-face-hurdles-in-running-for-office. Accessed May 1, 2020.

Shalby, Colleen. 2018. A Record Number of Women are Running for Office. This Election Cycle, They Didn't Wait For an Invite. *Los Angeles Times*. October 10, 2018. https://www.latimes.com/politics/la-na-pol-women-office-20181010-story.html.

Shear, Michael D. and Eileen Sullivan. 2018. "Horseface, Lowlife, Fat, Ugly: How the President Demeans Women." *New York Times*. October 16, 2018. https://www.nytimes.com/2018/10/16/us/politics/trump-women-insults.html. Accessed March 15, 2020.

Shear, Michael D. and Mervosh, Sarah. 2020. "Trump Encourages Protest Against Governors Who Have Imposed Virus Restrictions." *New York Times*, April 17, 2020. https://www.nytimes.com/2020/04/17/us/politics/trump-coronavirus-governors.html. Accessed April 21, 2020.

Shear, Michael D. and Ron Nixon. 2017. "New Trump Deportation Rules Allow Far More Expulsions." *New York Times*. February 21, 2017. https://www.nytimes.com/2017/02/21/us/politics/dhs-immigration-trump.html. Accessed April 29, 2020.

Sheth, Sonam. 2020. "Trump Says He Thinks Some Americans Are Wearing Masks to Show They Disapprove of Him and Not as a Preventative Measure during the Pandemic." *Business Insider*. June 18, 2020. https://www.businessinsider.com/trump-americans-wearing-masks-show-disapproval-not-as-preventive-measure-2020-6?r=MX&IR=T. Accessed November 15, 2020.

Silva, Christianna. 2020. Hospitalizations Surge In Dakotas: 'It's Like We Opened Up A Spigot.' NPR, SHOTS: Health News from NPR, November 14, 20207. Accessed November 15, 2020. https://www.npr.org/sections/health-shots/2020/11/14/934185297/covid-19-hospitalizations-surge-in-dakotas-its-like-we-opened-up-a-spigot.

Silva, Daniella. 2018. "Trump Calls for Deporting Migrants 'Immediately' Without a Trial." *NBC News*. June 24, 2018. https://www.nbcnews.com/politics/immigration/

trump-calls-deporting-migrants-immediately-without-trial-n886141. Accessed April 29, 2019.

Silverman, Hollie, Konstantin Toropin, Sara Sidner and Leslie Perrot. 2020. Navajo Nation surpasses New York State for the Highest Covid-19 Infection Rate in the US. *CNN* May 18, 2020. Accessed November 14, 2020 https://www.cnn.com/2020/05/18/us/navajo-nation-infection-rate-trnd/index.html.

Sinclair, Harriet. 2017. "Is Donald Trump 'Obsessed' With Barack Obama." *Newsweek*. October 14, 2017. https://www.newsweek.com/donald-trump-obsessed-barack-obama-685143. Accessed April 29, 2019.

Singer, Ross. 2020. "Toward Intersectional Ecofeminist Communication Studies." *Communication Theory*, qtz023, https://doi.org/10.1093/ct/qtz023.

Smith, Leef and Wendy Milillo. 1996. "If It's Crowd Size You Want, Park Service Says Count It Out". *Washington Post*, October 13, 1996. https://www.washingtonpost.com/archive/politics/1996/10/13/if-its-crowd-size-you-want-park-service-says-count-it-out/0ec7dcf4-3206-48ee-b062-1459e4ddc28c/. Accessed April 4, 2020.

Smith, Sharon G., Xinjian Zhang, Kathleen C. Basile, Melissa T. Merrick, Jing Wang, Marcie-jo Kresnow, and Jieru Chen. 2018. The National Intimate Partner and Sexual Violence Survey (NISVS): 2015 Data Brief—Updated Release. Atlanta, GA: National Center for Injury Prevention. Accessed November 14, 2020. https://www.cdc.gov/violenceprevention/pdf/2015data-brief508.pdf.

Smooth, Wendy G. Tamelyn Tucker. 1999. "Behind But Not Forgotten: Women and the Behind-the-Scenes Organizing of the Million Man March. In *Still Lifting, Still Climbing: African American Women's Contemporary Activism*. New York University Press: New York.

Snyder, R. Claire. 2008. "What Is Third-Wave Feminism? A New Directions Essay." *Signs*, 34(1): 175–196. https://www.jstor.org/stable/10.1086/588436.

Soboroff, Jacob. 2019. "Emails Show Trump Administration Had 'No Way To Link' Separated Migrant Children To Parents." *NBC News*. May 1, 2019. https://www.nbcnews.com/politics/immigration/emails-show-trump-admin-had-no-way-link-separated-migrant-n1000746. Accessed April 29, 2019.

Southern Poverty Law Center. 2011. *Ku Klux Klan: A History of Racism*. https://www.splcenter.org/20110228/ku-klux-klan-history-racism. Accessed April 29, 2019.

Southern Poverty Law Center. 2016. "Ten Days After: Harassment and Intimidation in the Aftermath of the Election." https://www.splcenter.org/20161129/ten-days-after-harassment-and-intimidation-aftermath-election. Accessed April 29, 2019.

Starr, Barbara, Zachary Cohen and Jim Sciutto. 2017. "US Joint Chiefs Blindsided By Trump's Transgender Ban." *CNN*. July 27, 2017. https://www.cnn.com/2017/07/27/politics/trump-military-transgender-ban-joint-chiefs/index.html. Accessed April 29, 2019.

Stanford Open Policing Project, The. 2020. Available at https://openpolicing.stanford.edu/. Accessed December 3, 2020.

Steinhauer, Jennifer and Matthew Rosenberg. 2016. "Donald Trump's Remarks Show He's Mistaken on Sexual Assault in Military." *New York Times*. September 8, 2016.

https://www.nytimes.com/2016/09/09/us/politics/donald-trump-sexual-assault-military-women.html. Accessed November 24, 2020.

Steinem, Gloria. 2016. After the Election of Donald Trump, We Will Not Mourn. We Will Organize." *Guardian*, November 10, 2016. https://www.theguardian.com/commentisfree/2016/nov/10/after-donald-trump-win-americans-organizing-us-politics.

Steverns, Maggie and Katy O'Donnell. 2020. "House Members, Senate Aides Traded Stocks in Early Days of Coronavirus" *Politico*, March 21, 2020, updated March 23, 2020. https://www.politico.com/news/2020/03/21/coronavirus-trading-house-senate-140260. Accessed April 29, 2020.

Stoller, Robert J. 1968. *Sex and Gender: On the Development of Masculinity and Femininity,* New York: Science House.

Sturgeon, Noël. 1997. *Ecofeminist Natures: Race, Gender, Feminist Theory and Political Action.* New York: Routledge.

Subramanian, Courtney. 2020. "How a Frantic Trek to a McDonald's Parking Lot Shows the Scramble States Face for Coronavirus Supplies." *USA TODAY*, April 18, 2020. https://www.usatoday.com/story/news/politics/2020/04/18/coronavirus-creates-ppe-bidding-war-states-like-illinois-new-york/5144652002/. Accessed October 22, 2020.

Suh, Krista and Zweiman, Jayna. 2016. "The Pussyhat Project." https://www.pussyhatproject.com. Accessed April 4, 2020.

Suh, Krista and Zweiman, Jayna. 2016. *The Pussyhat Project Manifesto*. https://drive.google.com/file/d/0BwBjtQGbV7gEZU1TdUd2b1JIZGM/view. Accessed April 30, 2020.

Suh, Krista. 2020. "The Pussyhat Project: A Yarn about How We Got Started." Illustrated by Aurora Lady. https://kristasuh.com/the-pussyhat/. Accessed April 16, 2020.

Sutton, Jazma. 2019. "Beyond Harriet: African American Work in the Underground Railroad." October 13, 2019. Process: a blog for American History. https://www.processhistory.org/sutton-beyond-harriet/. Accessed December 1, 2020.

Tamman, Maurice. 2016. "Clinton has 90 Percent Chance of Winning: Reuters/Ipsos States of the Nation." *Reuters*. November 7, 2016. https://www.reuters.com/article/us-usa-election-poll-idUSKBN1322J1. Accessed August 22, 2020.

Tate, Julie, Jennifer Jenkins and Steven Rich. 2020. Fatal Force. A Database of Every Fatal Shooting by an On-Duty Police Officer in the United States. Last updated, Dec. 1, 2020. *Washington Post*. Accessed December 3, 2020. https://www.washingtonpost.com/graphics/investigations/police-shootings-database/.

Taxin, Amy. 2018. "Immigrant Children Describe Treatment in Detention Centers." *Associated Press*. July 17, 2018. https://apnews.com/1a8db84a88a940049558b4c450dccc8a.

Taylor, Dorceta E. 1997. "Women of Color, Environmental Justice, and Ecofeminism." In *Ecofeminism: Women, Culture, Nature*, edited by Karen Warren, 38–81. Indiana University Press: Bloomington.

Taylor, Dorceta E. 2002. "Race, Class, Gender, and American Environmentalism." Gen. Tech. Rep. PNW-GTR-534. Portland, OR: U.S. Department of Agriculture,

Forest Service, Pacific Northwest Research Station. 51 p. https://www.fs.fed.us/pnw/pubs/gtr534.pdf.

Terborg-Penn, Rosalyn. 1997. "African Women and the Vote: An Overview." In *African American Women and the Vote, 1837–1965*, edited by Gordon et al. University of Massachusetts Press: Amherst, MA.

Tessum, Christopher W., Joshua S. Apte, Andrew L. Goodkind, Nicholas Z. Muller, Kimberley A. Mullins, David A. Paolella, Stephen Polasky, Nathaniel P. Springer, Sumil K. Thakrar, Julian D. Marshall, and Jason D. Hill. 2019. "Inequity in consumption of goods and services adds to racial-ethnic disparities in air pollution exposure." *Proceedings of the National Academy of Sciences of the United States of America.* March 11, 2019. https://www.pnas.org/content/116/13/6001. Accessed November 19, 2020.

The Southern Poverty Law Center. 2011. *Ku Klux Klan A History of Racism and Violence,* Sixth edition. Edited by Richard Baudouin. Printed in the United States of America.

Thompson, Krissah and Scott Wilson. 2012. "Obama on Trayvon Martin: 'If I Had a Son, He'd Look like Trayvon.'" *Washington Post*, March 23, 2012. https://www.washingtonpost.com/politics/obama-if-i-had-a-son-hed-look-like-trayvon/2012/03/23/gIQApKPpVS_story.html. Accessed April 10, 2020.

Timm, Jane C. 2020. "Trump Pushes False Claims about Mail-In Vote Fraud. Here are the Facts." *NBC News*, April 10, 2020. https://www.nbcnews.com/politics/donald-trump/trump-pushes-false-claims-about-mail-vote-fraud-here-are-n1180566. Accessed May 2, 2020.

Tobin, Jacquelin L. and Raymond G. Dobard. 1999. *Hidden in Plain View: A Secret Story of Quilts and the Underground Railroad.* Anchor Books. New York.

Tonko, Paul and Brian Schatz. 2019. "Trump Administration's 'Scientific Oppression' Threatens US Safety and Innovation." *USA Today*. July 23, 2019. https://www.usatoday.com/story/opinion/2019/07/22/donald-trump-war-on-science-hurts-america-and-americans-column/1765301001/. Accessed April 29, 2020.

Torgrimson, Britta N. and Christopher T. Minson. 2005. "Sex and Gender: What Is the Difference?" *Journal of Applied Physiology*, 99: 785–787. https://journals.physiology.org/doi/pdf/10.1152/japplphysiol.00376.2005. Accessed April 29, 2020.

Trump, Donald J. "It Snowed Over 4 Inches This Past Weekend in New York City. It is still October. So much for Global Warming." *Twitter*, Nov 1, 2011. https://twitter.com/realdonaldtrump/status/131456348822061056?lang=en. Accessed April 30, 2020.

Turner, B.L. and Marina Fischer-Kowalski. 2010. "Ester Boserup: An Interdisciplinary Visionary Relevant for Sustainability." *Proceedings of the National Academy of Sciences*. December 2010.

Union of Concerned Scientists. 2018. "Scientists Agree: Global Warming is Happening and Humans Are the Primary Cause." August 3, 2018. https://www.ucsusa.org/global-warming/science-and-impacts/science/scientists-agree-global-warming-happening-humans-primary-cause. Accessed April 29, 2020.

United Nations. 1968 "Universal Declaration of Human Rights." https://www.humanrights.com/what-are-human-rights/universal-declaration-of-human-rights/. Accessed April 29, 2020.

United Nations. 2018. "UN Rights Chief Slams 'Unconscionable' US Border Policy of Separating Migrant Children From Parents." *UN News*. June 18, 2018. https://news.un.org/en/story/2018/06/1012382. Accessed April 29, 2020.

UN—United Nations. 2020. "Recognition, Justice and Development: The Midterm Review of the International Decade for People of African Descent." https://www.un.org/en/observances/end-racism-day. Accessed April 14, 2020.

USAFacts.org 2020. 4.4 million Households with Children Don't Have Consistent Access to Computers for Online Learning during the Pandemic. September 28, 2020 4:00PM PDT | Updated Mon, October 19, 2020. Accessed November 14, 2020. https://usafacts.org/articles/internet-access-students-at-home/.

U.S. Const. The United States Constitution, Amendment XIII, section 1.

Valdez, Roger. 2020. "COVID-19 and Eviction: Government Action Uneven Across the Country". *Forbes*, April 1, 2020. https://www.forbes.com/sites/rogervaldez/2020/04/01/covid-19-and-eviction-uneven-actions-across-the-country/#48b8ca183d05. Accessed May 1, 2020.

Vanden Brook, Tom. 2019. "Shanahan Calls for Reforms as Military Sexual Assaults Rise by 38%; Highest for Young Women." *USA Today*. May 2, 2019. https://www.usatoday.com/story/news/politics/2019/05/02/military-sexual-assaults-climb-2016-2018-pentagon-army-navy-marines-alcohol/3625405002/. Accessed April 29, 2019.

Varanasi, Anuradha. 2020. "Over 14 Million People of Color in the U.S. Live in Counties with High Air Pollution." *Forbes*. April 27, 2020. https://www.forbes.com/sites/anuradhavaranasi/2020/04/27/over-14-million-people-of-color-in-the-us-live-in-counties-with-high-air-pollution/?sh=3c3a16cf5301. Accessed November 18, 2020.

Victor, Daniel. 2017. "'Access Hollywood' Reminds Trump: 'The Tape Is Very Real.'" *New York Times*, November 28, 2017. https://www.nytimes.com/2017/11/28/us/politics/donald-trump-tape.html. Accessed April 4, 2020.

Villalobos, Briana. 2017. "Intersectional Ecofeminism: Environmentalism for Everybody." *IWW Environmental Unionism Caucus*. February 26, 2017. https://ecology.iww.org/node/2100?bot_test=1. Accessed May 1, 2020.

Viñas-Nelson, Jessica. 2017. Interracial Marriage in "Post-Racial" *America. ORIGINS: Current Events in Historical Perspective,* 10(12). https://origins.osu.edu/article/interracial-marriage-post-racial-america/page/0/1.

Vogels, Emily A. 2020. "From Virtual Parties to Ordering Food, How Americans Are Using the Internet during COVID-19." *Pew Research, Internet and Technology*, April 30, 2020. https://www.pewresearch.org/fact-tank/2020/04/30/from-virtual-parties-to-ordering-food-how-americans-are-using-the-internet-during-covid-19/. Accessed May 2, 2020.

Vogels, Emily A. Andrew Perrin, Lee Rainie, and Monica Anderson. 2020. "53% of Americans Say the Internet Has Been Essential During the COVID-19 Outbreak." *Pew Research Center, Internet and Technology*, April 30, 2020. https://www

.pewresearch.org/internet/2020/04/30/53-of-americans-say-the-internet-has-been-essential-during-the-covid-19-outbreak/. Accessed May 2, 2020.

Volcovici, Valerie. 2017. "Trump Administration Tells EPA to Cut Climate Page from Website: Sources." *Reuters*. January 2, 2017. https://www.reuters.com/article/us-usa-trump-epa-climatechange-idUSKBN15906G. Accessed April 29, 2019.

Wallace, Tim and Alicia Parlapiano. 2017. "Crowd Scientists Say Women's March in Washington Had 3 Times as Many People as Trump's Inauguration." *New York Times*, January 22, 2017. https://www.nytimes.com/interactive/2017/01/22/us/politics/womens-march-trump-crowd-estimates.html?_r=0. Accessed April 30, 2020.

Warren, Karen. 1990. "The Power and the Promise of Ecological Feminism." *Environmental Ethics,* 12(2): 125–146.

Warren, Karen J. 2000. *Ecofeminist Philosophy*. Rowman & Littlefield: New York.

Warren, Tom. 2020. "Zoom Grows to 300 Million Meeting Participants Despite Security Backlash." *The Verge, Tech*, April 23, 2020. https://www.theverge.com/2020/4/23/21232401/zoom-300-million-users-growth-coronavirus-pandemic-security-privacy-concerns-response. Accessed May 1, 2020.

Wathen, C. Nadine. 2019. "Gender-Based Violence: Being Not Male Increases Risk of Victimization." *Phys.Org*. August 30, 2019. https://phys.org/news/2019-08-gender-based-violence-male-victimization.html. Accessed April 29, 2020.

Watters, Jessica. 2017. "Pink Hats and Black Fists: The Role of Women in the Black Lives Matter Movement." *William & Mary Journal of Women and the Law*, 24(1): 199–207. https://scholarship.law.wm.edu/cgi/viewcontent.cgi?article=1466&context=wmjowl. Accessed March 19, 2020.

Waxman, Olivia B. 2020. "'It's a Struggle They Will Wage Alone.' How Black Women Won the Right to Vote. *Time*. August 17, 2020. https://time.com/5876456/black-women-right-to-vote/. Accessed August 20, 2020.

Webb, Gary. 1996. *Dark Alliance: The CIA, the Contras, and the Crack Cocaine Explosion*. Seven Stories Press: New York.

Weiss, Penny A. 1987. "Rousseau, Antifeminism, and Woman's Nature." *Political Theory*, 15(1): 81–98. https://www.jstor.org/stable/191721.

Wernick, Adam. 2019. "A New EPA Rule Will Require Confidential Health Records for Scientific Studies." *NPR*. December 19, 2019. https://news.wbfo.org/post/new-epa-rule-will-require-confidential-health-records-scientific-studies-0. Accessed April 29, 2019.

Westcott, Lucy. 2017. "Trump Team Considering Cuts to Federal Violence Against Women Program: Report." *Newsweek*. January 19, 2017. https://www.newsweek.com/donald-trump-violence-against-women-federal-funding-budget-cuts-544710. Accessed April 29, 2019.

Westwood, Sarah. 2020. "Despite Trump Executive Order, Meat-Processing Plants Struggle to Stay Open." *CNN Politics*, May 1, 2020. https://www.cnn.com/2020/05/01/politics/executive-order-meat-processing-plants-open/index.html. Accessed May 2, 2020.

Wetli, Patty. 2016. "Chicago Knitters Unite for Pussyhat Project, To Cap Off With D.C. March." *DNAinfo-Chicago*, December 21, 2016. https://www.dnainfo.com/

chicago/20161221/north-center/pusshyat-project-trump-dc-march-protest-knitters-january-21/. Accessed April 16, 2020.

Whyte, Chelsea. 2020. "Strong Support for Trump Linked to Willingness to Persecute Immigrants." *New Scientists*, September 2, 2019. https://www.newscientist.com/article/2214987-strong-support-for-trump-linked-to-willingness-to-persecute-immigrants/. Accessed May 2, 2020.

Wilkerson, Isabel. 2020. *Caste: The Origins of Our Discontents*. Random House: New York.

Williams, David. 2020. "Health Workers Face Anti-Lockdown Protesters in Dramatic Photos." *CNN*, April 20, 2020. https://www.cnn.com/2020/04/20/us/coronavirus-colorado-health-care-trnd/index.html. Accessed April 26, 2020.

Williams, Rhonda Y. 2008. Black Women and Black Power. *OAH Magazine of History*, 22(3): 22–26. https://www.jstor.org/stable/25162182. Accessed December 2, 2020.

Wilson, Jason 2020. "The Rightwing Groups Behind Wave of Protests against Covid-19 Restrictions." *Guardian*, April 17, 2020. https://www.theguardian.com/world/2020/apr/17/far-right-coronavirus-protests-restrictions. Accessed April 26, 2020.

Wingrove, Josh. 2020. "Trump Tells Three Democratic States to 'Liberate' Themselves." *Politics, Bloomberg*, April 17, 2020. https://www.bloomberg.com/news/articles/2020-04-17/trump-tells-three-democratic-states-to-liberate-themselves. Accessed April 26, 2020.

WM—Women's March Inc. 2017. *Women's March Annual Report* 2017. https://static1.squarespace.com/static/5c3feb79fcf7fdce5a3c790b/t/5c422af80e2e725f8f0ea8f8/1547840252450/2017%2BWM%2BAnnual%2BReport_LoRes.pdf. Accessed April 4, 2020.

Wolf, Z. Byron. 2017. "Is There Something Wrong with this White House Photo?" *CNN* March 24, 2017. https://edition.cnn.com/2017/03/23/politics/mike-pence-patty-murray-photo/index.html. Accessed November 24, 2020.

Wolf, Z. Byron. 2018. "Trump is Obsessed with Undoing Obama's Deals, But Now He's Working On One of his Own." *CNN*. May 9, 2018. https://www.cnn.com/2018/05/09/politics/trump-obama-deals/index.html. Accessed April 29, 2019.

Wolf, Zachary B., Curt Merrill, and Daniel Wolfe. "How Voters Shifted during Four Years of Trump America Has Chosen Joe Biden as its 46th President. Here's an Idea of How Voters have Changed since 2016." *CNN Politics*. November 7, 2020, Updated November 10, 2020. Accessed November 11, 2020 from https://www.cnn.com/interactive/2020/11/politics/election-analysis-exit-polls-2016-2020/.

WOM-Worldometer. 2020 United States Coronavirus Cases. Accessed May 3, 2020 from https://www.worldometers.info/coronavirus/country/us/.

Wong, Edward. 2016. "Trump Has Called Climate Change A Chinese Hoax. Beijing Says It Is Anything But." *New York Times*. November 18, 2016. https://www.nytimes.com/2016/11/19/world/asia/china-trump-climate-change.html. Accessed April 29, 2019.

Wong, Julia Carrie. 2016. "Dakota Access Pipeline: 300 Protesters Injured after Police Use Water Cannons." *Guardian*. November 21, 2017. Accessed December

16, 2020. https://www.theguardian.com/us-news/2016/nov/21/dakota-access-pipeline-water-cannon-police-standing-rock-protest.

Woodstock, Molly. 2018. "The Trump Administration Says It Wants To Define Sex 'On a Biological Basis.' It Gets the Science Wrong. *Washington Post*. October 29, 2018. https://www.washingtonpost.com/outlook/2018/10/29/trump-administration-says-it-wants-define-sex-biological-basis-it-gets-science-wrong/. Accessed April 29, 2020.

Worldometers. 2020. COVID-19 Coronavirus Pandemic. Last updated: November 15, 2020, 21:49 GMT. https://www.worldometers.info/coronavirus/. Accessed November 15, 2020.

Wu, X., R. C. Nethery, M. B. Sabath, D. Braun, and F. Dominici. 2020. Air Pollution and COVID-19 Mortality in the United States: Strengths and Limitations of An Ecological Regression Analysis. *Science Advances*, 6(45): eabd4049. Accessed November 14, 2020. https://projects.iq.harvard.edu/covid-pm.

WXYZ 2020. "Whitmer Orders All Shut-Off Water to be Restored during COVID-19 Outbreak." *WXYZ*, March 28, 2020. https://www.wxyz.com/news/coronavirus/whitmer-orders-all-shut-off-water-to-be-restored-during-covid-19-outbreak. Accessed May 1, 2020.

Yan, Holly. 2020. "200,000 People Have Died from COVID-19 in the US. That's More Than Battle Deaths from 5 Wars Combined." CNN. September 22, 2020. https://edition.cnn.com/2020/09/22/health/us-coronavirus-deaths-200k/index.html. Accessed September 28, 2020.

Zapotosky, Matt and Sari Horwitz 2017. "Sessions Tells Prosecutors to Bring More Cases Against Those Entering U.S. Illegally." *Washington Post*. April 11, 2017. https://www.washingtonpost.com/world/national-security/sessions-tells-prosecutors-to-bring-more-cases-against-those-entering-us-illegally/2017/04/11/9fc6e964-1eb7-11e7-ad74-3a742a6e93a7_story.html Accessed April 29, 2020.

Zernike, Kate. 2018. "Female Candidates Break Barriers, Except When It Comes to Money." *New York Times*. October 30, 2018. https://www.nytimes.com/2018/10/30/us/politics/women-campaign-fundraising.html. Accessed May 1, 2020.

# Index

# About the Authors

**Lydia Rose** is an associate professor in the Department of Sociology at Kent State University. She earned a PhD in Sociology from Purdue University. Her research centers on environmental justice, ecofeminism, and inequality. Rose's teaching and scholarship emphasizes the intersectionality and impact of race, class, gender, and other inequalities in our social institutions including education, family, economy, food systems, and the environment. Her praxis emphasizes the connection of theory, research, and social action to alleviate the injustices created by social inequalities from micro and macro levels.

**Teresa M. Bartoli** is an independent scholar and activist. She earned an MA in Speech Communications from California State University, Fullerton. Her areas of research include ecofeminism, agnotology (culturally induced ignorance), and inequality. She specializes in youth issues and leadership inspired from her time as the director of a youth program that served youth in Los Angeles County. She was instrumental in designing and organizing youth leadership opportunities that addressed homelessness and other social issues. Bartoli is a public speaker, and while working for California State University, Fullerton, she taught public speaking and held a position at the Social Science Research Center.